Pioneer of the Catholic Revival

Pioneer of the Catholic Revival

The ideas and influence of Emmanuel Mounier

Michael Kelly

Sheed and Ward
London

Copyright © 1979 by Michael Kelly. First published 1979. All rights reserved. *Nihil Obstat* Anton Cowan, Censor. *Imprimatur* David Norris, Vicar General, Westminster, 10 July 1979. Printed in Great Britain for Sheed and Ward Ltd, 6 Blenheim Street, London W1Y 0SA by the Bowering Press, Plymouth and London.

Contents

Introduction		vii
1	The Formation of a Leader (1905–1931)	3
2	The Foundations of Personalism (1931–1935)	27
3	The Politics of Personalism (1935–1938)	55
4	War (1938–1944)	81
5	Battle for the Minds (1944–1947)	111
6	The Struggle for Survival (1947–1950)	146
Conclusion		167
General Bibliographical Notes		177
Index of Names		180

For Jo

Introduction

Emmanuel Mounier is a key figure in the development of modern Europe. His work in the 1930s and 1940s was decisive in setting in motion many far-reaching innovations which have become the political and ideological background of our own time. A courageous and outspoken thinker, he played a leading role in transforming the attitudes and alignments of the catholic community in his native France. But his influence can still be felt in many countries of the world. His pioneering work did much to prepare the momentous changes of the second Vatican Council, to lay the basis for a new social and political orientation among christians, and to introduce a revived personal and spiritual dimension into socialist thought.

When he died in March 1950 at the early age of forty-four, Mounier was one of France's most respected writers and intellectuals. Not only was he a leading figure in the political and cultural life of French-speaking Europe and Africa, but his commitment to friendship and reconciliation in the post-war world also earned him an international reputation which extended into Eastern Europe and across the Atlantic. Mounier's work was many-sided. As founder and director of the influential review *Esprit*, he was active in all the important debates and controversies of the thirties and forties. He made important contributions to christian social doctrine, philosophy, psychology, political thought, education, journalism, literary and cultural criticism, among other things. His life came to an abrupt and premature end at a time when his thought was still developing, and when he was entering into full intellectual maturity. Even so, the range and diversity of his writings make it difficult to sum up completely the nature of his achievement and the extent of his influence.

Mounier was a man of transition living in a period of transition. The few years before, during and after the second world war were a time of radical and often brutal transformations in all spheres of human activity. The bulk of Mounier's work was produced in this short period of less than two decades. He played a prominent part in the developments of his time, and the interest of his work on a historical level is itself considerable. The growth and decline of Mounier's personalist philosophy is a fascinating chapter in the history of ideas. His writings have an important place in the history of political thought. His analyses of contemporary events are still valuable sources for understanding the recent history of France. His studies of writers, movements, societies and civilisations are significant contributions to modern cultural criticism. The review, *Esprit*, which he developed into a unique and influential organ, has its own historical importance. And Mounier's own trenchant reappraisals of christian thought and action in the world have an assured place in the history of modern christianity. In these and other fields, Mounier's importance must first be understood in terms of the historical conditions which gave rise to his work, and determined its context and meaning.

Time and events have eroded the relevance of many of Mounier's writings. Many of the principles he fought hard to defend have gained general acceptance, many of his concrete objectives have been realised. But in one important respect, Mounier's influence has continued to operate long after his death: on a political level, his work has remained both relevant and controversial. For this reason, above all, the interest of his thought is more than historical.

In response to the succeeding crises of the 1930s and 1940s, Mounier developed a form of revolutionary socialism which he offered as being wholly compatible with both the letter and spirit of catholic doctrine. In so doing he obtained the consent and, increasingly, the support of the French catholic hierarchy, despite the uncongenial atmosphere of the intensifying cold war. Similar in many ways to the utopian socialists of an earlier century, Mounier played the role of vanguard, exploring little-known and hazardous territory in advance of the main body of the army. Although he did not succeed in producing a fully coherent and practical form of socialism, he found many elements within the catholic tradition which tended towards socialism, and located within the socialist tradition many elements conducive to christian values. These he drew together in a loose and provisional synthesis which prepared the way for later, more developed syntheses, and helped to equip a new generation to carry the work forward.

French catholicism has moved over a period of fifty years from a virtually monolithic right-wing stance to a pluralistic and increasingly left-wing position. Mounier's role was to encourage and facilitate this change on the level of ideas and attitudes. It is not surprising, therefore, that his work should continue to arouse opposition and hostility in right-wing quarters long after his death.

An indispensable component of Mounier's socialism was a growing assimilation of marxist analysis. Marxism was, and continues to be, the strongest, most coherent and most comprehensive current within socialism. Aware of this, Mounier undertook to adapt such aspects of marxism as would strengthen his own form of socialism. Though his interest was mainly in learning from marxist social and economic theory, Mounier began a cautious exploration of all areas in which marxism might hold useful lessons. As a result of this intellectual encounter, and as a result of political developments within France, Mounier entered into the beginnings of a dialogue with the French communist party. The courage and intelligence with which Mounier carried out his vanguard role are well shown in this instance. Though it was often a difficult and thankless task, his success in maintaining dialogue in an open, public manner enabled the ground to be marked out in some degree, preparing more satisfactory contact under later, more favourable conditions.

Mounier's readiness to establish relations, however strained, between catholics and communists, and his ability to find common ground, however limited, between christianity and marxism, have remained the most fruitful and contentious aspects of his work. His efforts have proved a source of help and inspiration to christians grappling with serious social and political issues in places as different as Spain, Poland and Latin America. Equally he has incurred hostile reactions in conservative circles, anxious to prevent a dialogue and contacts which could not be in their interests. Questions of marxism and communism continue to pose fundamental problems and to arouse corresponding degrees of passion among christians. For all its misgivings, however, the catholic church never intervened to curtail Mounier's activities. and subsequent events have served to increase rather than diminish the value of the dialogue he initiated.

During his life, Mounier never shirked unpopular positions on controversial issues, so long as he felt that his stance was consistent with his catholic faith. Later developments have most often tended to confirm the wisdom of his choices, and it is therefore not always easy to appreciate their originality or difficulty. Since his death, many of Mounier's most distinctive and most fiercely argued options have become commonplaces among wide sections of the catholic community. His part in forming their ideas is no longer obvious, and his books, though widely read, appear now as classics rather than as avant-garde manifestos.

Mounier often said that the best fate he could wish for his thought was that it should merge, unremembered, into the everyday assumptions of everyman. In many ways this wish has been fulfilled among European christians. The aim of the present study is to retrace Mounier's seminal role in the historical development of attitudes and opinions, and to examine the ways in which he still remains a pathfinder.

During the preparation of this study I have received help and support from many people. To Professors Donald Charlton and Richard Coe I owe a long-standing debt of gratitude. To Professor Anthony Levi I am indebted for his advice and guidance. I am particularly grateful to Mme Paulette Mounier and M. Jean-Marie Domenach, who gave ungrudgingly of their time and offered both their invaluable help and their friendship. If I were to thank individually my family, my friends and the many people with whom I have discussed this work, or who have given their help in other ways, I should need many pages, though I owe them most. I wish, however, to thank especially Jo Doyle, my wife, to whom the book is dedicated.

Michael Kelly
Dublin, June 1979

Pioneer of the Catholic Revival

CHAPTER ONE

The Formation of a Leader
(1905-1931)

France after the Great War
As it emerged from the Great War, France, though victorious, was on the brink of collapse. The four years of struggle had exhausted the country's resources, leaving it massively in debt, with only a remote chance of obtaining the reparations demanded from a shattered Germany. The western front had cost two million French lives, and the ten North-Eastern departments had been laid waste. The task of economic reconstruction was long and difficult, but was largely achieved by the mid-1920s thanks to the return of Alsace-Lorraine, the survival of basic infrastructures over most of the national territory, the extensive modernisation of agriculture, and the accelerated growth of industrialisation. Despite its financial instability, the ultra-conservative *Bloc national* government saw production reach and exceed pre-war levels, a success which was only achieved with considerable inflation and indirect taxation. That meant an increased prosperity for the industrial bourgeoisie, for the urban middle classes and for large and medium farmers, but provoked rising militancy in the industrial and agricultural working-class who now faced more acute problems of poverty and working conditions than before. Politically, the ruling class bolstered its position with an intensified nationalism, directed mainly against defeated Germany and bolshevik Russia. It was opposed by a divided left, newly split into communist and socialist parties, both sympathetic to the working class movements in Russia and Germany. Between right-wing nationalism and left-wing socialism lay a cluster of groups who for various reasons resisted both. They represented middle-class interests but were anxious to reduce political and sectarian polarisations. This 'moderate' group was strengthened by the emergence of the French communist party in 1920, which rapidly asserted itself as the 'extreme left', pushing the reconstituted socialist party towards the centre. The moderates were strengthened on

the other flank by the church's disavowal in 1926 of *Action française* and by the succeeding polemic which impelled many catholics to reconsider their traditional nationalism. From the fall of the *Bloc national* in 1924, it was the moderate parties who in one combination or another effectively occupied power until the *Front populaire* twelve years later.

The ideological complexion of the country reflected these changes. The growing urban proletariat was beginning to assert its economic strength through stronger trades union organisations, and its political strength through the socialist and, increasingly, communist parties. Corresponding to this was a shift from the syndicalist tradition of Proudhon to the more powerful, hard-headed socialism of Marx and Lenin. As communism became increasingly established in the working class, so liberal socialism found a stronger power-base in the lower strata of the petty-bourgeoisie, leaving its upper strata to continue the traditional liberalism of the radical parties. The landed and propertied classes continued to support the nationalism and conservative republicanism traditionally associated with the catholic church. But inside catholicism changes were taking place. There were the first signs of disquiet at the fact that the working class was now largely non-christian. There were signs of a desire to confront seriously the ideas of socialism. There were also signs of an attempt by christians to find an alternative political ideology to replace *intégrisme*, the extreme right-wing catholicism which sought a return to the *Ancien Régime*. Since the war, a new generation of catholics had begun to emerge, who felt themselves to have a legitimate role to play in the national development. They had not known the violent sectarian divisions of before the war, and they felt more affinity with Marc Sangnier, the turn-of-the-century catholic leader of the democratic republican *Sillon* movement, than with Charles Maurras, the anti-semitic editor of the *intégriste* paper *Action française*. Entering republican politics for the first time they found an early expression in christian democracy, which was consolidated into a modest political party, the *Parti Démocrate Populaire*, in 1924.

Childhood and youth
Born on 1st April 1905, Emmanuel Mounier came to manhood in these years of the mid-1920s, when the franc was finally stabilised, when the country seemed set for a new era of growth and prosperity, when national divisions seemed to be abating, and when France seemed to be reasserting her greatness in a world largely at peace. His hometown, Grenoble, had been relatively cushioned from the

effects of the Great War, thanks to its setting in the mountains of the South-East, nearer to Italy and Switzerland than to Germany, Belgium or the war-torn North-East of France. In many ways, Grenoble was typical of provincial France. It participated in the economic expansion as a local capital and as an industrial city in its own right. Socially it experienced the creation of working-class ghettos, swelled by Italian and North African immigrant labour, and it saw the increasing growth of the more prosperous central and suburban areas. Ideologically it also reflected the same divisions as the rest of the country, situated in an area of varying religious and political commitment.

Mounier was the second child of a pharmacist: he had one elder sister, Madeleine. His parents came from artisanal and farming stock and raised their son and daughter in the values of the provincial catholic petty bourgeoisie. They enjoyed a comfortable, though not affluent standard of living, and respected the virtues of thrift and industry, without knowing hardship or want. They held their unquestioning catholic faith from their forebears, from whom they also took a strong sense of the independence and integrity of the family.

Although the Great War left no apparent mark on his childhood, a series of personal misfortunes rendered Mounier totally deaf in one ear and virtually blind in one eye at an early age. At school he was a conscientious and methodical pupil, who, having lost a year's schooling for reasons of health, came to dominate his fellows both in ability and maturity. Although his final year at the Lycée Champollion in Grenoble revealed his substantial gifts in philosophy, his attention had been directed largely towards the sciences, and on leaving school in June 1923 he was encouraged by his parents to study medicine. The young man of eighteen was torn between his taste and competence for more contemplative activities and his family's desire that he should make his career as a country doctor, a course he half persuaded himself to embrace. The confusion and uncertainty was Mounier's first serious experience of mental suffering and he later recalled a feeling of 'désespoir, jusqu'aux goûts de suicide'.[1] In March 1924 he attended his first religious retreat, during which he became convinced of the need to abandon medicine for philosophy. At the same time he underwent what he regarded as a religious conversion. It took the form of a new enthusiasm and earnestness in his christian faith, which he felt to be 'le passage d'un piétisme traditionnaliste et bourgeois à la vie véritablement chrétienne'.[2] As a result of this experience, his father decided to entrust him to a young philosophy teacher at the University of Grenoble, Jacques Chevalier, with whom the Mounier family were distantly acquainted. The intention was that Emmanuel should 'faire de la philosophie en vue de l'apostolat'.³ Chevalier agreed to become Mounier's mentor and take charge of his intellectual and spiritual formation.

Catholic Bergsonism
Jacques Chevalier, who was born in 1882, had followed a highly successful academic career. After three years at the Ecole Normale Supérieure and second place in the philosophy *agrégation* of 1903, he held grants and taught both in England and in France. His doctorate in 1914 on the concept of necessity in Aristotle and Plato had been highly praised. Since his arrival in Grenoble in 1919, not only had he established a high reputation as a teacher, but he had also published a number of books on major thinkers, and many articles on religious and philosophical questions. His reputation as a philosopher rested mainly on his two major works, *Descartes* (Paris, 1921), and *Pascal* (Paris, 1922), and he was also a close friend and admirer of the eminent philosopher Henri Bergson, which added lustre to his name. His thought was inspired by orthodox catholicism and combined with conservative political and social views. He was particularly opposed to liberal individualism, which he saw as springing from the renaissance, enthroned by the French revolution of 1789, and leading to the ruin of the family by pernicious laws on divorce and the distribution of property.⁴ Doctrines and institutions were equally undermined by individualism, he argued. The only remedy was for the individual to renounce his own interests and submit to the higher interests of religion, society, law and order.

Chevalier's views determined much of the content of his teaching, and it would be misleading to see him as entirely characteristic of French philosophy teachers of the 1920s. His narrowly parochial approach to modern philosophy was certainly typical of provincial France: German philosophy, including Kant, was almost entirely ignored and even British thinkers of the status of Hobbes, Locke, Hume and Berkeley were presented as little more than caricatures. On the other hand his treatment of Greek, Latin and French thinkers appears to have been thorough. He dealt at length with Plato, to a lesser extent with Aristotle, allowed some time for selected philosophers of the seventeenth century, but above all dwelt on catholic thinkers. A large part of Chevalier's teaching centred on religious questions. While much of the discussion stemmed readily from the thinkers studied, lectures and seminars were also devoted to topics of doctrinal interest in themselves. The immortality of the soul, miracles, the power of truth, God and morality, sin and grace, these and many other subjects of christian concern occupied his philosophical attention. However, the most distinctive feature of Chevalier's thought was the christian form of Bergsonism which he had developed.

Henri Bergson was the best-known and most influential French thinker of the early twentieth century. He offered a possible resolution to the acrimonious struggles between science and religion, between reason and faith, which had preoccupied the leading thinkers of the nineteenth century. Acknowledging the wave of agressive positivism and other-worldly forms of spiritualism, he put forward a doctrine which claimed to reconcile the best of both opposing views. While accepting the findings of rational enquiry and science, Bergson stressed the importance of intuition as a privileged form of knowledge, giving access to the deeper levels of reality which intellect could not fathom: the human self and its transcendence of nature; the mystery of human freedom in a material universe; the distinction between measurable mechanical time and the experience of duration; the limitations of intellect and system in understanding movement, invention, creation and life. Bergson therefore proposed to accept in full the findings of modern scientific enquiry, but to complete them with a further dimension which science could not comprehend.

Although Bergson was of Jewish origin and professed no explicit belief in God, his thought plainly offered many points of interest to christians seeking to reconcile their spiritual beliefs with the modern world. Chevalier perceived this, and in his book, *Bergson* (Paris, 1926), he presented the philosopher as a modern Plato, whose thought could be seen as the preparation for an authentically religious experience. Bergson's later development confirmed the value of this interpretation. His book *Les deux sources de la morale et de la religion* (Paris, 1932) anticipated his eventual acceptance of catholicism, and his thought in many ways served to exemplify the conception of philosophy as a discovery of God.

Bergson's thought was central to Mounier's own development, and it was the christianised form of it that he adopted. In early 1926, Mounier wrote, and had published, lengthy, detailed summaries of Chevalier's lectures on Bergson.[5] At the same time, he was also acting as a kind of unofficial secretary to Chevalier and worked hard to help in the preparation of his teacher's book on Bergson.

Mounier's own writings at this period were often little more than developments of Bergsonian themes along the lines of the christian Bergsonism he took from Chevalier. This tendency was even further emphasised by his encounter with the writings of Bergson's disciple, Charles Péguy.

Chevalier
Mounier's debt to Chevalier, however, goes beyond his Bergsonism. When he had first been entrusted to Chevalier, Mounier's normally timid character had been in an extremely impressionable condition since his recent upheaval. Chevalier's teaching was in complete harmony with what Mounier had been brought up to believe, and in a provincial university where intellectual mediocrity was often the rule, Chevalier's reputation and ability made him a great man by local standards, and an object of admiration for his students. The extent of Mounier's discipleship can be judged by an article of uncritical eulogy which he wrote on the subject of Chevalier and his teaching in 1926, attributing to him qualities of genius, personal magnetism and humility.[6] By the end of his studies in Grenoble he was on intimate terms with his teacher, assisting not only in Chevalier's *Bergson,* but also in an edition of Descartes' *Discours de la méthode* (Paris, 1927), and in organising study groups and seminars for him. In his turn, Chevalier was gratified by the effect he had on this bright pupil, and returned the affection offered. For three years he had almost complete control of Mounier's development, and found him anxious to assimilate everything his master taught him. The relationship between the two was by no means accidental or unusual. It is a good example of the way in which a lay élite was formed within the catholic church. No formal arrangement existed, but a certain number of catholic intellectuals undertook to supervise, with special personal care, gifted young men who came under their tutelage. This mechanism of élite-creation is not confined to the church, but the kind of spiritual patronage involved was particularly highly developed in the French catholic church between the wars. Chevalier was the first, but not the only patron to guide Mounier's steps, and Mounier was not Chevalier's only protégé. When Mounier left Grenoble the spell slowly faded. His own strong and independent character began to assert itself, and within a year he was able to suggest to his mentor that the period had been 'trois années de convalescence et de bonheur trop calmes'.[7] Despite the undeniable mark he left, Chevalier also had the effect of a cocoon, which, having outlived its usefulness, was left behind.

Academic philosophy

In addition to the distinctive influence of Chevalier, Mounier assimilated many other currents of thought during these formative years and already began to lay the basis for the wide-ranging eclecticism which came to characterise his own thought. From Plato, an early enthusiasm of his, he learned ways in which a non-christian philosophy could be used to elucidate or support the catholic faith. Platonic psychology contributed to the construction of Mounier's notion of the human person, and the Platonic theory of forms was influential in his conception of values and value-hierarchies. He also took something of the Greek philosopher's project of moral education and adapted elements of his criticism of forms of society.

Pascal, the seventeenth century moralist whose *Pensées* were Mounier's bedside reading, formed much of his thinking on the spiritual and transcendent dimensions of human existence. The intensity of Pascal's christian faith and his near-obsession with purity made a lasting mark on the young Mounier. It was at this time also that he made his first acquaintance with the medieval scholastic, St Thomas Aquinas, who was enjoying a renewal of interest since the recommendation of his work by Pope Leo XII. St Thomas provided him with a foundation of theological orthodoxy, and fostered a facility for theological discussion which informed many of his later analyses, including major studies on anarchism, property and the problem of war and peace. Maine de Biran, the catholic spiritualist philosopher of the early nineteenth century, inspired some of Mounier's enquiries into the nature of personal identity, with God as the ultimate basis, into the relation between philosophy and religion, and into the intimate relation between life and thought. Maurice Blondel, the catholic academic philosopher of the early twentieth century, helped to stimulate Mounier's thought on the problem of action and the spiritual roots of human activity generally.

Descartes

The culmination of Mounier's university studies was his dissertation for the *Diplôme des Etudes Supérieures*, entitled 'Le conflit de l'anthropocentrisme et du théocentrisme dans la philosophie de Descartes', which he presented on 23 June 1927.[8] Initially he was to have included Descartes, Pascal and Malebranche in his subject, but the two latter were eventually omitted through lack of time. The title was suggested by Chevalier, though Mounier drew also on the work of Henri Bremond, whose *Histoire littéraire du sentiment religieux en France* (Paris, 1916–1933) was, and remains, a major study of conceptions of spirituality in the sixteenth and seventeenth centuries, examining the main themes and figures in devotional literature during that period. He also took much of the analysis set out in Jacques Maritain's recent book *Trois réformateurs* (Paris, 1925), which castigated the damaging errors of Descartes, Luther and Rousseau.

In his study, Mounier examined the relationship between man and God, their respective functions and their place in the order of things. Descartes' thought served as a starting point for a wide-ranging meditation which drew together the threads of what could be called a form of christian humanism. Mounier tried to chart an acceptable path between the flamboyant humanism of the Renaissance which exalted man against God, and the anguished anti-humanism of the Reformation which totally submitted the creature to God. He saw the merit in Descartes' acknowledgment of God as central to the human self and as the necessary foundation and guarantor of all knowledge, and he affirmed the sincerity of Descartes' christianity. The major criticisms levelled at the philosopher were his failure to envisage God as a final end as well as a first principle; his exclusion of divine intervention from the natural world and from the operations of reason; and his reliance on the human will and on reason to construct a practical morality. Although he gave God all the honours on a theoretical level, Mounier emphasised, the practical result was that Descartes relegated him to a realm where he was completely excluded from contact with human reality or the natural world, leaving man as the master of all he surveyed. While he admitted the considerable strength of the Cartesian system, Mounier pointed out that this internal principle of division entailed the risk of engendering successors who, with scant regard for the coherence of the original system, would not hesitate to base their thought on the suppression of one of the terms. In Mounier's eyes, Descartes was therefore responsible for those who regarded him as the father of rationalism and the founder of scientific humanism.

There was little originality in Mounier's study, but his strength never stemmed from original thought. The value of his dissertation lay in Mounier's increasing facility for identifying elements of a thought-system which supported, or were compatible with, orthodox catholic belief and could therefore be assimilated. He showed a firm grasp of the principles of catholic philosophy and a confident ability to apply them theoretically. The specific problem of finding a christian humanism which could synthesise both theocentrism and anthropocentrism remained a driving inspiration of Mounier's own thought in its many forms. Along with a growing number of christians he was driven to define the relevance of his faith and his church in a world which was finding them increasingly dispensable.

The catholic community
Mounier's university studies in philosophy complemented and reinforced the other aspects of his personal and intellectual development. He was brought up to be a conscientious and devout member of the catholic community, and by personal choice he took upon himself an active commitment to defend and further the cause of his church. His philosophical studies armed him for the struggle intellectually, but the most vital part of his training took place outside the academic world. He fulfilled his religious obligations with seriousness and enthusiasm, entering into long and frequent discussions with laity and clergy on matters of faith. He spent long hours in meditation and helped to organise discussion and study groups to deepen his and others' understanding of catholicism. Along with his sister, Madeleine, and a group of like-minded young people, he sought out opportunities and ways of winning over friends, acquaintances and other students to the church. Before long he became a prominent figure in Grenoble's young catholic circles.

One local priest who took an interest in Mounier's development was Father Emile Guerry, who later rose to high office in the French hierarchy. As well as encouraging Mounier in his meditations and his evangelical activities, Father Guerry encouraged him to take an active part in the *Association Catholique de la Jeunesse Française* of which the young priest was an organiser. Founded in 1886, the ACJF was almost entirely a middle-class, and largely student-based organisation, which sought to awaken social and civic awareness among its members, with the more specific aim of forming catholic students to take leading roles in social organisations and public life. Several of Mounier's contemporaries in it became leading members of the post-war christian democrat MRP party, and held government posts. Much of its work consisted in study groups and discussions, and there is no doubt that Mounier received his early political formation in this context. His first two published articles were in the christian democrat newspaper, *La Vie Catholique*, which had close connections with the ACJF, though neither article was political in intention. At this time Mounier was much more preoccupied with moral and metaphysical issues than political or social ones. The comfortable environment in which he lived was further cushioned by the relative stability of the country in the mid-1920s. Politics appeared largely as a matter of reintroducing catholic principles into public life and seemed a long-term project which posed no insoluble problems and possessed no special urgency.

Sharing some of the social concerns of christian democracy was the *Société Saint Vincent de Paul,* an organisation of more traditional stamp which had flourished in the previous century under Frédéric Ozanam, a staunch catholic with a strong social conscience who had led the society energetically from its foundation in 1833. It aimed at uniting catholics of all classes, and reconciling social antagonisms. To this end it undertook charitable works in poor quarters, home-visiting, providing hostel accommodation, improving housing for the workers, christian education for the young, Sunday schools and the like. Although it was generally middle-class, conservative and paternalistic, it did have contact with some poorer sections of the population. Mounier belonged to the Grenoble *conférence,* as the local branches were called, and his involvement in its activities gave him some experience of poverty in the working-class areas of Grenoble, and helped him to understand the intolerable social conditions in which much of the working class lived. Nonetheless, the working class remained a foreign and slightly exotic territory, far removed from the comfort and security of the world in which Mounier and his circle belonged. Though they were concerned and distressed by the misfortunes they witnessed, they were not led to ask any far-reaching questions about them. Poverty was seen as an inevitable and permanent condition which offered an opportunity for the exercise of virtue: charity from the fortunate, forbearance from the unhappy victims. In neither case did it pose any serious problems, nor did it call for urgent remedy.

In his class background, in his personal development and in his social outlook, Mounier shared the experience of young catholics throughout the country. Nothing significantly differentiated his environment from the pattern which prevailed all over France, and for that reason he found so much in common with his contemporaries in the early 1930s. He was singled out in his late teens for an intellectual training which was not accessible to all of his generation, but most of his later associates had been through a comparable process to become the new catholic élite. His attitudes and his skills prepared him to take a leading role in defending the vital interests of the catholic church on an intellectual level. He was groomed to play the part of an avant-garde, with the task of enabling the church to adapt its teachings to the complex and challenging conditions of twentieth century ideological struggle without abandoning the basic values it stood for, and without losing its power and authority over people's minds. Having reached the highest intellectual level Grenoble could accommodate, Mounier's next step was to graduate from his provincial cradle to the intellectual crucible of the capital.

Paris
Though Grenoble was a large provincial town, it fell far short of Paris in the facilities and experiences it could offer. Since the Middle Ages, Paris had come increasingly to monopolise a disproportionate part of French life. It was the centre of wealth and industry; it was there that social conflicts were the most acute; politically and administratively, France had long been ruled from and by Paris; it was the acknowledged international meeting-place for writers, scientists, artists, scholars, musicians and thinkers. In scale and variety the capital dominated France on every level of activity.

On 29 October 1927 at the age of twenty-two, Mounier arrived in Paris to prepare the *agrégation,* the highest academic competition in the French education system. The bewilderment and insecurity he felt at the change was compounded with his suffering as a result of the death in early January 1928 of his only close friend, Georges Barthélemy. This event first provoked religious doubts, but he soon eliminated them and threw himself into preparing the examination. His resulting loneliness eventually drove him to an energetic search for human contact, from which his future role at *Esprit* arose.

He spent the academic year 1927–1928 studying on his own and attending lectures at the *Ecole Normale Supérieure.* He seems to have been little attracted by the teaching but this did not prevent him from being awarded second place in the philosophy *agrégation.* The first place went to Raymond Aron, who later became a prominent right-wing political philosopher and sociologist. The future father of French existentialism, Jean-Paul Sartre, took the examination for the first time in the same year and, against all expectations, failed. Mounier mentioned him in a letter, but it is unlikely they ever came into contact at this time.[9] The experience of his first year in Paris left Mounier with an implacable loathing for all that the Sorbonne represented, for the academics he met there, and for the sophistication, the hypocrisy, the superficiality, and the decadence which seemed to him to distinguish Paris from the provinces. Despite his own position as an intellectual and a philosophy teacher, he remained hostile to the values he associated with the university, and with Parisian intellectual life.

Initially, hostility was a defensive reaction. Some of the most prestigious intellectual circles were dominated by non-catholics, and even the catholic intellectuals had mostly abandoned the woolly mysticism of comfortable nineteenth century piety. Paris was an environment open to a wide range of different currents of thought. The traditions of French rationalism and materialism flourished in new forms; Kantian critical philosophy and Hegelian idealism were still influential; positivism survived in a more subtle guise than the second empire had known; scholastic thought had been revived and updated by the neo-thomists; advances in the natural sciences were once more challenging established ways of thinking; developments in the new human sciences of psychology and sociology were revolutionising existing concepts of man; the first stirrings of existentialism were being felt from Russia, Germany and belatedly, Denmark; marxism was fast emerging as a dynamic and comprehensive intellectual, social and political movement, powerfully supported by the results of the October revolution, now ten years old.

Faced with this intellectual turmoil, Mounier sought the safety of the familiar. His links with Grenoble were still strong, and he maintained a copious correspondence with Chevalier, his own family and his old friends. He struck up a friendship with an old pupil of Chevalier's, Jean Guitton, who later became an eminent catholic scholar and *académicien*. Guitton was a near contemporary whom he had first met in 1924, but who now helped him to settle to Paris life, introducing him to new friends and putting him in contact with some of the Parisian catholic community. Mounier also met Jean Lacroix, a philosophy teacher from Lyon, who was already establishing his reputation as a man of letters. He later joined Mounier's review, *Esprit,* and remained a life-long friend. More influential was the old priest to whom Chevalier sent Mounier at the beginning of his stay and with whom Mounier had a close relationship until the old man's death.

Guillaume Pouget, a Lazarist priest of peasant origin, was gifted with an extraordinary knowledge of scripture and an unusual talent for biblical exegesis. He took upon himself the role of teacher, and in his old age taught a number of young catholics, many of whom became well-known, and among whom figured Jean Lacroix. Though he wrote little, he impressed many who knew him with his wisdom and saintliness. He later played an important part in bringing Bergson to accept catholicism: an act which bears witness to the force of his personality. When Mounier met him in November 1927, Pouget was in his eightieth year and had been blind for twenty years. Mounier was immediately impressed and for nearly five years he worked privately with Pouget two afternoons a week, amassing a considerable documentation on a wide variety of subjects, principally the bible, religious history, mystic saints (notably the two saints Teresa of Avila and John of the Cross) and themes of meditation and action. The old priest's work in helping to form a catholic élite certainly bore fruit in Mounier, who gained from him a deeper knowledge and self-assurance in questions of catholic faith and dogma, which served him well in later years. To these can be added the intangible effects of the humility, simplicity, poverty and wisdom which were later recorded in Jean Guitton's *Portrait de M. Pouget* (Paris, 1941).

Projects
Despite Mounier's dislike of the university, his success in the academic exercise which most typified the Sorbonne assured him of considerable advantages in whatever he chose to do. He saw it as the first step in a traditional academic career, for which he had no inclination, but he was also aware that it opened many other doors. In effect the *agrégation* was a certificate of entry into an intellectual élite. A high placing in the results conferred respect and prestige, as well as a guarantee of secure employment, well remunerated, and offering attractive prospects for advancement. Although he refused a university career, Mounier did not hesitate to use his qualification in other ways, whether to obtain a scholarship or a teaching post, or to establish himself as an intellectual journalist. Even his refusal of a university career was far from clear-cut, since he did accept a three-year grant to prepare a doctoral thesis. Uncertain of his choice of subject, he spent much of his time discussing different topics with various Sorbonne philosophy tutors, who advised him on subjects ranging from Greek stoicism through Spanish mysticism and eighteenth-century moralists to Nietzsche. At the end of his first year he decided to concentrate his efforts on the Spanish mystic, Juan de los Angeles, and with him in mind spent three weeks in the spring of 1930 visiting a number of Spanish cities. Later, he projected a major study on the problem of personality, approached from a biological, juridical, theological, psychological and moral point of view, dealing with the origins and theory of individualism, and with the role of the individual in mystical experience. The ultimate aim of this work was to contribute to a moral renewal, since he considered

that morality had undergone a continuous decline since the middle of the nineteenth century.

Mounier discussed his projects with his professors and with a variety of informal advisers, but his interest was less than whole-hearted. His feeling of alienation was increased by the conflicting advice of different tutors as to which direction he should take, and by his failure in two successive years to be accepted by the Thiers Foundation, a wealthy academic institution which offered research facilities, grants, prestige and other advantages. Though he detested the traditional university system, Mounier recognised its intellectual superiority with a confused mixture of admiration and mistrust. He felt no commitment to the institution and felt only half-hearted about pursuing his research in isolation. Gradually he came to realise that he would not be able to complete his doctorate, and that he was academically lost. But if he was floundering in the world of the university, which he was soon to leave, the three years of his doctorate grant proved both fruitful and decisive on another level. During this time he began his career as a writer, as a journalist and as a teacher, and made important friends.

Catholic politics
The end of the 1920s marked the beginning of a new era in French catholicism. The condemnation of *Action Française* in December 1926 was a political development of great importance, but it was the result of more far-reaching changes. *Intégrisme,* the strongest political movement among catholics, was traditionally strong in more isolated rural and provincial areas, among the aristocracy, the peasantry and to some extent among the liberal professions and students. Nationally, these groups were declining or changing as France moved from an agricultural to an industrially based economy concentrated in larger units and centralised in Paris. Rural depopulation, urbanisation, the proletarianisation of the peasantry, the changing nature of the petty bourgeoisie, and the growth of the industrial working class meant that the new and growing sections of the population were not catered for by the church's dominant tendency. The gradual reconciliation of catholics to parliamentary politics within the republican constitution, albeit of a generally conservative nature, contributed to the situation, as did the restoration of French relations with the Vatican, and the election in 1922 of a more forward-looking pope, Pius XI. A gradual revival of the progressive tendencies within the catholic community was already under way in the immediate post-war years. The survivors and

successors of the liberal and social catholics, of the modernists, and of the catholic republican *Sillon* movement were joined by a new generation which had not lived through the bitter years of the Dreyfus case and the separation a quarter of a century earlier. The condemnation of *Action française* seriously weakened the *intégriste* cause, strengthening in the first instance the conservative republican catholics, but in the longer term aiding progressive catholics, among whom a christian democratic tendency was already emerging as the dominant current.

Mounier had never been attracted to *intégrisme*, and although his mentor, Chevalier, was of conservative republican leanings, Mounier had had more contact with progressive elements among his own generation. He had, as yet, little interest or experience in political matters. Appropriately, he was introduced to politics by his next mentor, an eminent philosopher for whom the condemnation of 1926 had been a traumatic event, Jacques Maritain.

Maritain

Maritain, born in 1882 of a Protestant family, had been converted, with his wife, to catholicism in 1906. During his successful career as a scholar and philosopher, he had acquired a high esteem in catholic circles, and contributed much to the Thomist revival in France. He had also been heavily involved with *Action française* and, in the wake of its disavowal by Rome, was beginning to grope for a new political philosophy compatible with his catholic faith. He set down his first conclusions in a book, *Primauté du spirituel* (Paris, 1927), which had a great influence on many young catholics. His argument was directly inspired by the lessons of 1926. On the one hand the church, he said, having jurisdiction in all ethical and spiritual matters, was superior to politics in the hierarchy of values. In so far as moral and metaphysical questions were involved in politics, he argued, the church had an indirect power over temporal affairs, and the right to define the extent of its own intervention. On the other hand, he insisted, the church must never be subordinated to, or annexed by any political party or ideology, right-wing or left-wing, since the temporal had no jurisdiction in spiritual matters. The church in its wisdom left it to the conscience of the individual to choose his political preferences, he argued, though it had the right to condemn those it saw as incompatible with the faith. He insisted that there was a difference between action *en chrétien* and action *en tant que chrétien*, which meant that a particular political commitment could be inspired by but not necessitated by christian principles. In many respects Maritain's political philosophy was an articulation of the currents of thought underlying the ACJF. Later it was taken widely to offer a theoretical basis for christian democracy, though Maritain always took care to keep a distance from that movement, which he regarded with critical sympathy.

Mounier was strongly influenced by *Primauté du spirituel* and made its basic ideas his own, while remaining reticent about Maritain's simultaneous call for a return to the principles (though not the institutions) of the middle ages. In this way there was much common ground between them when the two men eventually met towards the end of 1928. By virtue of his eminence and the wide-ranging network of personal relationships which he and his wife had established, Maritain held the key to an important section of the christian intellectual milieu in Paris, as well as part of the provincial intelligentsia. The monthly gatherings at the Maritains' home in the Paris suburb of Meudon were centres of debate and information which attracted a wide variety of thinkers and artists. As well as meeting many of his own contemporaries, Mounier there met writers of the stature of Gabriel Marcel, the dramatist, critic and christian existentialist philosopher; Charles du Bos, the art historian, literary critic and essayist; Marcel Arland, the journalist, novelist and man of letters; and Nicolas Berdyaev, the expatriate Russian orthodox mystic and existential philosopher. Through Maritain, Mounier had an early and privileged introduction to the most energetic and influential of the christian and particularly catholic laymen. In this way he quickly established a network of sympathy and support which stood him in good stead during the rest of his life. Once again, the mechanisms of catholic élite-formation operated efficiently, and Maritain, the last of Mounier's living mentors, proved to be his most useful patron. The extent of Maritain's value was repeatedly demonstrated both in Mounier's own career and in the success of *Esprit* in its early years.

The 'Davidées'

At the same period, Mounier also made contact with a catholic group, which, though humbler than the parisian intelligentsia, was in its way just as valuable to him. At Easter 1929, Jean Guitton introduced him to a movement among primary school teachers. Based in Aix-en-Provence, the *Davidées,* who took their name from the heroine of René Bazin's novel, *Davidée Birot,* were a group of catholic teachers in state schools. As well as forming a circle of friendship, they held devotional and intellectual retreats, and published a monthly bulletin entitled *Aux Davidées*. Their aim was to enrich their intellectual and spiritual lives, to sustain each other in their religious beliefs, and to explore ways of putting their beliefs into legitimate forms of action within their professional lives. In this they received considerable support from the clergy. The initiator and inspiration of the movement was Mlle Silve, a teacher whose spirituality made an immediate impression on Mounier, and whose simplicity and serenity led him to return several times to the movement's meetings. Not only did he find peace, however, he also saw there a first tentative solution to the problem of action. Until this time he had seen two possibilities—either to remain a sedentary intellectual, with unsullied integrity but without effective influence, or to commit himself to effective action and accept the accompanying party discipline, lies and erosion of spiritual life. With the *Davidées* he saw a pure, discreet, but apparently effective form of action based on spiritual values and carried out through personal contact.

Mounier was so enthusiastic that he offered to write a regular column in the monthly bulletin. The offer was gratefully accepted, and from November 1929 under the heading *Lettres philosophiques* he contributed a series of articles some five or six pages long, intended to provide the reader with a means of approaching philosophical subjects, usually in the form of an edifying discourse expressed in simple language. Written under the pseudonym of Jean Sylvestre, they are of no great interest outside their immediate context, but reflect the preoccupations he was also expressing elsewhere. Descartes and themes of meditation were gradually replaced by Péguy, Maritain and themes of action, but since his contributions were all aimed at a devout catholic audience, they tended to fall too easily into pious homily. Mounier was aware of his prestigious position and like many other intellectuals conceived himself as an intermediary between the people and the truth. The tendency for French writers to consider themselves as a kind of lay clergy was implicit in many of the debates between the wars, though it was by no means unique to the period. Julien Benda's book *Le trahison des clercs* (Paris, 1927) is a characteristic example. Sartre, as he described himself in *Les Mots* (Paris, 1964), also had a similar conception.

Despite the apparent innocence of their activities, the *Davidées* were operating in a sensitive and politically contentious area. After the revolution of 1789, education in France was taken over by the state, and religious teaching was forbidden. Since that time successive governments had given a varying amount of freedom to religious orders to administer their own schools, but the principle of secularity in the state system remained. The question of religious education was a constant source of conflict, though much of the bitterness which followed the separation of church and state in 1905 had abated by the mid-1920s. It was indicative of the new climate that so many young catholics were willing and able to teach in state schools, though they were at times viewed with suspicion by non-catholic colleagues. In the spring of 1930, the *Davidées* came under attack from a teachers' organisation, the *Ligue de l'enseignement,* which was pledged to defending the principle of secularity. A leading member of the *Ligue,* the socialist Marceau Pivert, accused them of subverting the laicity of public education. They were, he said, a secret society intent on infiltrating among and converting primary school teachers with the active support of the catholic hierarchy and its various organisations.[10]

Although he exaggerated the strength of the *Davidées* and overestimated their effectiveness, Pivert's interpretation of their action as 'une entreprise de noyautage' was quite compatible with the facts. Amid the controversy that raged for some months afterwards, Mounier wrote an article in their defence.[11] Speaking under a pseudonym, he held that their action was valuable from a catholic point of view, entirely consistent with the principle of secular education and protected by the constitutional right of freedom of thought. His long, closely documented and argued article was reproduced separately and distributed in some quantity. It may have helped the movement to weather the crisis, and certainly won Mounier friends among catholic teachers, many of whom later helped to form the hard core of *Esprit* subscribers. The substance of his defence was to reject Pivert's suspicions as implying an unreasonable degree of Machiavellian intention on the teachers' part. The posture of wounded innocence was, however, too ingenuous to be plausible, and although he was probably right in asserting that the letter of the law had not been transgressed, he could not convincingly argue that the *Davidées* were observing the spirit of secularity in education. At all events, the group survived the attack though they were obliged to exercise more caution in their activities. Mounier drew from this affair a new experience of public controversy since he was for the first time seriously embattled on an important political issue. He also gained valuable training in the skills of philosophical and political journalism, on which much of his later influence depended.

Professional training
During the same period, Mounier had a similar, though less controversial, involvement with another publication for provincial teachers. With the title *Après ma classe, revue de culture générale*, the first half of which was later dropped, the magazine was aimed at an audience roughly half of whom were catholic, and reached a circulation of about 2,500. Published in the Gard region, it was founded in January 1929 for the benefit of young primary school teachers, with the intention of contributing to their personal education and development, particularly since they often found themselves teaching in isolated surroundings. As an *agrégé*, Mounier's own teaching posts were at a much higher level: he taught on a part-time basis, to supplement his grant, in a series of secondary schools in France and Belgium. Nonetheless he was happy to offer his philosophical talents and after two confused, self-satisfied and condescending pieces, signed *un ami*, Mounier contributed a regular column from early 1929 to the Summer of 1932. The articles dealt with a wide variety of philosophical and moral topics, generally reflecting his own current preoccupations. Writing them helped Mounier to define his own thought, to develop his powers of expression and to adjust to a partly non-catholic audience. These articles and those he wrote for the *Davidées* all strengthened his confidence as a member of the intellectual élite and enabled him to explore the rôle of spiritual leader which he already saw as his vocation.

A less edifying, but equally necessary, experience completed Mounier's apprenticeship in journalism. From late 1929 until the end of 1931, he contributed forty book-reviews to *La Quinzaine critique*, a new fortnightly which undertook to review new publications. His regular appraisals of philosophical works were largely devoted to uninteresting original works and editions of well-known texts, since Jacques Chevalier, the other philosophical reviewer, was given the choice of all major works. Apart from three of Chevalier's works, Mounier saw little of interest, though he was occasionally able to draw from this reading for his other writings. The staff of the review also included Gabriel Marcel and Jean Bruller, who later won fame in the resistance as 'Vercors', but since the context afforded him little contact with either, the only benefits he drew from this work were a few francs and a lot of experience in book-reviewing.

Péguy

The last and most decisive element in Mounier's early intellectual formation was undoubtedly the work of Charles Péguy. Péguy, who was killed in 1914 in action at the battle of the Marne at the age of 41, was a poet and journalist who had moved from an early socialism to a highly individual form of catholicism. A leading *dreyfusard* and a staunch republican, his main work was published in the *Cahiers de la Quinzaine,* a periodical which Péguy edited and directed. His socialism was of the utopian kind, expressed in visions of a future harmonious society which served as a touchstone for moral denunciations of the present imperfect one. His conversion to catholicism infused his social and political commitments with a mystical dimension which tended to subordinate reason to moral intuition. Péguy soon discovered a close affinity with Bergson and declared himself a disciple of the philosopher, taking his defence in a succession of controversies. The religious lyricism which animated much of his poetry was associated with fervent patriotism, a combination which he saw as being embodied in the French national martyr, Jeanne d'Arc, beatified in 1909. The curious mixture of Péguy's thought made him an ambiguous figure during his lifetime, and ensured that he was claimed by both right and left after his death. His ardent followers in the 1920s included writers like Henri Massis and Maurice Barrès, both closely associated with *Action française,* and also people like Robert Garric, journalist and youth organiser, and Maurice de Gandillac, philosopher and critic, both identified with the liberal, more socially conscious elements of the catholic intelligentsia. This division among those who felt themselves to be sympathisers, if not followers, of Péguy stemmed from the ambiguities, and frequently the contradictions, which coexisted within his thought, laying it open to conflicting interpretations. Péguy was alternately annexed by nationalists and by democrats with apparent ease, and it seemed that almost any shade of political opinion could find support in his writings.

In the spring of 1929, Mounier re-read some of Péguy's works, and was immediately filled with enthusiasm for him. He developed the idea of writing a book on him. Maritain, who was responsible for editing a series of philosophical and religious books for Plon's *Roseau d'Or* collection, asked Mounier, along with two other young men, Marcel Péguy, the writer's son, and Georges Izard, a young lawyer, to prepare manuscripts on Péguy for him.

Mounier, in undertaking the task, examined the relation between eternal spiritual values and the problems of their expression in the temporal, physical world. Though he saw the weaknesses and contradictions in Péguy's proposed solutions to the decay and ultimate destitution of the material world and social life, Mounier stressed the importance of the moral transformation Péguy called for, the purification of the temporal by the effects of a spiritual revolution. Throughout his book, Mounier raised problems which were central to his own preoccupations. His analyses developed themes which had been central to his education as well as issues arising from the career in intellectual journalism which he now saw as his vocation.

The importance of Péguy, however, lies less in his specific ideas than in the effect of his example. By his training and inclination, Mounier was disposed to welcome much of Péguy's thought, as did many catholics of his generation. Péguy combined an imaginative interpretation of Bergson with a clear development towards catholicism, and thereby found an immediate response in the young Mounier, imbued as he was with Chevalier's teaching. But he particularly admired Péguy as a person, for he seemed to embody the heroic and spiritual virtues of catholicism and focus all that Mounier held valuable into a striking and attractive model. This deep affinity emboldened Mounier to explore the dangerous paths which led away from the traditional conservatism of provincial piety, without feeling that he was betraying the essence of his faith. The political dimensions of Péguy's writing, his utopian socialism and his republican *dreyfussisme* could be translated twenty years later into revolutionary personalism and anti-fascism without too much difficulty. The terms had changed, but the same spirit presided. Péguy's slogan 'La révolution sera morale ou elle ne sera pas' became Mounier's motto, occurring most strikingly at the head of his first article in *Esprit*.[12] It sums up the essence of the utopian socialism which both men shared: that the transformation of society should and would be produced by a prior commitment to truth, justice and spiritual values, arising within men's minds and hearts. Mounier was permanently marked by his encounter with Péguy. Consciously and unconsciously he followed his example on innumerable occasions. As time passed Péguy's domination of his thought decreased, but it was powerful during the most formative years of Mounier's intellectual development, and more than any of his living patrons, Péguy can be considered as Mounier's mentor.

The book, *La pensée de Charles Péguy,* appeared after some delay in January 1931. Despite the economic slump, which was affecting book-sales, it was bought in good numbers, and the critics received it favourably. Warm reviews in the influential literary review *Nouvelle Revue Française,* and the authoritative Jesuit monthly journal, *Etudes,* indicated the quality of Mounier's work. More revealing, though, was the heavily sarcastic attack which it provoked from Henri Massis in the long-established journal of the extreme right, *La Revue universelle.* This led to a polemic between Mounier and Massis, taking up a heated exchange they had already had after a lecture given by the young right-wing journalist Jean-Pierre Maxence, who had just written a book on Péguy.[14] Massis and Mounier each vehemently contested the validity of the other's interpretation of Péguy, and the incident marked Mounier's first real conflict with the right-wing catholic groups. Mounier earned the undying malevolence of Massis, but, more important, began to see his own political standpoint clarified in practice.

The formation of an intellectual
The spring of 1931 is an appropriate time to pause and assess Mounier's development, since in many ways it marked the end of his apprenticeship. At the age of twenty-six he was approaching the end of his formal studies, having decided not to pursue his doctorate. He had published his first book and a large number of articles; he was having his first taste of public controversy, with Massis and the *Davidées* affair; and he was already laying firm plans for founding a new review.

Mounier's sheltered upbringing in a pious, petty-bourgeois, provincial home led easily to a narrow but intensive philosophical training. He was a talented and serious student, receptive to the friendly guidance of a philosophy professor for whom he felt a strong intellectual and personal attraction, but who could only offer him limited intellectual nourishment. Mounier was taught the great classics, a handful of nineteenth-century catholic thinkers and Bergson. He was virtually ignorant of recent movements within France and of most non-French thought. Apart from peripheral involvement in student organisations with a limited social orientation, his world was virtually restricted to philosophy and religion. Political events and social movements, in or out of France, made no noticeable impact on him: he was cushioned by a comfortable social position in a period of relative prosperity, by the provincial insularity of Grenoble, and by his choice of contemplative pursuits.

Leaving home, he found Paris a foreign, hostile place. Naturally he sought out people who would sympathise with the ways of his home environment and for two or three years he lived protected by a strong defensive mechanism which excluded many ideas and experiences which were now offered to him. During this time he acquired a basic training in the skills of a writer, journalist and intellectual; he met and was accepted by a small intellectual circle; he consolidated his ideas without significantly enlarging them; and he began to grope towards some idea of what he was going to do with his life. Maritain and Péguy were beginning to form in him some basic notions of political philosophy, preparing the groundwork for a form of catholic socialism, which as yet was remote and unformulated. Though he hated the university and disliked intellectuals, he was by the spring of 1931 a fully-fledged, university-trained, catholic intellectual, supported by experienced patrons who were anxious to groom him and smooth his way to establishing himself as a member of their élite. All he lacked was experience. But already he was taking the first steps in his public existence as an intellectual and was becoming aware of a wide range of issues which gradually began to draw him out of his cloister.

Notes

1 E. Mounier, *Oeuvres*, 4 vols (Paris 1961–1963) IV p417. (Hereafter, this work is referred to simply as *Oeuvres* with volume number.)
2 *Esprit*, décembre 1950, p940, in a letter to his sister dated 19 décembre 1925.
3 *Esprit*, décembre 1950, p941.
4 See particularly Chevalier's pamphlet, *L'individu, souverain maître de la vie* (Lyon 1923).
5 These summaries appeared between March and July 1926 in the journal *Revue de cours et de conférences*.
6 'Un penseur français, Jacques Chevalier', *La Vie Catholique*, 3e année, no79, 3 avril 1926, p1–2.
7 *Oeuvres* IV p422–423.
8 Only one copy survives, kept in the Bibliothèque Mounier at Châtenay-Malabry.
9 *Oeuvres* IV p435.
10 The speech, delivered on 7 June 1930, was reprinted under the title 'Une entreprise de "noyautage" de l'enseignement public—les Davidées', in *L'Ecole Libératrice*, 28 Juin 1930, p553–554.
11 'Une amitié spirituelle: Les Davidées', *La Vie Spirituelle*, no139, avril-juin 1931, p66–91, signed "François Chauvières".
12 *Oeuvres* I p137.
13 A. Thibaudet, 'Réflexions—Péguy et Bergson', *Nouvelle Revue Française*, no211, avril 1931, p580–592; Gabriel Marcel, 'Compte rendu', *Nouvelle Revue Française* no212, mai 1931, p747–750; P. Defrennes, 'Chefs de file', *Études*, tome 208, 20 juillet 1931, p169–188.

14 See Henri Massis, 'Charles Péguy et l'Agrégé', *Revue Universelle*, tome XLIV, no24, 15 mars 1931, p742–747; and Henri Massis, 'Péguy et l'Agrégé (suite)', *Revue Universelle*, tome XLV, no2, 15 avril 1931, p227–230.

Bibliographical Notes

The historical material is widely available, but particularly useful studies are: A. Cobban, *A History of Modern France*, vol 3 (London 1965); D. W. Brogan, *The French Nation 1814–1940* (London 1957); G. Wright, *France in Modern Times* (Chicago 1960); T. Zeldin, *France 1848–1945*, vol 1 (London 1973). Valuable studies of the religious developments are: A. Dansette, *Histoire religieuse de la France contemporaine* (Paris 1965). A. Dansette, *Destin du catholicisme français 1926–1956* (Paris 1957); R. Kothen, *La pensée et l'action sociale des catholiques, 1789–1944* (Louvain 1945); J. -B. Duroselle, *Les debuts du catholicisme social en France* (Paris 1951); G. Le Bras, *Études de sociologie religieuse* (Paris 1955). A detailed examination of Grenoble is contained in P. Barral, *Le département de l'Isère sous le Troisième République 1870–1940* (Paris 1962).

There is no standard biography of Mounier. The major source of information is the anthology of letters and notebooks edited by his widow Mme Paulette Mounier as *Mounier et sa génération* (Paris 1956), reprinted, with alterations, in E. Mounier, *Oeuvres*, IV (Paris 1963) p407–831. This material is incomplete, however, and is partly complemented by the special number of *Esprit* devoted to Mounier (décembre 1950, no174, 721–1080) particularly the article compiled by Albert Béguin as 'Une vie', *ibid*, p923–1060. Additional information can be gleaned from the twice-yearly *Bulletin des amis d'Emmanuel Mounier* which contains much otherwise unpublished material.

Many studies exist on Bergson, the most useful being Ian Alexander, *Bergson* (Cambridge 1957) and Vladimir Jankélévitch, *Bergson* (Paris 1959). Little has been written on Jacques Chevalier, but a useful short study is A. Guy, *Métaphysique et intuition: le message de Jacques Chevalier* (Paris 1940). Le père Pouget has been well served by Jean Guitton's *Portrait de M. Pouget* (Paris 1941), and there is interesting material on his part in Bergson's conversion in Jacques Chevalier's *Bergson et le père Pouget* (Paris 1954). A good study of Maritain's philosophy is J. Croteau, *Les fondements thomistes du personnalisme de Maritain* (Ottawa 1955); a useful work is Joseph Amato, *Mounier and Maritain* (Alabama 1975); Jacques Petit's edition of the correspondence is also valuable, *Maritain-Mounier 1929–1939* (Paris 1973). There is much information in Maritain's own autobiographical *Paysan de la Garonne* (Paris 1966). The intellectual milieu of 1920s Paris is well conveyed in Raissa Maritain's *Les grandes amitiés* (Paris 1962); Nicolas Berdyaev's *Dream and Reality* (London 1950); and Helen Iswolsky's *Light before Dusk* (New York 1942). A useful account, which reprints Mounier's article defending the group, is Jean Guitton's study *Les Davidées* (Paris 1967), to which should be added the article by M. Silve & A. Germain, 'Les Davidées', *Cahiers universitaires catholiques*, mars 1961, p410–416. There are many studies of Péguy, the most thorough being Jean Delaporte, *Connaissance de Péguy* 2 vols (Paris 1944; revised edition 1959).

CHAPTER TWO

The Foundations of Personalism (1931–1935)

The crisis of the 1930s
After the relative tranquillity of post-war recovery, France was gradually feeling the effects of the international economic crisis. The Wall Street crash of October 1929 had shaken the structures of international trade and finance, and initiated the great depression, but France was cushioned from its immediate effects and only seriously began to suffer two years later. The resulting social disruption affected all aspects of French life, and no one from the year 1931 onwards thought to deny that there was a crisis however they interpreted it. The growing problems of inflation, declining standards of living, and unemployment, with all that entailed, began to strike not only at the working class, who were accustomed to them, but also at the more privileged social classes. With the crisis spreading rapidly to all sectors of the economy, it was not long before repercussions became visible in political life and thought. There was a growth in the strength of movements which undertook to bring radical and, if necessary, violent remedies to the major social and economic problems. The increasing polarisation between the extremes of left and right threw the more moderate traditional parties into disarray, obliging them to seek new solutions if they could.

The traditional right, grouped around the extreme monarchist newspaper and movement, *Action Française*, was expanding into a number of small but related leagues. They were fiercely nationalistic and often modelled on a military pattern. Increasingly they were looking to Italy and Germany, where impressive fascist movements were already attracting international attention. The left had split into two after 1920. The communist party was committed to the Soviet-led third international and professed a strict marxist-leninism. The socialist party had kept its national exclusiveness and followed the syndicalist tradition within French socialism. The communists had increasingly won the support of the urban working class and looked to the bolshevik revolution for their inspiration, whereas the socialists had their base in the middle classes and rural areas, and offered a more moderate social democratic programme for political change. Between socialism and nationalism were all the centrist currents which had developed from the successive controversies of the third republic. Largely conservative and pragmatic in their attitudes, they found their most characteristic expression in the post-enlightenment liberalism of Alain, which particularly animated the 'radical' parties. Alain (1868–1951), a philosophy teacher from Normandy, had not constructed any systematic political philosophy, but his short aphoristic essays, the *Propos,* put forward a mistrust of central government, calling for a limitation of state power. Broadly within this body of political attitudes was a small christian democratic current. It grouped many catholics who accepted the republic but mistrusted the major republican parties which tended to keep to the anti-clericalism of their origins.

The church had, from the earliest days of the republic, been identified politically with the anti-republican, monarchist, nationalist right. There was no theoretical obligation on catholics to take this position, but in practice the majority had done so. At the turn of the century an evolution had begun away from this position, taking some impetus from Leo XIII's encyclical *Rerum novarum,* which was published on 15th March 1891. Devoted to the condition of labour, it was the first major statement from the church on the position of workers in modern industrial societies. Although the same pope had warned against the dangers of christian democracy in his encyclical *Graves de communi,* of January 1901, there was at least a genuine attempt on the part of the church to understand the modern problems of democracy and social justice. The way was left open for catholics to explore political positions other than the traditional right. The decision in 1926 to place *Action française* on the index of prohibited books made it more urgent for catholics to look elsewhere for solutions to the problems posed by the post-war state of society. In May 1931, in the middle of the economic and social crisis, Pius XI issued the encyclical *Quadragesimo anno* which spoke out sharply against the evils and abuses of the capitalist system and attempted to lay down structures for a solution to some of the problems, strongly inspired by corporatist theory. Despite its shortcomings, the encyclical had the effect of calling catholics to a reappraisal of their social thought, and although it continued to anathematise socialism and communism, it did suggest a limited measure of political reform.

Political developments were accompanied by less dramatic, but equally far-reaching ideological developments. The crisis sharpened the need for French intellectuals to produce a serious conceptual framework for understanding their times. The old middle-class secular ideologies of liberal individualism were being found inadequate to deal with urgent social problems. Positivist and rationalist methods were incapable of analysing the movements, changes and conflicts of which even intellectuals were becoming increasingly aware. The major alternative secular ideology was an aggressive marxism which brought new concepts and methods of analysis but was politically revolutionary and socially working-class. The old religious ideology of the catholic church was also under pressure. It had already virtually lost the urban working class to marxism. An increasing proportion of its members belonged to the middle-classes and were strongly influenced by the liberal individualism there. If the church was to retain its strength it had to speak to the working-class, rural and urban, it had to purge itself of the contamination from decaying middle-class ideologies, and it had to address itself to the acute social issues, offering a plausible analysis and general guidelines helpful to all classes.

In *Quadragesimo anno* Pius XI restated the church's rejection of individualism as well as of collectivism. He spoke on issues such as the nature of property relations, the relations between capital and labour, trade unions and the role of the state in social and economic affairs. In each case he tried to make constructive suggestions based on the church's traditional understanding of the nature of man in society, but also taking into account the extremes of social inequality and injustice which existed in modern societies. As a practical plan, the pope's suggestions were generally ignored; but for catholics of the rising generation the encyclical had the effect of asserting the relevance of the church's social doctrine and of impelling them to re-examine its theoretical foundations.

The new movements
To Emmanuel Mounier, a young catholic in the spring of 1931, it was difficult to avoid feeling the need to participate in the search for new political, social and ideological solutions. His participation was solicited from many sides. Maritain encouraged him to join in the rethinking, which he himself was undertaking independently. Maritain also put him into contact with a number of young men who

were already engaged in similar work, for Mounier was something of a late-comer to this scene. Something of the energy and urgency of this rethinking can be judged from the explosion at this period in the number of new periodical reviews appearing in France, not restricted to catholics, but most of them under the impulse of men and women who had been too young to fight in the Great War, and who now had reached adulthood. Late in 1932, the influential *Nouvelle Revue Française* published an anthology of essays which aimed to represent the views of the main currents, ranging from the young communist intellectuals Paul Nizan and Henri Lefebvre to the young Maurrassien Thierry Maulnier.[1] The elements they shared in common were a denunciation of the existing state of society and a determination to renew the intellectual traditions from which they came. Nizan and Lefebvre rapidly dissociated themselves from any sort of solidarity with the rest, seeing them as a refurbished form of the old bourgeois intelligentsia, anti-marxist and probably in some cases crypto-fascist.[2] Otherwise, the group, dominated by young catholics, shared a refusal to participate in any of the established political categories, adopting the slogan *ni droite ni gauche* to emphasise the point. This was combined with radical social and spiritual transformations, a desire to elaborate an intellectual blueprint for the new world, and a total lack of practical experience in applying their abstract conceptualisations.

The young writers represented, including Mounier, were characterised by a desire for innovation which tended to mask their differences. Not all were catholics, but the ideology which provided their main point of reference was catholic, and their vocabulary was drawn from this common inheritance. Politically, they were relatively innocent and had not yet been forced by events to define their positions in practice, but already three groups were distinguishable. The *Jeune Droite* did not hide the political tradition to which it felt closest, and the names of its characteristic reviews, *Réaction* and *La revue française*, clearly marked it out as 'reactionary' and nationalistic. Its spokesman, Thierry Maulnier, who advocated violent revolution, since spiritual means were ineffective, was a close friend and collaborator of Jean-Pierre Maxence and Jean de Fabrègues, the leading figures of the movement. Though their views derived mainly from Charles Maurras, they were concerned to escape from the narrow orthodoxy of *Action Française*, which had lost much support. The second group, and the one most heavily represented in the NRF anthology, was known as *Ordre nouveau*, though it should not be confused with the fifth republic fascist group of the same name.

Catering for apolitical and independent young intellectuals, it sought, under the inspiration of a young lawyer-turned-librarian, Arnaud Dandieu, to build an original philosophy, cutting across the old divisions and making friends from the communists to the monarchists. The third group, and the most politically progressive of the young catholic movements, was centred on the review *Esprit*, of which Mounier was by this time the director. Close to *Ordre nouveau* both in personnel and in general orientation, *Esprit* appeared more determined to give its views practical political implementation and was anxious to dissociate itself from any connexion with the rightwing tradition. None of the three groups offered a distinct conceptual framework nor any basis for an independent political ideology. The future of the *Jeune Droite* was a complete assimilation into the traditional right, the future of *Ordre nouveau* was an increasingly irrelevant abstraction, leading to a brief flirtation with fascism and an early dissolution. The future of *Esprit* was longer and more complex than either.

The emergence of 'Esprit'
The notion of founding a new review had arisen during discussions with Maritain and his circle. Two of Mounier's contemporaries were following a similar development to himself: Georges Izard, the young lawyer who was contributing to the book on Péguy, and André Déléage, a librarian at the Sorbonne and later in Toulouse. Independently Mounier on the one hand and Izard and Déléage on the other were contemplating ways of giving their thought a practical expression which might influence not particular events but the spiritual fabric of modern civilisation. All three thought, partly under the influence of Péguy's example, that a new review might provide the solution. So when on the night of 7th December 1930 Izard asked Mounier to direct the review he and Déléage had decided to found, Mounier had no hesitation in agreeing to abandon his reluctant teaching career to take on the task.

Material difficulties made progress slow but through Maritain the young men had access to a large sector of the catholic intelligentsia, and found there an important pool of sympathy. By the end of 1931 they had promises of aid from philosophers of the stature of Nicolas Berdyaev, Maurice Blondel, Paul Archambault, Etienne Gilson, Henri Bremond, René Le Senne and Louis Lavelle. Maritain himself adopted the rôle of guarantor to the review, which soon acquired the name *Esprit,* probably Mounier's suggestion. The catholic communication network, lay and clerical, was a valuable instrument in making contacts, enlarging the mailing list and soliciting support. Once it was generally known that the project was considered important by respected intellectuals and churchmen, there was a vital fund of goodwill and energy made available. Financial difficulties were never easy to resolve, but with energy, initiative and strong sponsorship they were eventually overcome.

Throughout the first half of 1932 preparations continued. Publication, which had first been planned for late 1931, then for Easter 1932, was fixed for October 1932. The delay, while provoking some frustration, gave time for the financial situation to improve but, more important, allowed Mounier the leisure to collect a substantial fund of material and promised contributions to choose from in his first issue. Helpful though Maritain was, he tended to suggest mainly writers of his own generation whose reputation was already established. Mounier did not wish to be burdened by too many older men who might tend to turn the review into a pale reflection of existing periodicals. His main problem was to discover writers of his own age group of sufficient calibre to maintain high literary and intellectual standards while offering fresh and adventurous analyses which would distinguish the review from its respected, but staid predecessors. In the time at his disposal he was able to gather around him an impressive team of young intellectuals. Mounier, Izard and Déléage were joined by Louis-Emile Galey, a young architect and journalist; Jean Daniélou, a Jesuit seminarian who eventually rose to become a Cardinal; Jean Lacroix, the young philosopher; André Ulmann, the political and economic commentator; Edmond Humeau, the poet and literary critic; Denis de Rougemont, the Swiss protestant critic and journalist, who also brought many of his *Ordre nouveau* colleagues to contribute in *Esprit*. Though they did not all remain with the review, these young men assured it a high level of analysis and comment in the crucial days when it was establishing its reputation.

Having assured the quality of the contributors and sufficient finances, the editors had to face the first of a long succession of political problems which, even before its appearance, beset *Esprit*. It had been agreed from an early date that the review should not be just another theoretical magazine, but that it should be co-ordinated with a movement and eventually, possibly, a political party. Déléage and Izard had originally intended the review to be the theoretical organ of the movement, whereas Mounier, encouraged by Maritain, was primarily concerned with establishing a review which would inspire a movement founded on its principles.

THE FOUNDATIONS OF PERSONALISM (1931–1935)

In the autumn of 1931 a number of study groups were set up, from which there grew two tendencies. The one, centred on Mounier, was concerned with creating a new doctrine; the other, centred on Déléage, was concerned to initiate action, Izard providing the liaison between the two. Throughout the early months of 1932 the debate simmered, Mounier and Déléage both intransigent in trying to impose their conflicting visions. The struggle, however, was unequal, for Mounier had powerful support from Maritain and his associates, who felt they could trust only Mounier to put sufficient emphasis on spiritual and theoretical questions. It was therefore Déléage who, through Izard's diplomacy, yielded. It was agreed that the review should be independent of the movement, but that the movement should remain faithful to the doctrines elaborated by the review, except in so far as the tactical demands of concrete action prevented their strict application. It was implicit that the Mounier-Izard combination would keep both sections together: Izard being a member of Mounier's editorial board, Mounier being a member of Izard's central committee. This solution survived a turbulent but decisive confrontation at the review's pre-publication conference of Font-Romeu in the Alps in August 1932. In theoretical terms it meant the priority of principle over practice, of the spiritual over the material and of philosophy over politics. In practical terms it meant the separation of thought and action, which was at the root of *Esprit*'s perpetual inability to give its principles any concrete implementation.

Nonetheless, the August conference produced two tangible results. First, a political movement was constituted under the name *Troisième Force*, to provide a radical alternative to capitalism and communism. It was intended that it should work closely within the doctrinal limits laid down at Font-Romeu, and that it should seek new and effective means of implementing spiritual principles in a temporal context. Second, the review was launched with its first issue settled for the following October. As its director, Mounier was in a strong position personally. Control of a substantial intellectual undertaking was in his hands, and since the *Troisième Force* initially had a public existence only through the review, he could expect to exercise a considerable influence on its development, even though it was nominally independent. In addition, this crucial victory had conferred on him a substantial measure of authority both in his own eyes, and in the eyes of the entire group. He was master in his own house, and enjoyed the trust of a large section of the catholic intelligentsia, many of whom looked back with nostalgia to the early years of the century when a succession of prominent intellectuals and writers were converted to catholicism, including Maritain and Péguy. Mounier was widely expected to lead another similar spiritual revival, Such expectations could be excused, since many of Mounier's ideas and aims seemed to encourage them. But Mounier himself was slowly developing and, more important, the situation in France in the 1930s called for a quite different approach.

The spiritual revolution

When the first number of *Esprit* appeared in October 1932, it was dominated by a lengthy article by Mounier with the title 'Refaire la Renaissance'.[3] It was a re-worked version of the paper which had been accepted at Font-Romeu as defining the spiritual directions of the review. In effect it was a detailed statement of basic principles. The renaissance, evoked by the title, was generally held by catholics to mark the beginning of an individualism which wantonly destroyed the medieval catholic order and undermined both the church and spiritual life. The project of remaking the renaissance situated Mounier's concerns in the broadest possible field, not merely philosophical, nor political, nor religious, but encompassing the movement of an entire civilisation. The motto from Péguy heading the article, 'la révolution sera morale ou elle ne sera pas', recalled the *Cahiers de la Quinzaine* and asserted that a moral and spiritual revolution was the prerequisite to any worthwhile social and political transformation. The first lines declared the conviction that *l'esprit,* or *le spirituel,* was the fundamental motive principle of the world, but did not stop to define these crucial terms. There was no new theory of reality involved, however, for Mounier was using a vocabulary which would command easy recognition and a ready acceptance in the predominantly catholic milieu to which he was addressing himself. *Le spirituel* could refer at the same time to the Bergsonian concept of the spirit, to the christian notion of spiritual forces, to the church in its temporal manifestations, to the values of mind and intelligence, and to the intelligentsia in general, be it religious or secular.

The present crisis, he continued, was provoked by material factors, and while that crisis was real enough, it was only the visible sign of a profound disorder in the spiritual world which, though less apparent, was more far-reaching. Mounier made it clear that his main battle was not to be fought in the political arena, nor were his goals primarily political; but since politics and spirituality were historically linked, he felt he could not evade the problem. He suggested first that the traditional identification of the spiritual and the reactionary had to be destroyed, but that the spiritual should be saved from falling into the contrary and equally erroneous identification. Mounier regretted that the opposition between left and right had arisen, particularly since it was a misleading oversimplification, but he appreciated that it had to be taken into account, even though it had eventually to be dissolved. He saw his task as twofold: on the one hand to wean the spiritual community away from the right; on the other to wean the left away from its aggressive anti-spiritualism.

At this point he confronted the marxist critique. He admitted that those who traditionally defended spiritual values had too often sought to avoid their temporal responsibilities, and by their default had left the world to its material mechanisms. He agreed that marxism was an accurate account of the world as it had been allowed to become, but insisted that materialism only saw the surface workings of things, whereas reality could only be adequately understood by accepting that there was a spiritual principle which was far more basic. His uncritical assumption that marxism was an accurate account of the material forces operating in the world was a little surprising, but reflected Mounier's almost complete ignorance of it and his early tendency to regard as largely irrelevant any non-spiritual agencies. This was adequately demonstrated when he went on to consider the difficult question of what action was to be undertaken to change the degenerate world.

A spiritual crisis, he argued, demanded spiritual action. This consisted essentially in the elucidation of truth as the basis for a spiritual revolution consisting of a transformation of the values of humanity at large. He was led therefore to formulate a 'politics of sanctity', by which he understood a pure spiritual action which, by personal example and patient teaching, would win adherents to the truth. He was, of course, aware that pure spirituality did not remove urgent temporal problems, but he was more concerned that spiritual values should not be compromised and subverted in the impurity of political action. His own view of action owed something to Maurice Blondel, who had advanced a complex view which founded action on participation in the divine presence. Mounier saw it as a spiritual process, the conjunction of a man radiating truth and a man being changed by the truth radiated. His efforts were therefore to be directed at changing men's minds and hearts.

Many of these ideas were the common currency of the catholic tradition and Mounier was able to give an abstract formulation of them since he felt he could legitimately leave more specific problems to the politically oriented *Troisième Force*. On two points, though, he was touching on new and contentious ground. The first was Mounier's firm determination to end the situation in which right wing politicians were parasitic on catholicism, and to open the way for catholics to choose a political commitment elsewhere in the political spectrum. The second point was his almost incidental acceptance that marxism provided an accurate account of the world as it had been allowed to become in the absence of a firm action by spiritual forces. In this latter he was largely following Nicolas Berdyaev whose article on the subject also appeared in the first issue of *Esprit*.[4]

Briefly, Berdyaev's position was that communism was a religion which set itself to replace the christian religion. Owing its success to the failure of christians, Berdyaev suggested, it proposed a messianic appeal to the soul of the masses, and an ethic of devotion. Philosophically, he argued, it was based on rigid economic determinism, denying the importance of ideological, spiritual or cultural activities and offering a secular equivalent for all the powerful 'myths' of christianity. The truth of marxism lay, he said, in its critique of the exploiting capitalist system, of formal democracy, of nationalism, and in its determination to ally theory and practice to build a new world. The lie which outweighed these truths, he insisted, was the denial of God and therefore of man, the deification of society and the proletariat in particular, in short, its materialist collectivism. Berdyaev held that the strength of communism lay in the fact that it contained truths mixed with error. The best tactic, therefore, he argued, would be to admit the true parts while rejecting the errors, rather than merely attacking the whole of it. Berdyaev's analysis, adopted by Mounier, became a classic statement of *Esprit*'s position on marxism and lies at the root of its often complex and widely criticised relations with French communism.

A spiritualist humanism
Though *Esprit* was largely based on a catholic readership, one of its primary aims was to express the church's teaching in a new and relevant form that would be attractive and accessible to as wide an audience as possible, including non-catholics. Mounier attempted to achieve this by formulating an underlying conceptual framework in harmony with catholic doctrine but not specifically limited to catholics. The church's social doctrine was based on a view of man's

essential nature; it held that society was made for man, and man was made by God in his own image. It therefore proposed a normative account of man, and sought to elaborate the social structures and relationships which would best suit him. Mounier followed the church's method, basing himself largely on its teaching, with which he was well acquainted. He set himself to elaborate a vision of man, on which to found his social and political theory. The foundations for this spiritualist humanism were set out in the second part of his essay 'Refaire la Renaissance'.

Analysing man's relationships with the material world, Mounier felt that medieval christianity had established an intimate link between man and nature, which was shattered during Descartes' lifetime and replaced by a new dualism which encouraged man to regard nature as an inert and foreign object. Man was then able to manipulate nature, quantifying it for his own convenience. The solution, he suggested, was to reaffirm the spirituality of matter, thereby giving the world a soul and a solidity which permitted man to have a genuine and valuable relationship with it.

Examining the social dimension of man, Mounier denounced both individualism and collectivism as half-truths. The renaissance, he argued, saw the birth of the individual as the central metaphysical value, cut off from everything, aggressive and entirely self-regarding. This brand of humanism, he went on, now dominated the western world, and had provided the excuse for brutality and oppression by invoking the values of liberalism. The contractual relationship and the politics of *laissez-faire* legitimised and facilitated the tyranny of the strong, he said, and liberty and toleration were dangerous unless tempered by discipline and justice. More briefly, he examined the rise of collectivism since the mid-nineteenth century, with its culmination in the marxist subordination of the individual to society. He declared that he would defend the human person against its assimilation into a communist state machine but would not fall into the opposite error of defending liberal individualism. His solution was to emphasise the necessary interplay between the private and public poles of the human self, fulfilled only by a freely chosen and wholehearted participation in the world. In practice, he suggested that contemplation and self-purification should be coupled with social action and work, and that one should cultivate an openness to other people, particularly strangers, a fresh, youthful vitality, and a liberating spiritual and material poverty.

The third dimension which Mounier attributed to man was spiritual. He dissociated himself from the idealist tradition which sought to reduce everything to spirit in a comfortable homogeneity. Since there could only be contact between distinct beings, he thought it essential to introduce a principle of spiritual distance to establish the possibility of communion without confusion. The basic experience which expressed this principle was the *rencontre,* he said, where two distinct beings perceived the real presence of each other and came together in a spiritual union without losing their individuality. Associated with this was Mounier's determination to foster a sense of mystery in the world and a responsiveness to the solicitation of events. He saw the sense of mystery as an awareness of the infinite complexity and the ultimate spirituality of the universe. Events he saw as privileged occurrences where the universe outside the self most closely interacted with the self. In view of their spirituality, he said, they should be regarded as a form of communication and discipline from the spiritual world.

This description enclosed both a metaphysic and a theory of knowledge. The metaphysical spiritualism was fundamental to Mounier's thought, but always taken for granted, and without any coherent attempt to establish an ontological basis. This lack of precision allowed him to avoid lengthy scholastic debate, but with the later accretion of new analyses to his thought it also left him vulnerable to the accumulation of implicit contradictions. In Mounier's epistemology, the knower and the known were defined neither as separate entities nor as one indissoluble reality, but as being both distinct and united participants in a spiritual universe. The terms, while unclear, had the advantage of laying the groundwork for the introduction of a more dialectical account of the human person. At the same time, they encouraged the development of a phenomenological view of perception not always compatible with the implicit metaphysic on to which Mounier grafted it. Suggestive though these analyses were, they were clearly unsatisfactory as an independent philosophy.

Though Mounier seemed to discourage the connection with any specific religion, his thought was comprehensible only in the context of a pre-existing and familiar framework of christian beliefs. There were two main reasons why Mounier should omit any reference to God and to his own religious commitment. First, he was conscious of writing, not so much to represent his own beliefs in detail, as to lay down a more general doctrine for the review, which was based on his own catholic views, but which did not exclude non-catholics or non-christians with a spiritual view of the world. Hence all specifically catholic dogma was set aside and the remaining philosophical

THE FOUNDATIONS OF PERSONALISM (1931–1935)   39

positions, though clearly intended to be compatible with it, were offered as a basis of common agreement. Second, Mounier was aware that a non-confessional stance would allow greater liberty of thought to his contributors, where an explicit affiliation to catholicism might lead to embarrassing interventions from the church hierarchy, or at least oblige him to pay excessive attention to the orthodoxy of opinions expressed. The wisdom of this was often proved in his relations with the catholic hierarchy. It is unlikely that his readers were perturbed to any great extent by the absence of specific reference to catholicism. They were predominantly catholics, who shared Mounier's frame of reference, and they generally assumed that *Esprit* was, in an important sense, a catholic review. A third, unforeseen advantage of Mounier's vagueness was to open up an initially catholic exposition to a fertilisation from other currents of thought which were also grappling with the problem of formulating a new philosophy of man.

The ideas of 'Refaire la Renaissance' represented the first major crystallisation of Mounier's own thought, the product of his thorough catholic training and an attempt to make a creative response to the crisis. They were also the culmination of intense collective reflection within the group of young catholics around *Esprit*. But if these analyses appeared at the time as an end-product, the next few years revealed them increasingly as a starting-point. The pressure of events and the influence of a variety of men and ideas produced a rapid evolution in the political and philosophical positions of Mounier and *Esprit*.

The 'Third Force'
The most serious crisis to face the review arose from the simmering disagreements, which had been papered over at Font-Romeu, concerning the relationship between the doctrinal and the political wings of the movement. The *Troisième Force*, once formally constituted, issued a manifesto,[5] in which it reiterated the spiritualist doctrine Mounier had outlined, and went on to define itself as an alternative to both capitalism and communism. It particularly launched a strong attack on the evils of the capitalist system, predicting its imminent collapse, presaged by the current crisis. It called for a revolution to set up a just economic and political order, suggesting such steps as the socialisation of credit, workers' control of their workplaces and the decentralisation of political power and economic production. At the same time it was careful to point out what it considered as the failure of the Soviet Russian revolution and

to distinguish itself from communism. The manifesto was a strange blend of abstractions on a spiritualist theme and radical political intentions. Whereas its philosophy clearly came from catholicism, its political aims were decidedly socialist and even Trotskyist in affinity. The difficulties involved in sustaining this uneasy synthesis emerged slowly in the following months.

By early 1933 the *Troisième Force* had acquired a headquarters, organisational structures and soon an organ of its own. Its activities were largely confined to Paris, particularly the Latin Quarter, where it engaged in various forms of combat with right-wing groups. At its height its numbers were probably eight to nine thousand. As the movement developed it began to grow away from the review. Many of its members treated Mounier's spiritual preoccupations with friendly derision. Their lack of respect for the doctrinal pronouncements of *Esprit,* and in many cases their ignorance of it, were paralleled by Mounier's basic lack of interest in political action, and the outright suspicion in which the movement was held by many of his editorial team. Izard and Mounier tried to patch up the original relationship along the lines adopted at Font-Romeu. For a short time matters improved, but the contradictions were too deeply rooted. Ideally, Mounier wished the movement to invent an entirely new form of political expression, independent of the old left-right opposition. The movement, however, was moving distinctly to the left and felt antagonised by Mounier's attempts to limit its field of action. By early 1933 it had come to accept the possibility of cooperation with the communists in undertaking a collectivist revolution, after which it would initiate a further revolution on behalf of human and personal values. Maritain was outraged and threatened to dissociate himself publicly from the review, a damaging step, unless Mounier separated *Esprit* definitively from what he felt to be no more than a *Force 2-bis,* an adjunct to communism.[6] Maritain's criticism struck a deep chord in Mounier, and served to add to his own misgivings. He held disillusioned negotiations with Izard, and within a few days they agreed that the movement and the review should separate definitively. The July number of *Esprit* carried a joint declaration to this effect,[7] insisting that the reasons were doctrinal, giving the impression that a separation had been the original intention, and adding that there was no *dessous* to the affair. This last claim was a tactical dishonesty, aimed at doing the least possible damage to either side. Mounier continued to attend meetings of the movement but felt it had died finally when, in the autumn of 1934, it merged

THE FOUNDATIONS OF PERSONALISM (1931–1935)   41

with another movement, Gaston Bergery's *Front commun*, to form a united *Front social* party which played a part in the formation of the *Front populaire*. The separation of *Esprit* from the *Troisième Force* meant the failure of Mounier's first attempt to solve the besetting problem of his life: how to translate spiritual values into acceptable political action without abandoning their purity.

Reactions

For all the caution and soul-searching it had undertaken, *Esprit* rapidly found itself under attack for its political position. The right made no mistake in sensing a hostile force. *Action française* smelt bolshevism and particularly took Berdyaev to task for his neo-Stalinism,[8] while *La revue française*, a review of the *Jeune Droite* group, derided the ambiguity of its spirituality and the abstractness of its revolutionary intentions.[9] François Mauriac, the celebrated novelist, writing in a leading nationalist daily, issued a sharp reprimand, warning the deluded men of *Esprit* that after they had facilitated the revolution they would be ruthlessly suppressed because they were catholics, and that they should therefore have no truck with revolution.[10] The left, although generally indifferent to what it regarded as nothing new, offered one or two criticisms. *L'étudiant socialiste* regretted the obvious antipathy shown towards marxism, but did not altogether dismiss *Esprit*, hoping that a closer contact with the proletariat might save it from its tendency towards an aristocratic socialism of intellectuals.[11] Paul Nizan, the young communist writer, took up Mauriac's point to reassure him that *Esprit* was no danger to the bourgeoisie, since it only sought to defend traditional bourgeois values in a new disguise.[12] The centre was generally silent with the notable exception of the small christian democratic tendency, which expressed a guarded sympathy but offered serious criticisms. A leading journalist, Paul Archambault, criticised *Esprit* for its vagueness and for its failure to produce a constructive alternative to the many things it refused. He felt that their hearts were in the right place but regretted that they did not tell him who he should vote for.[13] Another leading christian democrat, Robert Garric, was worried that *Esprit*'s pessimism as to the present state of society was unwarranted and that the young team was wasting its time preparing for a revolution which was never going to materialise.[14]

These reactions indicated the approximate area of sympathy available to *Esprit*. Its predominantly catholic audience was absent from the Maurrassien right and the communist left, it extended in a small degree to the socialists and the conservative republicans, but was strongest in the centrist christian democratic tendency. Mounier always insisted in keeping a critical distance from the established political parties and at times had harsh comments to make about the catholic-dominated ones in particular. But he was careful to make it clear that he felt himself part of the same christian family and wanted only to bring them to a sharper awareness of their spiritual obligations.

At the same time it was important that *Esprit* should appeal to a wide non-catholic audience if it was to fulfil its role of spreading the spiritual values it was based on. Mounier deliberately avoided any aggressively catholic declarations which might alienate other christians or even sympathetic non-believers. Some of the older supporters, including Maritain, were anxious to see catholic colours nailed to the mast. Mounier resisted these pressures. His attitude, as editor, was that he would not publish anything which recommended or implied atheism, nor would he consider any article attacking the church, or even in clear opposition to a papal encyclical. But he would not give space to interdominational squabbles. In the spring of 1933, the Cardinal Archbishop of Paris asked for a report on the review, showing some concern over its relations with the *Troisième Force,* the church and non-catholics. Thanks to the influence of Maritain and the judicious intervention of friendly clerics, Mounier was able to reassure the Archbishop and his *Comité de Vigilance* as to the value of *Esprit*. He was able to report the separation from the *Troisième Force,* but he strongly asserted his independence from the church hierarchy. Welcoming the close contact and advice of the church, he made it clear that catholic contributors would not truncate their faith but that he was not prepared to require other christians to renounce or hide their differences from Rome.[15] For the time being, any danger of official censure was averted. Mounier was aware that such censure would put an end to any influence he might hope to wield, and one effect of the incident was to make him conscious of the fragility of his position and of the need to avoid dangerous excesses in his material, unless they were accompanied by a firm editorial corrective.

Though it sought a wide appeal, *Esprit* was generally regarded as a catholic undertaking. The early subscribers were mainly catholic since they were recruited through catholic circles, and the presence of the names of catholic intellectuals and occasionally clerics among the published lists of subscribers would soon reveal the fact to an observant reader. Moreover, it is unlikely that anyone would subscribe to or buy regularly a review whose orientation he did not know. *Esprit*'s public was not all catholic by any means, but non-catholics were a minority. Reflecting this situation, one of the review's most influential early issues was based on the problems of christianity in the modern world. Mounier's own article set the tone.[16] Pointing out the massive desertion of spiritual values by christian people, he denounced the extent to which the church had compromised itself with the temporal forces of the world. The worst treason, he said, was its close identification with the most reactionary elements of the bourgeoisie, its alliance with power and money. Catholic doctrine, he continued, required obedience to temporal powers only so long as they did not constitute a tyranny. Western capitalism did constitute a tyranny, he insisted, and only the possibility of a worse, communist, tyranny should deter catholics from entering into revolution. The enemy was the bourgeois, which he saw as a moral rather than an economic category. Bereft of love or a sense of true existence, the bourgeois, he said, sought the order and tranquillity necessary to procure a mediocre contentment based on possessions, and therefore was a subtle representative of the Antichrist. The remainder of the issue of *Esprit* was devoted to drawing a firm line between christian values and their misappropriation in defence of modern bourgeois capitalism. Protestant, catholic and orthodox churches were represented by writers of stature, such as Berdyaev, Maritain, Denis de Rougemont and the young socialist André Philip. In all, the issue was an impressive contribution to the renewal of christian reflection on moral, political and social questions. It further advanced Mounier's attempt to apply the long-established principles of christianity to a complex and changing world.

The Friends of 'Esprit'

Despite the intellectual quality of its contents, *Esprit* was without any direct means of putting its ideas into practice. It was widely read, as its circulation figures show. Within three months of its appearance 500 subscriptions had been received, rising to 1100 in mid-1934 and probably reaching over 2000 by the late 1930s. Total sales probably averaged around 8000, a healthy figure for a monthly review. Since many of the sales were to families, study groups, schools, seminaries and other collectivities as well as to influential individuals such as teachers, priests, journalists and professional men, the readership was much higher than the number of sales and the ideas were much more widely communicated than actual copies of the review. On the basis of this extensive audience,

Mounier decided to initiate a new form of action to replace the *Troisième Force*. In July 1933 he announced the setting up of the *Amis d'Esprit*,[17] which was to be a network of groups of friends forming spiritual communities and study groups throughout France. On a practical level they were to safeguard the material conditions for the review's continuation, and eventually try to implement its judgements. Soon after this a young Belgian catholic, Raymond de Becker, interested him in a movement he was planning to found, based on a secularised version of religious communities. Mounier was enthusiastic, and the movement, soon entitled *Communauté*, aroused in him high hopes that he might at last have found the form of action to which he could unreservedly commit himself. The project, however, made little progress and Mounier turned back to *Esprit* as his best hope of achieving efficacity. The groups were slowly spreading, and in addition to regional gatherings, Mounier set up study groups to establish considered positions on various questions, with the ultimate purpose of preparing articles for the review.

No doubt Mounier was thinking back to his experience with the *Davidées* when he conceived the *Amis d'Esprit*. It was a similar but much larger scale of operation, aimed at organising the evident support enjoyed by the review, particularly in the provinces, which provided a strong base for *Esprit*. Using the groups, Mounier expected to ensure an effective agency for the propagation of *Esprit*'s ideology. In this expectation he was not mistaken. By carefully selecting correspondents and organisers in the provinces and in the French-speaking areas of Switzerland, Belgium and North Africa, by publicising them regularly in the back pages of *Esprit*, and by the frequent visits he and other leading figures of the editorial staff made to these areas, he was able to build up an efficient network of groups. By late 1934 there were groups in over thirty French towns, seven Swiss and five Belgian towns as well as a dozen groups in various other countries. The number of groups expanded to a peak of over sixty in France alone by the late 1930s, but before then it had become clear that the nature of the groups was corresponding less and less to Mounier's hopes. Originally conceived as the militant, active wing of a spiritual revolution led by *Esprit*, the groups once formed tended to lose momentum, and after a first rush of enthusiasm settled into a pattern of study groups and friendly gatherings. The groups in their final form were far short of Mounier's ambition, but they were still a valuable assistance to *Esprit*, then and later, on a material and an ideological level, forming a stable, loyal and reliable clientele. Although most of the militants in the provinces were otherwise unknown local enthusiasts, several of them were, or became, known on a national level. The most distinguished was probably the philosopher Maurice Merleau-Ponty, but others were Pierre-Henri Simon, the literary critic; Max-Pol Fouchet, the poet; Maurice de Gandillac, the philosopher; Jacques Ellul, the political commentator; Roger Secrétain, the journalist; Bertrand d'Astorg, the poet; Jean-Marie Soutou, the diplomat, and many more of lesser distinction. These men formed the core of a solid and influential support group which served *Esprit* well.

During the early months of the *Amis d'Esprit* experiment, the groups were invited to contribute to a collective reflection on the problem of action, which *Esprit* had not successfully solved. The results were synthesised by Mounier and presented in a series of articles.[18] Refusing both impotent purism and cynical realism as dangerous and inadequate responses, he suggested the elaboration of a range of non-violent action which would only be replaced by violence under the strictest of conditions. He declared that the militants of the revolution must submit to a strict self-discipline and self-examination to ensure that they were as pure as possible in all their actions and that their commitment included dedication to spiritual values before material success. Rejecting political action as impure, and institutional changes as ineffective, he outlined the nature of the actions which he encouraged as long as the choice remained open. These included publicly exposing and denouncing the oppression and injustices of the established disorder; refusing to participate, even indirectly, in it; passive disobedience by boycotting and obstructing its operations.

It was essentially a personal ethic, intended to bear witness to a daily refusal of complicity. It called for a thorough and long-term *dépouillement*, but was not to be understood as replacing the more specific responses required by the development of events. Nonetheless, this conception of action was abstract and removed from direct contact with reality, however satisfying it was on a moral or philosophical level. Mounier later conceded that it was excessively dominated by a desire for purity.[19] Mounier never disavowed his concepts of spiritual revolution or his search for purely spiritual forms of action, but already events were prompting the emergence of a more concrete political commitment. For his principles to become an effective ideology it was necessary to combine them with a practical response to the historical situation. In the event, the second half of the 1930s left Mounier and everyone else with little alternative but to take specific political positions.

The philosophy of the human person
Parallel with the political development of *Esprit* in the early thirties went a gradual evolution in the spiritualist humanism which was offered as the philosophy of the review. 'Refaire la Renaissance' had focussed on a concept of man as the free, creative agent at the intersection of the material, the human and the divine manifestations of the spirit. In catholic terminology this agent was usually referred to as the human person. It was in part through the revival of interest in St Thomas Aquinas that the person became a focal point of discussion in France during the 1920s and 1930s. In his discussion of the persons of the Trinity, Aquinas took up Boethius' definition of the person as an individual substance of rational nature.[20] Jacques Maritain developed this, opposing the person, characterised by reason and wholeness, to the individual, characterised by matter and incompleteness. As early as 1925, in a study on Luther, he argued that the individual, but not the person, was subordinate to society, and he was influential in establishing a distinction between the person and the individual which within ten years became a well-worn commonplace. In Maritain's view, the individual, man considered in his material aspect, was at the service of the community, which was in turn at the service of the person, man considered in his spiritual aspect, who was in turn at the service of God. For this reason, he could argue that his vision of society was 'aussi fondamentalement anti-individualiste que fondamentalement personnaliste'.[21] A closer definition of the person was difficult, he explained, since it was the most perfect thing in nature, but it was possible to say of it that it had God at its centre. The person therefore appeared as approximately equivalent to what might be called the spiritual dimension of man, though it was understood that it was inseparable from the material dimension. At the same time it was a goal of human aspiration, the embodied form of perfection, and therefore held strong moral implications. Maritain gave the classic neo-Thomist definition in his important work *Les degrés du savoir* (Paris, 1932):

> Une personne est un centre de liberté, fait face aux choses, à l'univers, à Dieu, dialogue avec une autre personne, communique avec elle selon l'intelligence et l'affection. La notion de personnalité, si complexe qu'elle soit, est avant tout d'ordre ontologique. C'est une perfection métaphysique et substantielle qui s'épanouit dans l'ordre opératif en valeurs psychologiques et morales.[22]

Primarily a metaphysical reality, the person was for him the source of moral and psychological values, though in Maritain's own thought, the establishment of a metaphysical foundation predominated.

During the 1930s the concept of the person was also receiving attention in other quarters. The most lucid representatives of non-Thomist personalism in France at this time were the members of the movement *Ordre nouveau*, and in particular their leading theorist Arnaud Dandieu. Dandieu drew his personalism from many sources, and while taking much from Bergson, he allied a Nietzschean individualism with a deep-rooted Proudhonian socialism. Dandieu had made a considerable study of the German phenomenological writers, who were still relatively unknown in France, and was attracted particularly to the thought of Max Scheler. Scheler, taking Kant as his ethical starting-point and heavily imbued with Nietzsche, developed the analyses of Brentano, Husserl and Meinong to construct a theory of the person as a spiritual being ontologically attached to an objectively existing hierarchy of values. The example of Scheler encouraged Dandieu, and consequently *Ordre nouveau*, to develop a personalism in which the moral and the metaphysical implications were scarcely distinguished. Scheler's thought was also being made known in France by an ex-pupil of his, Paul-Louis Landsberg, who had left Germany after Hitler's rise to power. Landsberg had already formulated a christian-based notion of the person drawing on Scheler's analysis, and was making a considerable impact on Parisian catholic circles.

The development of personalism

These philosophical developments held a strong attraction for Mounier, who experienced a convergence of many currents of thought on the concept of the person. The catholic Bergsonism he took from Chevalier already contained the elements of a personalist theory, though Bergson himself drew a stronger distinction between mind and matter than his catholic followers; the analyses of Maritain appeared reliable and cogent; those of Scheler and Landsberg seemed new and exciting; he was surrounded by close friends who had adopted the personalism of *Ordre nouveau*; and he was in search of a coherent theory of man on which to base his spiritual revolution. The category of the person increasingly seemed to offer a fertile and flexible centre of reflexion and exploration, though it also held the less obvious danger of leading to a philosophical eclecticism if the disparate currents were not adequately synthesised. In the spring of 1934 a study group was organised to define a personalist and communitarian philosophy for *Esprit*. Mounier organised it, but it was largely dominated by Landsberg. In late 1934 Mounier presented the fruit of this collective reflexion in two essays which represent the main lines of the personalist philosophy with which he rapidly became identified.[23]

Taking up Maritain's point, Mounier distinguished the person from the individual; the individual was taken to mean the purely material, and therefore lowest dimensions of the human self. The person was equally distinguished from consciousness of the self such as it might be perceived in prolonged introspection, Mounier said, for it ultimately escaped even the deepest scrutiny. It was like an invisible centre to which everything was attached, he suggested, but was not a psychologically isolable phenomenon, nor was it localised in space. 'Personal', he suggested, was synonymous with 'spiritual', and to speak of a person was to designate a spiritual presence in a man, beyond time, space or consciousness, which constituted a moral absolute. Reworking the analysis of man in 'Refaire la Renaissance', Mounier distinguished three dimensions of the person: incarnation, communion and vocation. 'Incarnation' designated the link which bound man inseparably to his material environment through his body: Mounier emphasised that man should not seek to deny this condition of his existence, but should use it to fulfil and transcend himself. 'Communion' designated his situation as a part of one or several human societies. 'Vocation' designated the aspiration which led man to discover what would most fulfil his deep spiritual nature. To each of these dimensions Mounier allocated a fundamental exercise which would allow a man to realise his person more completely. To incarnation corresponded commitment, the recognition of one's materiality and the effort to spiritualise it. To communion corresponded self-denial, the determination to live in and for others. To vocation corresponded meditation, the persevering quest for a greater knowledge of oneself and of the spiritual reality beyond oneself.

The person was, for Mounier, in the first instance a metaphysical entity. But it also provided a normative model embodying these ethical values which must be promoted or defended. This meant that an action was to be judged according to the extent to which it encouraged or prevented a man's development towards becoming more fully a person as characterised by Mounier. Furthermore, he used the person as a yardstick for judgement in social, economic and political matters. Every state, he argued, had the duty to promote and protect the fullest development of all its citizens as persons, and ought never to treat a person as other than an end in himself. This doctrine differed from defending 'the liberty of the individual', he declared, in that it refused to accord liberties which did not both comply with the moral obligations placed on the individual, and conduce to the spiritual development of his neighbour.

The concept of community

Mounier dwelt at some length on the dimension of 'communion', examining those values embodied in society. In this, he drew heavily on Scheler's phenomenological sociology to supplement his catholic training. If the first renaissance established the individual as the central value, he argued, a second renaissance now in progress aimed at establishing society as central. Just as individualism was a vicious caricature of the personalist humanism it failed to attain, he explained, so nascent collectivism threatened to fall short of the communitarian socialism it ought to strive for. He suggested that a primary distinction was to be made between a society and a community. Societies were mere agglomerations of individuals, he said, but a community was a bond between persons. There were, he added, degrees of attainment in the establishment of the true community. Mounier established and described at some length a hierarchy of types of society and community which closely corresponded to Scheler's analysis. The lowest degree of community was the mass, the anonymous, impersonal herd. Strictly speaking, it was not a degree of community at all, but rather its absence, corresponding to what he called the 'monde de l'On',[24] Heidegger's *das Man*, Berdyaev's *objectivation*, the modern ad-mass, depersonalised and irresponsible. A higher stage was what Mounier termed 'les socéités en nous autres',[25] which occurred when a section of the mass acquired a collective will and a sense of identity. This included political parties but, Mounier said, for all the dedication they inspired, they could not encourage the development of the person, nor therefore be counted as genuine communities. The first degree of real community, he thought, were life-groups, based on race, nationality, kinship, geography or any other natural accident which, being organic in essence, tended to foster both individuation and social awareness in their members. Though at worst they could become closed and aggressive, he thought, at best they could provide a dynamic base for the preparation of true community. Above these, Mounier found the 'société raisonnable',[26] an association of men based on an intellectual principle. In practice, however, he saw this ideal as tending to fall into impersonal detachment and hence evade the personal development necessary to true community.

The highest form of community, Scheler's *Gesamtperson*, was what Mounier was really concerned to promote. Referred to alternately as 'la communauté personnaliste' and 'la personne de personnes',[27] it had the same role on a social level as the person itself on an individual level. It could only be founded on the values of the person, Mounier argued, and was the logical outcome of those values. In his view, the true community was a series of interlocking love relationships which taken together presented the same characteristics as a single person. He stressed, however, that the perfect community was not to be found in this world, but rather to be seen as an ultimate goal which was only reached in, for example, the communion of saints and, most eminently, in the Holy Trinity, which should be the model for an aspiring community. The conclusions implied in the analysis, Mounier argued, were that nothing should be allowed to hamper the development of the person, which alone could ensure the development of true community, but that this priority should not be used as a disguise for the selfish egoism characteristic of the individual. In practice, he said, it meant a rigorous self-discipline on the part of the person, and a decentralised, pluralist state, whose structures *Esprit* was striving to establish. The community, like the person, and all the more so since it depended on the person, was first of all a metaphysical entity, whose ontological foundation was an unspecified mixture of catholic theology and German phenomenology. Second, and more important, the community, like the person, was a normative model. Each group, association or society was seen as being always at some stage below the level of true community, which by implication it should strive for.

Theoretical refinements

In establishing this comprehensive theory of man in society, Mounier was consciously trying to provide a metaphysical basis for a social doctrine which was firmly within the catholic orthodoxy, which was adequate to understand and respond to the urgent problems of modern industrial societies, and which was sufficiently cogent to command the assent of non-catholics. His account contained philosophical inadequacies, largely deriving from his eclecticism, and his reluctance to attach the person explicitly to a faith in the christian God, but he was less concerned with providing a logical account than with promoting a set of values. Nevertheless, during the year following the first statement of his personalism, he did add a series of small modifications to meet two serious objections. The first objection was: if the person is able to be perceived as a part of experience, why do some people deny its existence? To this Mounier replied that while the person was experienced as a spiritual reality, some people may be 'person-blind'. Just as others were blind to colour, these people did not perceive the person, he said, though this in no way detracted from its reality. The circularity of the argument is evident; it was a reasonable but not a persuasive reply. Fortunately Mounier did not often invoke the principle of personblindness. The second objection was: if everyone is a person, how can they also strive to become one? Mounier countered it in two ways. He defended his presentation of the person both as a descriptive and a prescriptive concept, resting the two connected aspects on an act of faith, a logically unsupported affirmation of the person as that which is ultimately and absolutely valuable in itself.

As a second defence, Mounier operated a shift in his description of the relation between the person and the individual: where previously there had been a straight opposition, he introduced a tension between two opposed movements. On the one hand, he argued, material constraints exercised a permanent tendency to dissipation and degradation; on the other hand, the spiritual dimension exerted a force for unification and perfection. It was, he said, the spiritual dimension which, in its purest form, was designated the person. But the person, as the spiritual part of man, was always beyond its concrete manifestation, he pointed out, and therefore never strictly attained. Hence he thought it more fitting to speak of it as a process of spiritualisation or, synonymously, a process of personalisation. The move from a static account of the person as essence to a dynamic account of the person as movement introduced a flexibility and generality which had not formerly been present. These modifications, introduced in the *Manifeste au service du personnalisme* of 1936, were taken from Landsberg and thereby indirectly from Scheler.[28] With them, Mounier's personalism was substantially complete and formed the substance of *Esprit*'s theoretical position.

Personalism as an ideology
As a philosophy in its own right, communitarian personalism was both unoriginal and inconsistent, the inconsistency deriving from the unoriginality. Its sources were numerous, and became increasingly so as time passed: rooted in Jacques Chevalier's catholic

Bergsonism, it grafted Scheler's phenomenology on to Maritain's neo-Thomism, forming an odd hybrid nourished by any other ideas which came to hand. The contradictions, implicit and explicit, the ambiguity of key terms, the lack of assignable intellectual content in others, the undeclared and unelaborated assumptions, all undermine its coherence and highlight its piecemeal eclecticism. Fortunately the strength and interest of *Esprit*'s personalism did not rest primarily on its intellectual coherence but on its success as a cultural and political ideology.

Personalism as an ideology embodied a set of values shared to a greater or lesser extent, more or less consciously, by an important section of the population. By virtue of its generality, personalism attracted a handful of non-believers, and a larger number of christians of other denominations, but by far the majority of its devotees were catholic. Mounier based his thought firmly in the values and doctrines which catholics shared and recognised. Much of his theoretical writing would command an easy assent from catholics who recognised the language of their church and the traditional values it stood for. By articulating these values in a rough synthesis, personalism drew the people concerned into more conscious solidarity, thereby increasing their capacity for concerted activity.

Having established a corpus of doctrine, Mounier could hope to draw consequences from it which would direct the actions of his audience into channels which they had not previously considered, but which could be shown as legitimate in terms of the basic values and doctrines. This was especially important in social and political matters, where the church left a wide margin of initiative to its members in their choice of action. By establishing personalism as a semi-autonomous philosophy within the catholic tradition, Mounier was preparing it to function as a sub-ideology of catholicism, but intervening in a wider range of human activities than the church, and gaining the support of people outside the church. In this way, Mounier could claim to be carrying forward the church's work of understanding and responding to the modern world particularly in the area of social problems.

Though personalism in its early months was eclectic in its philosophy, abstract in its political thought and lacking in any active commitment, it was these features which fitted it to become a latter-day utopian socialism. The utopian socialists of the eighteenth and nineteenth centuries had lacked the means for an adequate understanding of history, economy or society. Their theories were creatures of reason and fantasy, yet they formed the starting point for more scientific analyses of society; their experiences prepared the way for more effective forms of social intervention. Likewise personalism, rising within a religion which had opposed most of the intellectual, political and social advances of two centuries, began to prepare the ground for a renewal within the catholic church which would enable it to assimilate these very advances. But if *Esprit*'s utopianism grew from discussion and meditation, its socialism, as yet embryonic, grew from the pressure of events.

Notes

1 'Cahiers de Revendications', *Nouvelle Revue Française*, décembre 1932, p801–845, edited by Denis de Rougemont.
2 See Paul Nizan, 'Sur un certain front unique', *Europe*, janvier 1933, p137–146.
3 *Esprit*, no1, octobre 1932, p5–51, reprinted with sub-titles and later alterations in *Oeuvres* I p137–174.
4 N. Berdiaeff, 'Vérité et mensonge du communisme', *Esprit*, no1, octobre 1932, p104–128.
5 'Chronique du mouvement', *Esprit*, no1, octobre 1932, p129–136.
6 J. Petit (ed), *Maritain-Mounier. Correspondance 1929–1939* (Paris 1973) p78–96.
7 'Avertissement', *Esprit*, no10, juillet 1933, p454–456, signed by G. Izard and E. Mounier, reprinted in J. Petit, *Maritain-Mounier*, p95–96.
8 Anonymous, 'Communisme et Communion', *Action Française*, 1 décembre 1932.
9 Anonymous, 'Sous le signe d'Esprit', *La Revue Française*, 25 décembre 1932.
10 François Mauriac, 'Les jeunes bourgeois révolutionnaires', *Echo de Paris*, 25 mars 1933, p1.
11 Pierre Boivin, 'Esprit', *L'Étudiant Socialiste*, janvier 1933.
12 Paul Nizan, 'Les enfants de la lumière', *Commune*, no2, 1933, p105–112, reprinted in P. Nizan, *Intellectuel communiste* (Paris 1969) p219–225.
13 Paul Archambault, 'Esprit', *Politique*, novembre 1932, p1034–1036.
14 Robert Garric, 'Pourquoi nous acceptons', *La Revue des Jeunes*, 15 février 1933, p159–173.
15 See *Esprit*, décembre 1950, p982, and J. Petit, *Maritain-Mounier*, p83–89.
16 E. Mounier, 'Confession pour nous autres chrétiens', *Esprit*, no6, mars 1933, p873–896, reprinted in *Oeuvres* I p373–393.
17 'Constitution des Amis d'Esprit', *Esprit*, no10, juillet 1933, p457–462, unsigned.
18 E. Mounier, 'Pour une technique des moyens spirituels', *Esprit*, nos 26 ,27, 29, novembre & décembre 1934, février 1935, reprinted in *Oeuvres* I p314–360.
19 E. Mounier, 'Les cinq étapes d'Esprit', *Dieu vivant*, no16, 1950, p37–53, reprinted in *Bulletin des Amis d'Emmanuel Mounier*, no29, mars 1967, p9–24.
20 *Summa Theologica* Ia.29.1, Aquinas defined the person as 'substantia individua rationalis naturae'.
21 Jacques Maritain, *Trois réformateurs* (Paris 1925) p32.

22 Jacques Maritain, *Les degrés du savoir* (Paris 1932) p457–458.
23 E. Mounier, 'Qu'est-ce que le personnalisme?', *Esprit*, no27, décembre 1934, p357–367, reprinted in *Oeuvres* I p175–183; and 'La révolution communautaire', *Esprit*, no28, janvier 1935, p548–580, reprinted in *Oeuvres* I p184–209.
24 *Oeuvres* I p186.
25 *Oeuvres* I p198.
26 *Oeuvres* I p201.
27 *Oeuvres* I p202.
28 See P. L. Landsberg, *Problèmes du personnalisme* (Paris 1952) esp p13–27.

Bibliographical Notes

Good analyses of French politics at this period can be found in D. Thomson, *Democracy in France* (London 1946) and Roy Pierce, *Contemporary French Political Thought* (London 1966). The attempts to renew French Catholic political and philosophical reflection are described in detail by J. L. Loubet del Bayle, *Les non-conformistes des années 30* (Paris 1969) and J. Touchard, 'L'Esprit des années trente' in *Tendances politiques dans la vie française depuis 1789* (Paris 1960). The best general account of French catholicism during the period is A. Dansette, *Destin du catholicisme français 1926–1956* (Paris 1957). Catholic doctrine relating to the human person in society is well dealt with by A. Delmasure, *Les catholiques et la politique* (Paris 1960), H. de Lubac, *Catholicisme* (Paris 1941), J. Y. Calvez & J. Perrin, *The Church and Social Justice* (Chicago 1961). More specifically social teachings are well dealt with in A. Freemantle (ed), *The Social Teachings of the Church* (New York 1963) and R. L. Camp, *The Papal Ideology of Social Reform* (Leiden 1969). Political issues are examined in R. Rémond, *Les catholiques, le communisme et les crises* (Paris 1960); M. Darbon, *Le conflit entre la Droite et la Gauche dans le catholicisme français* (Toulouse 1953); and A. Latreille and others, *Histoire du catholicisme en France*, vol3 (Paris 1964). The most useful study of Scheler's thought is E. W. Ranly, *Scheler's Phenomenology of Community* (The Hague 1966). A valuable analysis of Maritain's personalism is J. Croteau, *Les fondements du personnalisme de Maritain* (Ottawa 1955).

CHAPTER THREE

The Politics of Personalism
(1935—1938)

Political crisis
Though the economic crisis shook France from the beginning of the 1930s, the political consequences only came to a head with the events of February 1934. A slow evolution of the French right had produced a growing number of small groups openly and explicitly aligning themselves with the fascist movements in Italy and Germany. The exposure of serious corruption in government circles sparked off a large protest meeting in the Place de la Concorde on the evening of the 6th February 1934. The demonstration, consisting mostly of nationalists, royalists and members of the various fascist leagues, turned into an anti-parliamentary riot in which several demonstrators were killed by police gun-fire. Though the action failed to achieve more than a change at the head of the government, it was a severe shock to the left, and prompted massive counter-demonstrations by both communists and socialists. By the following summer the two parties of the left had reached agreement on common political action against fascism, a step made more urgent by the dangers threatening from Hitler's Germany and Mussolini's Italy. It was soon followed by the unprecedented decision of the two parties to present a joint programme at the following elections of spring 1936. They were joined by a number of smaller groups, and even the traditionally centrist radical party expressed a guarded willingness to co-operate. From the huge demonstrations of 14th July 1935 up until the electoral victory of 3rd May 1936, the *Rassemblement populaire*, as it was officially known, won the support of an increasing number of organisations. Apart from the major parties, communists, SFIO socialists, independent socialists, republican socialists, radicals and radical socialists, the *Rassemblement* also included the christian democratic *Ligue de la Jeune République*, which had arisen from the pre-war *Sillon* movement; and the *Front social*

of Gaston Bergery and Georges Izard, a christian socialist movement which still had links with *Esprit*. Two of the main trade union organisations supported the *Rassemblement*: the communist-led *Confédération Générale du Travail Unitaire* and the socialist-led *Confédération Générale du Travail*. Significantly, the catholic-led *Confédération Française des Travailleurs Chrétiens* withheld its support, but there were few bodies in the labour movement or in the political left and centre to follow its example. The electoral programme was a series of thoroughgoing reforms based on national and international peace and freedom, with social justice and economic growth. Despite the intensity of right-wing and fascist opposition, the popular front movement emerged triumphant in the spring elections of 1936, representing the high point of the French left's achievement.

Mounier's initial reaction to the events of February 1934 was to deplore the proliferation of myths erected on both left and right to simplify and falsify judgements.[1] If this was the condition of revolution, he said, then he felt obliged to abstain, and to prepare a more long-term spiritual revolution free from unacceptable impurities. He was anxious not to be drawn into party politics, which he felt offered little better than a choice between fascism and communism.

As early as January 1934, Mounier had firmly refused the attractions of fascism.[2] Admitting its dynamism, he accused it of being founded on the distorted caricatures of genuine values, and rejected it as an easy, but pernicious option. Nevertheless, he agreed, in the spring of 1935, along with other young intellectuals, to attend an explanatory conference in Rome on the fascist conception of the corporate state. Making every effort to give his sympathetic understanding to the complexities of Italian ideology, he re-stated his objections and added that the major theoretical obstacles were its acceptance of the state as the primary value, its belief that all persons could be assimilated spontaneously into a harmonious uniformity within it, and its consequent identification of the leader with the true state.[3] After allowing some debate in *Esprit*, notably with the leading fascist theorist Georges de Santillana, Mounier brought the question to a definitive end, baldly refusing all moral complicity with the aims and the path of fascism.[4] Henceforth the review was unambiguously anti-fascist. In taking this position, Mounier was allying himself with almost the entire French left, who began increasingly to insist on their common task of anti-fascism in face of the rising wave of fascism throughout Europe.

Mounier's stance regarding communism, on the other hand, was less straightforward. It proved to be the single most important dialogue of his career, and was governed by one unpleasant, but unavoidable fact: the communist party was the single and consistent effective defender of the working class in France. Without this, Mounier would doubtless have been even more peremptory than with fascism. Without retreating from his earlier position, he increasingly granted the value of marxism as a method of enquiry, while condemning its totalitarian expression in the Soviet Union. He denied that communism was necessarily inseparable from the defence of the working class, and denied that criticism of it was therefore reactionary. Consequently, he said, he felt free to oppose its implicit materialism, but only because he also opposed the oppression of the working class.[5] In practice, this defensive acknowledgement of communism was as yet only a verbal curtsey. The build-up of the left-alliance and the new spirit of dialogue and cooperation, initiated by the communists, led many catholics to review their rooted mistrust of communism. Mounier and *Esprit* were not to be won over easily, and it was only as a result of three decisive political experiences that their attitude began to soften.

Political initiations
The first experience arose from the development of the *Troisième Force*. In the autumn of 1934, the left radical deputy, Gaston Bergery, proposed a merger with his *Front commun*. This involved a certain acceptance of the usual party political conventions, including action on the masses. Mounier, whose notion of action was more élitist, wrote a letter in protest to Izard.[6] It was his unshakeable belief that the only worthwhile change was that brought about by a militant minority who would inject their values, in all their purity, into the impure mass by a process of *rayonnement* based on personal conversion. In November 1934 the merger was nonetheless voted. Mounier instantly resigned from the new *Front social* in deep disappointment. This formation was one of the bases on which the *Front populaire* was founded, but Mounier felt that the measure of compromise involved was unacceptable, and that the movement was now open to assimilation by the communists with their unified and intransigent ideology. Events proved Mounier's fears to have been unjustified, and with the growing success of the *Rassemblement populaire* movement, this small current, for all its impurity, was the closest of any to representing *Esprit*'s values in French political life.

The second decisive experience was a polemic with the General de Castelnau, right-wing leader of the *Fédération Nationale Catholique*, a movement founded in 1924 to oppose the secular education policies of the *Cartel des Gauches* government. The General had been urging in the right-wing catholic daily, *Echo de Paris*, that the period of conscription be raised from one to two years, that young catholics be encouraged to enrol in the army, and that re-armament should be introduced as a major priority of government. Outraged by this war-mongering, Mounier wrote in *Esprit* reminding him of the pope's condemnation of war and, referring to Castelnau's three sons killed in the Great War, asked, 'Général, trois fils, n'est-ce pas assez?'.[7] The General was indignant and wrote a vehement attack in the *Echo de Paris* and an insulting letter to *Esprit*.[8] The conservative catholic press, shocked and angry, accused Mounier of pride, vulgarity and brutality, while he insisted that his words were prompted by sincere charity and generous concern. However that may be, the affair came as a rude awakening to those who still saw *Esprit* as a harmless, abstract, though occasionally extravagant publication. It also gave a considerable jolt to Mounier himself, who become aware of his tendency to indulge in vast, abstract meditations and resolved to express himself with more vigour in matters of controversial political import.

A few days later the third decisive experience arose from an attempt to implement this resolve. Parliamentary elections were being held in an overwhelmingly catholic quarter of Paris, and the only candidate to stand was Jean Chiappe, a monarchist sympathiser who had been dismissed as prefect of the police for corrupt and antidemocratic practices. He was suspected of collusion in the preparation of the attempted fascist coup of 6 February 1934, and of involvement in the *affaire Stavisky,* a seamy financial scandal. Determined not to let him pass unopposed, a group of young catholics of *Esprit* organised a last-minute campaign to elect Jacques Madaule, one of their number. Supported by a selection of respectable catholic intellectuals they did all they could to expose Chiappe's misdeeds and appeal to the community to reject his candidature as an insult. Hindered by his late arrival and by the total silence of the public media regarding his campaign, Madaule lost heavily. Mounier was disappointed, but in the face of palpable failure, he appreciated how much needed to be done before his mission bore substantial fruit. It had also come as something of a shock to him to see the power of the press and of even a corrupt politician like Chiappe over the minds of those who professed to stand for spiritual values. All the vigour and probity of a spiritually-based action had been fruitless, and Mounier came one step nearer to realising the conflict between two desirable ends, purity and efficacity.⁹

The popular front

The Castelnau and Chiappe affairs in particular made Mounier feel a greater sympathy and openness towards the forces at work in the construction of a left-wing alliance. From June 1935 onwards, he was regularly invited to meetings organised by one or other of the popular front groups to build cooperation and unity. He soon found himself sharing platforms with leading communist intellectuals like Paul Nizan, André Malraux, Marc Bloch and Louis Aragon, all of whom had previously shown him nothing but hostility. Mounier was initially dismayed by the artificiality of their welcome and felt that political expediency was destroying their integrity. But it can be taken as a sign of Mounier's success in establishing himself as recognisably 'of the left', that he should be regarded as a useful ally. Though he was bewildered and mistrustful of the sudden change, Mounier found in their unity an important and hopeful sign, particularly since the rigid dogmatism of the communists had now given way to a readiness to listen to and tolerate contrary views.

Despite the softening of *Esprit*'s hostility towards existing parties, its theoretical position remained intransigent. The question of political action was discussed at the second *Esprit* conference on July 1935 and the collective statement, drawn up as a result, declared that since no party fully satisfied its conditions, *Esprit* would work for the long-term constitution of a third force, independent of the *Front populaire*—as of the right-wing *Front national*—neither marxist nor fascist.¹⁰ It had harsh words about the popular front which, it said, was attempting to monopolise the defence of social justice, and attaching it to unacceptable ideologies. In this matter, *Esprit* was obliged to advance prudently, and any unseemly enthusiasm could easily lead to censure from the church, an eventuality Mounier wished to avoid. As the church's volunteer advance guard, he knew that it was imperative not to be cut off from the main body of the army. At the same time, Mounier's threat to find a middle way between the left and right was politically unreal. He rapidly modified his analysis to acknowledge that, in so far as it represented more than an electoral manœuvre, the popular front might in itself be a step towards the middle way he was seeking. As a man of the left, however he understood it, Mounier could not disown the *Rassemblement*, but he was unwilling to be drawn into a movement which contained much to disquiet him, even if it did group the working class and all politically progressive movements in France at that time.

Despite the many reticences felt by *Esprit*, the electoral victory of the popular front was acclaimed with joy by most of the review's militants. More surprisingly, Mounier went as far as to claim the victory as the vindication of his own position. He argued that the rejection of class or religious sectarianism, the dilution of marxism by transcendent human values, and the conquest of political power by legal means, all points of *Esprit*'s position, were responsible for the electoral success.[11] There was some justice in Mounier's claim, for the *Front populaire* met most of the conditions he laid down for a catholic to be able to work within it. The reason for this is clear: intellectually, Mounier stood as far to the left as it was possible to stand at this period without incurring the censure of the church. Any left-wing movement could reasonably regard his conditions as a minimum requirement in order to attract significant catholic support. It is therefore not surprising that all three main sectors of the *Front populaire* should at least pay lip-service to the main human and spiritual values Mounier defended. They could not expect electoral victory without a degree of support from catholics, and even the general secretary of the communist party, Maurice Thorez, had made a speech offering *la main tendue* to catholics. French catholics did not respond enthusiastically to this, but enough of them were persuaded to give the popular front its victory. Mounier could fairly claim to be a representative of the kind of catholic the *Front populaire* had to win over. There was no direct causal link between Mounier's ideas and those of the new government, though there was sufficient resemblance for him to be excused a little discreet preening.

Working on the principle that firm but fair criticism was likely to be more influential than unconditional support or overindulgence, Mounier was particularly intransigent towards movements close to his own thought, so in this instance he reserved the right to criticise harshly. The defenders of the oppressed were in power, he argued, and he was therefore excused the scruples which previously led him to attenuate his disagreements. The main target he singled out was the danger of a materialist dictatorship under a new Stalin, a danger all the more acute since orthodox communism was the most cohesive and effective single element of the new dispensation. Consequently he promised to help and encourage all constructive projects, both at the hub and on the perimeter of the government. At the same time, bearing in mind the undoubted repression in the USSR, he promised to fight to eliminate any signs of an incipient police or party dictatorship. While the terms of his approval may seem muted, Mounier's scepticism was tempered by a strain of anticipation which reflected something of the exhilaration which the whole French left felt in the spring of 1936.

The leadership of Leon Blum in the first popular front cabinet effectively blocked the influence of the communist party; the manifesto promises, after an initial burst of activity, were rapidly attenuated as the government lurched slowly towards the positions of its most conservative components. The reforming work of the government had been increasingly impeded by pressure from industrialists and property-owners, supported by the more conservative elements in the coalition. The communists had refused to cooperate in administering the compromises introduced into the initial programme, which they had considered as a minimum. The balance of power was shifting to the right, exposing all the contradictions which had gone unchallenged in earlier more enthusiastic days. The preponderance of the lukewarm radical party grew until, within one year, even the moderate socialist Blum was replaced by the conservative cabinet of Camille Chautemps, an experienced parliamentarian of dubious integrity.

Esprit, true to its commitment, followed the progress of the popular front with critical sympathy, approving developments in the early weeks, but showing a lucid awareness of the difficulties and failures. Aligning itself roughly along the line of the socialist party, *Esprit* deplored the gradual decline of its initial energy and influence, and called for a new upsurge of popular pressure to come to the front's rescue. Its assessments, confirmed by events, became increasingly pessimistic until, early in 1938, the review pronounced the final death of the front. For the March 1938 issue of *Esprit* Mounier wrote a long assessment,[12] in which he tried to clear away some of the dead wood of slogans, cliches, and stereotyped attitudes, the mythologies which he considered to falsify and distort the expression of left-wing politics. Because of the tenacity of these parasitic accretions, he said, he was not prepared to be crudely categorised as a left-winger, but was willing to work in cooperation with, and for the purification of, those forces which did call themselves left-wing. The failure of the *Front populaire,* he suggested, could be ascribed to its not having purged itself of its mythologies. As a result, he said, it has been polluted and diluted by both the mediocre liberalism of the 'radical' parties, and the harsh materialism of the communist party, to the point where it combined the worst, rather than the best of all sides. There are many possible explanations for the undoubted failure of the *Front populaire*. Mounier's was above all an ideological explanation. He accused the government of betraying the *mystique* which had brought it to power, and of failing to elaborate a coherent ideology which took honest account of differences. The willingness to sacrifice ideological purity for purely material gains, he thought, inevitably led to actions failing to achieve their objectives. He himself was not willing to make such a sacrifice; he refrained from adding that this position led to no action at all.

The consent of the hierarchy

Apart from Mounier's temperamental obsession with spiritual purity, there was another factor which contributed greatly to the apparent timidity of *Esprit*'s political ideology. Since the brief alarm, already mentioned, of the French hierarchy's early probings, *Esprit* had been the object of a campaign by the nationalist right, which aimed at securing official disapproval of *Esprit* by Rome. One tactic was to equate *Esprit* with the openly pro-communist review *Terre nouvelle*, in an attempt to discredit the more prudent position of *Esprit*. *Terre nouvelle*, organ of the *Union des communistes spiritualistes*, first published May 1935, bore the symbol of the hammer and sickle superimposed on the cross, and described itself as the 'mensuel des chrétiens révolutionnaires'. Its contributors, including Déléage, and the young protestants André Philip and Paul Ricoeur, advocated christian cooperation with the communists in making the revolution. It was first censured in February 1936 and put on the index in July of the same year. Despite his sympathy for many of their aims, Mounier was obliged on several occasions to draw a firm distinction between his own and the other review, and even had specifically to rebut the suggestion that he was less than whole-hearted in his adherence to the pope's ruling against catholic and communist collaboration. At the same time, he had opposed Italian imperialism in Ethiopia, a fact which was used to exert pressure against him in Rome. His support for the *Front populaire* was the culmination of a succession of positions which set him on the left, and his enemies, mostly in the *Action française* circle, sought to demonstrate that he had distorted and betrayed the church's teaching in this. At the end of May 1936, Mounier was shocked to receive a letter from Maritain warning of *Esprit*'s imminent condemnation. It was common knowledge that the right regularly circulated the cardinals of the church with copies of *Esprit* and commentaries presenting it as a bolshevik organ. In addition, Henri Massis, an established opponent of *Esprit*, claimed to have some influence with the Vatican's powerful secretary of state, Cardinal Pacelli (later Pope Pius XII). *Esprit* and its supporters lobbied and made strong representations within the church hierarchy. The danger was soon averted, thanks, in part, to the goodwill of the Cardinal Archbishop of Paris.

As his contribution to the campaign, Mounier prepared a lengthy and detailed report, setting out the review's position in a comprehensive survey. In this he offered a revealing assessment of *Esprit*'s achievements.[13] First, he claimed, it had begun to compete with communism on its own ground. By constructing a series of effective techniques for social renewal without a rigid materialistic metaphysic, it had taken some of the force from the communist hold over the oppressed, and seriously challenged the necessity for materialism. Second, he explained, *Esprit* had established such links between catholics and non-believers that the catholics had been brought out of their intellectual and political ghetto, and the non-believers had abandoned some of their suspicion and resistance to catholicism. Third, he claimed, *Esprit*, now established, was the only major review in the cultural field to be dominated by catholics, most of the others being directed by communists. Finally, in view of the rise of the left all over Europe at this time, he thought it essential that the church should not be cut off from the progressive movements and particularly from the working class, but that it should be in a position to influence both those in power and their supporters in the factories. This he thought *Esprit* could claim to promote. He concluded with a veiled warning about the disastrous consequences of the review's condemnation.

Mounier's assessment undoubtedly contained some over-statement and wishful thinking. The broad terms in which Mounier described the impact of *Esprit* need clarification. It was read in a limited milieu and certainly did not command an audience in the working class, but it was read by a number of trade union leaders—mostly catholics—and by some of the non-catholic intelligentsia. It could certainly claim to be one of the few catholic-dominated reviews to be read at all outside catholic circles. The three other leading cultural reviews, *Commune*, *Europe* and *Nouvelle Revue Française* were at that time dominated by communists or their fellow-travellers. *Esprit*'s claim to offer a social doctrine which inherently challenged communism is more debatable. Partly at least because it had not had time, *Esprit* had by no means established a powerful, effective or original alternative to marxism, though it certainly intended to. There is little to add to Mounier's analysis of the link established between catholics and non-catholics. The review certainly fostered a more open attitude, but it is arguable that its effects were far more influential on catholics than on non-believers. The contributors to the review were much more ideologically diverse than its readers, and included most of the christian denominations and even some agnostics. Thus the dialogue between believers and non-believers was largely one-way as far as the readership was concerned. There can be little doubt that the condemnation of *Esprit* might have caused an upheaval among progressive catholics, comparable to the censure of the christian democratic *Sillon* in 1910, and would surely have placed considerable constraints on those who, like Mounier, were attempting to lead catholics out of their traditional right-wing political ghetto. How far *Esprit,* or any other catholic organ, was influential in government circles, or even in the various left-wing groupings, is difficult to assess, particularly since the *Front populaire* was dominated by three traditionally non-christian parties (communist, socialist and radical). It is probably fairer to see its action as preparing the future time when catholics would wield effective influence on the left in power.

The personalist manifesto
The exaggerated optimism of Mounier's assessment can be attributed in part to the high hopes which the *Rassemblement populaire* aroused in 1936. It was these same high hopes that prompted the publication in that autumn of Mounier's *Manifeste au service du personnalisme* (Paris 1936). In effect this was a summary of all the positions *Esprit* had elaborated in its four years of existence. Its novelty was to outline in programmatic form the cultural and political aims of Mounier and *Esprit,* with a view to playing a role in planning the progressive reforms promised by the new government. The overall emphasis was on 'pluralism' and bore the clear imprint of Pierre-Joseph Proudhon. Proudhon, the nineteenth-century anarchist socialist, had proposed a decentralised syndicalist state. His influence on the French labour movement and French socialism was considerable, providing the main alternative current to marxism. His best-known work, *Qu'est-ce que la propriété?* held that property was theft, that the present property-based social order was immoral, that it should be overturned by violent revolution if necessary, and that it should be replaced by an order based on justice, liberty and equality, organised into federations of small,

self-governing, local units. Libertarian Proudhonism was strong in small, provincial craft industries particularly, and many of its principles were adopted by parts of the christian working and lower-middle classes. For them, it promoted the independence of their trade organisations, and the autonomy of their cultural and religious institutions, as well as harmonising with an opposition to state power inherent in catholic and liberal social doctrines. For the kind of utopian socialism Mounier was constructing, Proudhon, rather than Marx, was the major theorist.

On the vexed question of education, the *Manifeste* called for a pluralist system which would allow schools of all different creeds, with a limited degree of centralised supervision to maintain standards. Within the schools, he argued, it should be accepted that the object of education was to foster the free and creative development of the child, the better to fulfil his vocation as a person. This may appear unremarkable, but the significance appears more clearly when set against the backcloth of the sectarian strife which had accompanied discussion of education in France since the first setting up of a secular republic. The third republic had, since its earliest times, attempted to enforce a thorough-going secularisation of education, bitterly opposed by the catholic church which felt education to be an intrinsic part of its apostolic mission. Both parties had been anxious to instil their ideologies into their pupils. Mounier attempted by his pluralist and child-centred conception of education to escape the state of conflict, though ensuring an adequate margin of freedom for the church to pursue its interests.

Turning to the problems of private life, a subject to which Mounier always attached great importance, he attacked the unreflecting mediocrity of bourgeois comfort, pleaded for the recognition of women as persons in their own right, and laid down recommendations for the renewal and enrichment of family life as a free community of persons. Seen in the context of the conservative and authoritarian conception of women and the family traditionally held by the church, these considerations represented a considerable step towards liberation, though they seem somewhat timid forty years later.

Next, Mounier denounced the stagnation and sterilisation of culture induced by the spread of bourgeois values, and while refusing to admit state control, advocated greater state patronage of the arts. He also reminded artists and intellectuals that they were by no means dispensed from observing the moral and social values which bound other men. These conclusions are particularly interesting, for they anticipate several aspects of the development of artistic and intellectual concern in France, particularly in the matters of state subsidy for art and the rise of popular and committed literature, which was not new, but which particularly marked Mounier's generation.

He saw economics as conditioning, though not determining, human activity. Its practical importance was out of all proportion to its position in the hierarchy of values, he thought, but was such that he devoted much space to it. Condemning in some detail the complex mechanisms of modern technological capitalism, which alienate and depersonalise, he proposed a pluralist economy in which profit was subordinated to production, production to consumption, and consumption to human needs. The details were not closely elaborated, since that would have been futile, but the principles were firmly established, and in effect reversed the order of priorities prevailing in modern capitalism. It remained a moral critique, however, drawing not only on Proudhon but also on some of Marx's early analyses, centring on the concept of alienation, and on Scheler's formulation of value-hierarchy.

Partly deriving from this was his political position. Rejecting the centralised state, he outlined a pluralist and decentralised democracy in which a skeleton state, with constituent powers firmly separated, would accurately represent the will of the people. Again, no firm details were provided, but Mounier suggested that there was much scope for invention within the bounds of his personalist principles, and pointed to the Proudhonist rather than the marxist tradition as the current from which his state would take its inspiration. It was also clear that, in his political philosophy, Mounier's precursors were the eighteenth-century theorists Montesquieu and the utopians just as much as Proudhon and Tocqueville from more recent times.

In the field of international affairs, Mounier condemned a narrow and aggressive nationalism at the same time as a weak-willed and unrealistic pacifism, but argued that France should strive to become a strong, independent nation without colonial or oppressive ambition, but one which would be able to assert and defend its right to live in peace and cooperation with demilitarised neighbours. Even less than the previous discussions was this section developed in detail. Mounier was not proposing a blueprint for foreign policy, but rather suggesting long-term objectives which ignored the short-term measures necessitated by international expediency. The high principles put forward were unfortunately not supported by any serious analysis of the nature or context of international relations and, more than the other sections, lacked concrete reality.

The question of action
The method of the *Manifeste* was to analyse both the structures of contemporary society and those of the ideal personalist society. Once the lines of the directing personalist utopia were laid down, the outstanding question still remained: how to progress to it? The first step, Mounier said, was the purification of the revolutionaries and the establishment of their unconditional commitment to honesty, integrity and generosity. With this accomplished, he thought it would be possible to undertake revolutionary activity provided it was directed at finding new modes of action consonant with the emergence of a new personalist society. Only as a final resort, when every other means had been tried, did he think it permissible to consider the use of coercive violence, and then only under the strictest of conditions.

One last question remained to be answered: who was going to carry out the personalist revolution? Sectarianism was excluded, but at the same time he accepted that the harsh realities had to be faced: there were few people capable of the appropriate dedication, and no success would be possible without the support of the working class. The problem as he saw it was to unite the true spiritual values, so long usurped by the bourgeois establishment, with the rich fund of values preserved intact by the working class, thereby waging a concerted struggle against the totalitarianism which threatened on either side. In practical terms, this meant for Mounier that a small number of active and intelligent people must be formed, who by training and dedication would be able so to affect those around them that far-reaching movements of renewal would be set in motion. It was an accurate description of the ambitions of *Les Amis d'Esprit*, and also a statement of Mounier's mission as the education of a spiritual and cultural élite to provide the initiative and inspiration for the personalist revolution.

In the autumn of 1936 the hopes placed in the new government were still green, and it would have been absurd to call for a revolution against a government established and still supported by a greater part of the popular forces. Many of its principles were in harmony with Mounier's and it was a permissible ambition to exercise, by the judicious infiltration of men and ideas, a certain influence over its policies, giving them a more personalist bias. He felt that the government was probably keeping itself informed of developments in catholic thinking, if only from electoral self-interest. If he could command even that limited attention, he thought that the quality of his review's work was high enough to exercise an influence by the power of truth embodied in it. Successive numbers of *Esprit* reflected this attitude. Special studies laid down recommendations on trade unions, education, the law, popular culture and political and economic realism among other things. These were areas in which the review was able to offer serious analyses which might be listened to. The decay of the *Front populaire* prevented any progressive influence *Esprit* might have had, as the left-wing coalition was gradually taken over by those interests it was trying to attack. In addition, the political scene was increasingly dominated by the course of international events. Mounier could hardly hope to influence them, but he could try to modify their effects on French attitudes, and it was in this perspective that he addressed himself to the problems of international politics.

Although it carried the subtitle 'revue internationale', *Esprit* did not pay close attention to foreign affairs during its early years. Its position consisted of denouncing the faults of the treaty of Versailles, suggesting the strengthening of the League of Nations, and lamenting the lack of adequate international response to the rise of Italian fascism and German national socialism. It had called for an end to colonisation and its consequences, exemplified by the war in Indo-China, in which France was engaged. In 1936, when Italy invaded Abyssinia, *Esprit* became involved in the controversy which divided catholics first on the ethics of expansion, and later on the interpretation of Pius xi's speech on the subject. Placing himself firmly on the same side as the christian democrats, Mounier condemned Italian imperialism and called for peace initiatives in France such as were being made by the English churches. But he was consistently reluctant to exacerbate the controversy, particularly on the delicate question of sanctions, and sought a solution which would be acceptable to all catholics, without retreating from his demands for justice and peace. He displayed here the same mixture of caution and boldness as elsewhere. Nowhere did he show it more, however, than in the most passionately argued international issue of these years: the Spanish civil war. The Spanish war, a unique and central issue in its own right, is also worth close scrutiny as a model of Mounier's handling of controversial questions, particularly in foreign affairs.

The Spanish civil war

The situation in Spain in 1936 was complex. Briefly, the left-wing popular front government, with the support of the communist and anarchist-dominated labour movement, had taken power after legal elections, bringing to an end a long period of conservative, catholic-dominated government, often dictatorship. In its efforts to introduce radical reforms, including widespread nationalisation of land and industry, the government had met bitter opposition from the property-owners, supported by the catholic church. Right-wing para-military leagues were formed modelled on Italian and German fascism. The violence ensuing escalated until a group of catholic generals led a rebellion against the government. These were the nationalists, among whom General Franco emerged as the leader, supported not only by the church but by Italian and German military aid. For three years the war was fought with a proliferation of brutalities on both sides until eventually the nationalists won. In France catholics were invited to see Franco's action as a holy war, encouraged by stories of republican violence against churches and priests; whereas the left generally urged that active support be given to the republic, and many Frenchmen left to fight for it in the international brigades.

Mounier himself had visited and acquired a deep affection for Spain; one of his first international correspondents was José Maria de Semprun y Gurrea, a catholic university teacher of law and political science in Madrid. Since late 1933 Semprun had contributed periodical accounts of political and social developments, and in early 1936 commented on the February elections there, welcoming the overwhelming confidence of the people in the republican *Frente popular* government headed by Azaña, but regretting the lack of spiritual leaders as a result of the heavy commitment of the catholic hierarchy to reactionary politics.[14] In May he answered rumours of civil war by defending the government, condemning the violence of the fascist leagues, and drawing attention to the partiality of the French press in reporting on Spain.[15] Another Spanish friend of *Esprit*, the catholic theologian, José Bergamin, held a similar attitude, insisting that the republican cause was at least compatible with the church's teaching. After the outbreak of hostilities, Mounier pointed out the dilemma for a catholic caught between two opposed blocks: on the one side the nationalist rebels with nothing to recommend them but the official support of the church in Spain; on the other side the government with everything to recommend it but its anti-clericalism. He praised the courage of his friends' choice but was careful not commit himself clearly to that option.[16] This attitude was dictated by intellectual integrity: an honest and intelligent case could conceivably be made for the other side; and by prudence: he could not be certain what position the church would allow him without considering censure.

In France, public opinion was being inflamed by the appearance in the press of exaggerated stories and lurid photographs suggesting devastating atrocities committed gratuitously against churches, priests and catholics by the government. Mounier insisted on presenting in *Esprit* the positive aspects of the republic's achievement and the series of atrocities committed by the rebels. He firmly denounced the widespread appeal to consider Franco as a crusader fighting a holy war, and constantly reaffirmed his sympathy for the Spanish working class, the republican basque priests and such gestures as the philosopher Miguel de Unamuno's opposition to Franco. In this, he was in a minority among catholics. The christian democrats were critical of Franco but even less fond of the republicans, with the result that they tended to take a firmly abstentionist line, which was as near as most catholics came to Mounier's position. Even François Mauriac, despite his much-repeated attacks on Franco and the call to a holy war, and Bernanos, despite his denunciation of nationalist atrocities, had little sympathy for the government forces. In this state of isolation it is therefore not surprising that Mounier avoided committing himself to republicanism, but he did nothing to suppress the pro-republican views of many of his colleagues in *Esprit*.

On 26 April 1937, German aircraft fighting for the nationalists bombed and strafed the basque town of Guernica, systematically destroying it and massacring its inhabitants. More than any other event, this atrocity mobilised international indignation. Mounier felt able for once to give vent to his anger and roundly denounced Franco. There was no longer any question of political option, he argued, the massacre was to be condemned on moral grounds.[17] For the June edition of *Esprit*, he wrote a detailed account of the reporting of the bombing, revealing the system of lies and contradictions with which the nationalists and the press favourable to them had attempted to deny their responsibility, and establishing as far as possible the truth of the matter.[18] He also agreed to sit on a commission of enquiry into the bombing and on a committee for civil and religious peace in Spain, which also included Mauriac and Maritain. Neither body, however, had more than a protest value.

As a result of its attitudes to the Spanish conflict, *Esprit* was now coming under heavy criticism from the catholic press, particularly the *Echo de Paris*, which still nursed a grievance from the Castelnau affair, and *Action française*, under the aegis of Massis. Apart from scurrilous personal attacks, the most serious charge was the recurrent one of encouraging communism, made more grave because of the publication on 28 March 1937 of a papal encyclical, *Divini Redemptoris*, which reiterated in stronger terms than before the church's position that communism was intrinsically wrong and that catholics should not under any circumstances cooperate with it. Mounier was categorical in denying that he supported communism in any way, but he was nonetheless obliged to exercise increased caution in his statements. In the spring of 1938 Semprun wrote calling for firm support by French catholics, in the republic's struggle for survival against the combined force of Franco, Hitler and Mussolini.[19] He left the question of concrete action open, but implicitly suggested that pressure be exerted for French intervention on behalf of the legal government. In his highly nuanced reply, Mounier reminded Semprun of the passion and polemic which Spain aroused among French catholics, adding that, so long as there was in France no irreparable division in the church or state, it was his duty not to cut himself off from one part of his country or his religion, particularly with the spectre of civil war as a consequence of such an action. This duty seemed to him all the more urgent since, by the inevitable impurity of action, Semprun's position entailed more acceptance of communism and other undesirable elements than Mounier could willingly admit. He pointed out that his attitude was only valid for those few who, at *Esprit*, put clarity and justice above any commitment to concrete action, but he accepted that for the majority it was necessary to come down on one side or the other, and made it clear that, on this basis, Semprun had his support. This reply is a fine example of Mounier's subtlety, the despair of less patient readers, but indispensable in the context of the many-fronted action he was undertaking. It is hard to fault his scrupulous fairness on a literal level, but the informed reader could not fail to see a clear-cut choice being made. Despite the many reservations it advanced, the effect of the reply was to endorse Semprun, while avoiding the risk of conflict with the church.

Mounier's attitude to Spain was exemplary in several ways. First, the Spanish civil war was the central international affair of this period, though not the only one, and as such served as an important yardstick for situating any writer or movement in the increasing political polarisation which was imposing itself on France. While he deplored the polarisation and stressed the importance of values beyond politics, Mounier nonetheless firmly placed himself on the side of the working class and the non-communist left. Second, his attitude to Spain provides a pattern for his approach to every other major issue. He constantly surrounded his commitment with a full range of reservations which ensured that it was compatible with the teaching of the church. This rendered his writing difficult to approach through a straightforward reading. But he appreciated that for most purposes, and certainly for the purposes of action, a simpler position was vital, and was always careful to indicate what the lines of such a position were. Third, his own written thought has always to be taken in the context of other expressed positions either within or outside of *Esprit*. His statements were often only one half of a dialogue, frequently correcting or completing another's position. His use of contributors to *Esprit* was so conceived as to permit things to be said which he could not himself formulate as director. This resulted in his own statements often appearing far more cautious in isolation than the impression given by the review as a whole. Finally, by taking a position on Spain which ran counter to the overwhelming tendency of French catholics, Mounier was relying on the ideological influence, or moral authority, which *Esprit* had established for itself on other grounds. He was not tapping any substantial body of opinion among catholics, but rather adopting an avant-garde position in the attempt to introduce new attitudes into his readership. This was his work of education at its clearest, as he fought to stem the most regrettable effects of an international crisis on the attitudes of catholics. It was a stand which required considerable courage, particularly if there had been any foundation in the widespread fear that the war might spread to France. It is debatable whether Mounier had much success in his efforts in these two or three years, but, though he could not yet know it, it was ideologically important after the Liberation to have been identified as a pro-republican, however many reservations such a designation might conceal.

Anarchism
In addition to its political effects, the war in Spain also provided the spur for a further refinement of *Esprit*'s political ideology. The Proudhonist tradition, from which many of the review's analyses sprang, shared many common features with the strong anarchist current within the Spanish labour movement. The anarchists were

playing an important role on certain sectors of the battlefront. In France they became a focus of attention for those elements of the left who found the leading role of the Spanish and international communist movement disagreeable. The interest aroused by anarchism can be measured by the success of *Esprit*'s special number on the subject, which sold out within a few days of its publication.

Anarchism as a political ideology had risen to prominence in the latter part of the nineteenth century. Though a number of thinkers could be regarded as important theorists, there was no coherent central doctrine which could be taken as accurately summing up anarchism. It is almost true that there were as many forms of anarchism as there were anarchists. The defining theme was an opposition to the concept of the state, usually accompanied by a vigorous refusal to accept any form of authority or absolute, whether political, religious or intellectual. It combined a defence of individual freedom with spontaneous and militant political activity. Although most anarchists were animated by these concerns, the ways in which they developed and expressed them were varied in the extreme. The indiscriminate terrorist activity associated with turn-of-the-century French and Russian anarchists was far from representative of anarchism generally. Much more typical were the peaceful syndicalist streams within the European labour movement: nowhere was this clearer than in Northern Spain.

Mounier's aim in devoting a lengthy study to anarchism was first to show a close relationship between his own ideology and a well established current of working-class ideology, and second to present his thought as offering an effective synthesis of the most valuable elements of the anarcho-syndicalist tradition.[21] He attempted to isolate those features which were most operative in the labour movement, and those which could be assimilated to his own personalism. He therefore began by dismissing those forms of anarchism which had no basis in the working class: Max Stirner's egocentric individualism, Leo Tolstoy's idyllic ruralism, Sergei Nechayev's frenetic nihilism. He confined himself to the positive contributions of the theorists Proudhon, Bakunin and Kropotkin, whose work, he felt, might offer a viable basis for a new alternative to communism, and provide a means of wooing the workers from their entrenched allegiance to marxism. In this light, he offered a brief history of the first international from the anarchist point of view. Marx and Engels were presented as doctrinaire, power-hungry manipulators who ruthlessly crushed the authentic aspirations of the working-class as expressed by Bakunin and by the

French anarchist representatives. By this means Mounier tried to present the success of marxism as in part achieved by underhand dealings and not necessarily permanent.

Passing from history to ideas, Mounier suggested that the central point of anarchism was its critique of power and authority. In the first instance, he agreed, this took the form of a denial of God, but more essential was the refusal of political power. Basing his analysis closely on Proudhon, Mounier accepted the anarchist point that authoritarian and coercive power-structures implied a pessimistic view of man, and that it should be possible to create a just society which would not be disordered but, built on free exchange, would simply be different from the present social order, based on authority. He added, however, that there was perhaps a legitimate sense to the concept of authority, divine or human. Mounier distinguished two radically different meanings of authority, as spiritual pre-eminence or as mere coercive force. He suggested that the error of the anarchists lay in not appreciating that there existed hierarchies of spiritual ascendancy, which had the need and the right to be expressed in the visible world, even if it involved a limited degree of coercive force. He felt that the anarchist attack on power and authority was justified against the abuse of authority, but that it should not be allowed to detract from legitimate spiritual authority as exercised by God or by human persons. He argued that this view of authority retained the essence of anarchist thought, but integrated it into a higher, more complete account. Mounier was concerned as far as possible to reconcile catholic teaching with a plausible interpretation of anarchism, in order to acquire the broadest possible area in which to install his personalism. Since he could allow himself little latitude of interpretation with his catholic values, it is not surprising if he was less scrupulous in what he presented as the principles of anarchism.

Next, he turned to examine the anarchist denunciation of government and the state. Anarchists did not reject the principle of social order, he insisted, but they did reject the imposition of a specific form of order on the grounds that it bred oppression and alienation. States, in their view, were by their nature based on an alienation of liberty, he said, and even the most equitable of state machines remained a machine, generating power and its consequent abuse. Hence no government could be revolutionary, since revolution was against government by nature, and no historical government, however apparently progressive, had been other than reactionary. The only possible solution, he argued, was a federative, 'pluralist', state. He explained that the principle of federation implied a series of autonomous, freely associated members, each having the right of secession. Economic and industrial decentralisation followed logically from this, he pointed out, though centralised controls might be necessary to a limited degree. In this matter, Mounier agreed that anarchist thought suffered, by comparison with marxism, from imprecision and naivety. But he insisted that the spirit of freedom and generosity inherent in their thought more than compensated, since they were promoting the liberty and integrity of the person, and their basic values were the same as those dominating personalist political theory.

Going on to deal with the philosophical bases of anarchism, Mounier acknowledged that reconciliation with personalism in this sphere was more problematical, since anarchism's irreducible core was positivist materialism. The refusal of absolutes and the attack on spiritualism left anarchists without an adequate philosophy of man and led logically to metaphysical individualism, he argued. He added, however, that this was counter-balanced by a rejection of the impersonal determinism of marxism and a defence of three important values: human dignity, emancipation and revolt. They also offered, he said, a valuable account of the community, which provided a richer analogy with his own vision. Mounier pointed out that anarchists refused to accept mass society as the only form of collective existence and proposed a model of society which was decentralised and organic, rather than centralised and mechanical. They saw 'the people' as a complex and organic whole which could not strictly be defined, he argued, since any attempt to reduce it to simpler components, such as social classes, resulted in the destruction of its reality. If 'the people' were thus conceived, it was evident to Mounier that the emancipation of the proletariat, the only section remaining in servitude, must inevitably engender the liberation of the entire people. This he saw as the goal which anarchism proposed for itself.

In conclusion Mounier set out to summarise what he regarded as anarchism's positive contribution. In effect he pointed out the various ways in which the anarchist tradition had prepared working class socialism to receive personalism. Its major contribution, he said, was the refusal of the will to power as a temptation both on a personal and a political level. He explained that it combined this refusal with a thoroughgoing critique of politicians, who tended to be so engrossed in the struggle for power that they forgot the emancipation of the proletariat. The anarchists understood that even when the politicians were not of bourgeois origin, they soon become assimilated to a bourgeois power-élite, he said, with the consequent reluctance to abandon their positions of power and privilege. The same critique, he suggested, applied to the intellectuals who automatically parasitised the working class, and although they did not exclude them from the revolution, anarchists very properly insisted that intellectuals be put in their humble place, and not be allowed to attain preponderance in a movement they should serve without seeking to control. Although it became ridiculous when systematised, he argued, anarchism was a fertile and unsystematic movement best suited to defending those qualities it embodied in the libertarian and even utopian wing of the socialist movement. While it was not capable of constructing a coherent plan of action even on a theoretical level, he thought, it did at least prevent the working class from becoming closed in a rigid marxism, and thereby held the door open to personalism. Finally, Mounier drew two practical lessons. Anarchism had always insisted on the need for ideological propaganda, he said, recognising that men must be transformed, as well as institutions, if the revolution was to succeed. And anarchism was firmly committed to concrete and direct action, he added, realising that beliefs had to be implemented. Even if they had occasionally fallen into excess, their infallible presence in revolution either on the barricades or in the market place had, in Mounier's view, assured them of an influence out of all proportion to their number. It was clear to him that personalism would benefit by adopting similarly active commitments.

Mounier's study of anarchism was an attempt to establish personalism as a political ideology, with a base in the working class, offering an alternative to marxism. By comparing it with anarchism Mounier situated personalism as an ideology of like aspirations. He suggested that anarchism had been groping for values and truths which personalism clearly apprehended, and that anarchism's political and institutional aims were fully included in personalism, though given an improved formulation. There was therefore no reason, Mounier implied, why personalism should not supplant anarchism as the libertarian current of working class socialism. The success of his ambition is best judged by its practical consequences. Though personalism belonged in some ways to the anarcho-syndicalist tradition, its influence failed to extend much beyond a few leading figures of the catholic labour movement. It never acquired a base in the working class, but its ideas did contribute to the gradual development of working-class organisations such as the

Confédération Française des Travailleurs Chrétiens, which was beginning to move from outmoded catholic social doctrines and conservative industrial practices to a more combative industrial strategy linked to a renewed form of syndicalist social and political theory.

On an intellectual level, Mounier's work invites serious criticism. His presentation of anarchism was excessively selective, both in limiting his sources to three thinkers and in taking disparate elements from each. He relied heavily on Proudhon in the field of political theory and on Bakunin in metaphysics; Kropotkin was only introduced for occasional corroboration. He stressed in each case the divergences from Marx, ignoring the convergences. He described a total anarchism which corresponded to nothing a professed anarchist would recognise as his. The tendentiousness of some analyses may be attributed in part to the undoubted diffuseness of anarchist thought, but they are more seriously the result of Mounier's limited concept of dialogue. In this dialogue with anarchism, Mounier showed that he was unable to deal with atheism or materialism except by ascribing them to insufficient thought, and that he could not recognise them as serious or lucid positions. He was embarrassed by the firm assertion of any belief he did not share, and tended to assume that it was symptomatic of a deeper, often contrary, impulse. He was incapable of questioning his own beliefs in the spirit he asked of his interlocutors, since he considered himself to be possessed of the truth on essential matters, and his opponents at best groping for it. In view of these limits, Mounier failed to appreciate the full force of anarchist thought or to add to the understanding of it. The book was, however, a first attempt at ideological warfare with a serious socialist opponent, and as such prepared the ground for the more important battle he was preparing to engage with marxism. The stance from which Mounier judged the anarchists was common to the vast majority of his readership. His essay was immediately useful to those he wrote for, providing a safe approach and a ready response to an important current of political thought. Its qualities were those which made Mounier a successful publicist and ideologist, its failings were those which prevented him from becoming an important theorist.

1938

By the summer of 1938, Mounier had already fulfilled many of the tasks he was beginning to work on in the spring of 1931. On a personal level, he had established himself in the catholic intellectual élite as the leading figure of a respected journal, and as a serious spokesman for those catholics who were open to the political left. The philosophy of personalism which had been elaborated in the first two or three years of the review's existence was being put to use both as a basis for analysing other philosophies and theoretical problems, and also as the central doctrine of a new ideology which claimed to offer practical remedies to the political and social problems that were becoming urgent in the mid-1930s. Although ideology and philosophy are inextricably bound together, the driving force behind the philosophy was its function as ideology. Mounier was not interested in philosophy for its own sake, he was interested in it as doctrine which would direct people's minds and ultimately their actions. To accomplish this ideological mission he had *Esprit*, a successful review with a stable and receptive audience, a coherent body of doctrine and a record of outspokenness and integrity. *Esprit* was an impressive intellectual achievement, but its audience was more limited than its content suggested. The influence of the review was mainly felt in middle-class catholic homes and among a small circle of non-catholic intellectuals. Its commitment to action by a dedicated élite took account of this, but on the level of action the élite had proved surprisingly sterile. Its commitment to reflection also took account of its audience, but in the field of political ideology, *Esprit* found itself parasitic on the practically-oriented ideologies which were being developed independently of it by the main parties of the *Front populaire*. Its own doctrine was abstract and its detailed political programme virtually irrelevant in the absence of anyone to carry it out. Whereas its political analyses, its special studies and its sometimes courageous statements of principle were generally respected, the fact remained that it was still only interpreting the world, not changing it.

The extent to which Mounier had become aware of the need for political and social action was clearly expressed in his report to the July 1938 conference of *Esprit* at Jouy-en-Josas.[22] In it he abandoned his earlier taste for apolitism and non-conformism, considering that the need was now for concrete and constructive political action. He understood that actions spoke louder than words and felt that the review's concrete political commitments had had more real influence than its best doctrinal studies. This did not mean that a firmly worked out guiding doctrine was rejected, but that he realised it had to be constantly expressed, and if necessary, modified, in action. He recognised that the easy moralism which led to a vague and universal benevolence was a constantly lurking danger which had to be rejected in favour of a firm and virile commitment.

In practical terms Mounier felt that *Esprit* had some influence among socialists and christian democrats, and in the *Front populaire* as a whole, but while he thought that it should be exploited, he found it ultimately inadequate because of the imperfections inherent in these organisations. What he foresaw was a series of political flying columns with the immediate object of forming militants and undertaking specific action on important issues. Mounier had come a considerable way from the *Amis d'Esprit* discussion groups, and there was a sense of urgency about his proposals which only serious pressure from events could produce.

Since Hitler's spring *Anschluss* of Austria, the international situation had rapidly deteriorated. By the early summer of 1938 it was clear that the emergency situation over Czechoslovakia could easily lead to a major European conflict. *Esprit* was entirely sympathetic to the plight of the Czechoslovakian people and strongly opposed the injustice which was being prepared. The Munich agreement and its aftermath was a turning point for Europe, and Mounier's reaction to it marked a decisive turning point in the development of the review. Munich was a culmination and a beginning; henceforth the question of war and peace dominated everything.

Notes

1 E. Mounier, 'Les leçons de l'émeute, ou la révolution contre les mythes', *Esprit*, no18, mars 1934, p905–915. Reprinted in *Oeuvres* I p361–369.
2 E. Mounier, 'Les pseudo-valeurs spirituelles fascistes', *Esprit*, no16, janvier 1934, p533–540. Reprinted in *Oeuvres* I p223–228.
3 E. Mounier, '*Esprit* au congrès franco-italien sur la corporation', *Esprit*, no33, juin 1935, p474–480.
4 E. Mounier & G. de Santillana, 'Dialogue sur l'État Fasciste', *Esprit*, no35–6, septembre 1935, p725–751.
5 E. Mounier, 'Tentation du communisme, pour un certain sang-froid spirituel', *Esprit*, no21, juin 1934, p416–425. Reprinted in *Oeuvres* I p229–235.
6 *Oeuvres* IV p536–538.
7 E. Mounier, 'Les catholiques et la défense nationale', *Esprit*, no31, avril 1935, p133–134.
8 The texts and a commentary on them can be found in René Rémond, *Les catholiques, le communisme et les crises 1929–1939* (Paris 1960) p79–83.
9 See A. Ulmann, 'La candidature Chiappe, scandale public', *Esprit*, no30, avril 1935, p126–128; E. Mounier, 'Contre Chiappe', *Esprit*, no 32, mai 1935, p331–333; E. Mounier, 'Leçons d'une campagne', *Esprit*, no33, juin 1935, p457–460, and *Oeuvres* IV p569, in his notebook dated 17 May 1935.
10 'Notre humanisme (déclaration collective),' *Esprit*, no37, octobre 1935, p1–24.

11 E. Mounier 'Rassemblement populaire', *Esprit*, no45, juin 1936, p441–449.
12 E. Mounier, 'Court traité de la mythique de gauche', *Esprit*, no66, mars 1938, p873–890. Reprinted in *Oeuvres* IV p40–75.
13 *Oeuvres* IV p582–595.
14 J. M. Semprun y Gurrea, 'Espagne, le drame électoral', *Esprit*, no41, fevrier 1936, p839–843, and 'Après les élections en Espagne', *Esprit*, no43, avril 1936, p13–16.
15 J. M. Semprun y Gurrea, 'La guerre civile en Espagne, ou l'organisation du mensonge', *Esprit*, no44, mai 1936, p280–282.
16 E. Mounier, 'Espagne, signe de contradiction', *Esprit*, no49, octobre 1936, p1–3.
17 E. Mounier, 'Guernica', *Esprit*, no56, mai 1937, p327.
18 E. Mounier, 'Guernica, ou la technique du mensonge', *Esprit*, no57, juin 1937, p449–473.
19 J. M. Semprun y Gurrea, 'Lettre ouverte à Emmanuel Mounier', *Esprit*, no68, mai 1938, p235–243.
20 E. Mounier, 'Réponse à Semprun', *Esprit*, no68, mai 1938, p245–251, reprinted in *Oeuvres* IV p31–39.
21 E. Mounier, 'Anarchie et personnalisme', *Esprit*, no55, avril 1937, p109–206. Reprinted in *Oeuvres* I p635–725. The essay was also reprinted in two collections of Mounier's articles, *Liberté sous conditions* (Paris 1946) and *Communisme, anarchie et personnalisme* (Paris 1966).
22 E. Mounier, '*Esprit* et l'action politique', *Esprit*, no73, octobre 1938, p34–64.

Bibliographical Notes

The events in France at this period (1934–8) are well described by Alexander Werth, who was the Paris correspondent of the *Manchester Guardian*, in his books *France in Ferment* (London 1934) and *The Destiny of France* (London 1937). Catholic positions are examined in René Rémond, *Les catholiques, le communisme et les crises* (Paris 1960). The popular front period is well described and documented in L. Bodin and J. Touchard, *Front populaire* (Paris 1961) and G. Lefranc, *Le Front populaire* (Paris 1965). Useful studies of the Spanish civil war can be found in H. Thomas, *The Spanish Civil War* (London 1961) and F. Borkenau, *The Spanish Cockpit* (London 1937); interesting catholic reactions are given in A. Coutrot, *Sept* (Paris 1961) and G. Bernanos, *Les grands cimetières sous la lune* (Paris 1938). Anarchism is well studied in G. Woodcock, *Anarchism* (London 1963); J. Joll, *The Anarchists* (London 1964); D. Guerin, *L'anarchisme* (Paris 1965); H. Arvon, *L'anarchisme* (Paris 1968).

CHAPTER FOUR

War (1938–1944)

Munich and its aftermath
In March 1938 the German army marched into Austria; from that time on, war became a real possibility. European politics was dominated by the Czechoslovakian crisis. Hitler claimed the right to annexe the Sudetenland area of the country to Germany on the grounds of a large proportion of German-speakers in the population. The claim was strongly resisted by the Czech government. France and Britain, fearing that the situation might provoke a military confrontation, met the German and Italian leaders in Munich in September 1938 and came to an agreement conceding the German claim. Daladier, the French Prime Minister, and Chamberlain, the British, claimed a victory for peace in Europe. Public reaction in France was mixed, regretting the plight of the Czechoslovak nation, but welcoming the apparent assurance that war was averted. The agreement was received with a divided mind by every major political grouping in France, with the exception of the communist party, which vehemently opposed it.

Mounier's reaction was instantaneous and unequivocal. In a strongly worded leader article entitled 'Lendemains d'une trahison',[1] he roundly denounced the betrayal, condemning those who perpetrated it. Characteristically, he saw the action as stemming from a deeper cause than political mismanagement. The cowardice and decadence of the whole French nation were to blame, he argued. France, he said, was in the grip of a spiritual malady which impelled it to dishonour and disavow its tradition of heroism and justice, a corrupt bourgeoisie had injected its poison into the nation, and Munich was the culmination of its effects. Condemning both the agreement and its spirit, he declared that the essential need was to oppose fascism with strength in the full awareness of its easily discernible ambitions. He warned that anti-Germanism and purely negative anti-fascism were not the answer, but that what was needed was a national re-awakening on personalist lines. Only this, coupled with international disarmament, he said, could avert catastrophe. Mounier foresaw the likelihood of war and some of its consequences, and resolved to fight to attenuate its effects in the minds of the population, with the object of creating the best possible conditions for a successful aftermath.

Since the Munich agreement was accompanied by the mobilisation of French military reservists and by frenetic rearmament, Mounier had every inducement to produce an analysis of this nature. The acceptance that war was likely imposed a totally different perspective: that of a major historical catastrophe which would affect every aspect of life. From his position of helplessness, Mounier felt that all he could hope to do was to limit the moral damage. Faced with the urgency of events, it had been agreed at *Esprit*'s summer conference that an organ was needed which would be more capable of dealing with developments than was possible for a monthly review. To this end a fortnightly newspaper was created. Entitled *Le Voltigeur*, and directed by *Esprit*'s theatre critic, Pierre-Aimé Touchard, it was intended to concern itself with questions of immediate political importance, basing itself on the principles of *Esprit*, and run by the friends and contributors of the review. Mounier wrote a number of short articles for it himself, but the majority of the contributions came from those members of *Esprit* whose interests were more specifically political. The need for such a paper was soon demonstrated, for the proliferation of crises leading up to the declaration of war made it difficult even for the *Voltigeur* to keep abreast of events.

From the summer of 1938 until September 1939, Mounier's thought was dominated by the impending war. Apart from the moral issues involved, he was concerned at the attitude of the church and the recrudescence of fascism in France. In the *Voltigeur* he did what he could to prevent catholic opinion from following the conservative right in its sympathy for Hitler and its disregard for nazi victims. He stressed the papal condemnation of nazism, constantly referring to the encyclical *Mit brennender Sorge*, in which the pope had spoken to the church in Germany early in 1937 pointing out the inacceptability of certain basic nazi doctrines. In one particularly courageous article, he spoke out plainly against what he saw as cowardice in Pius XII's refusal to condemn atrocities committed by Hitler and Mussolini, and the explicit approval accorded to Franco's initiation of war in Spain.[2] The months preceding the war also saw an alarming proliferation of fascism in France, both in the tradition of the French extreme right, and imitated from the German and Italian models. Mounier's stand against it was determined. Fascism was a strong and seductive movement, he argued; like nazism, it showed no gratitude for concessions made, and could only be countered by a resolute and forceful affirmation of true values, particularly those which fascism sought eventually to suppress. Christians should not be deceived by the lip-service paid to religion, he warned, for it was purely temporary and tactical. At the same time, he said, the opponents of fascism should avoid the trap of setting up an alternative type of fascism, which would be just as totalitarian and would defeat the object. Radical regeneration and constructive resistance should not be abandoned for their caricatures of frenetic activism and shrill diatribe, he insisted, and opposition to nazi imperialism should not be a cover for French imperialist aspirations. Worse, he thought, was the fatalistic acquiescence before the displays of power presented in Italy and Germany, the paralysis of the will which was a prelude to servile imitation and, eventually, cheerful subjugation. Mounier's analysis was lucid and thorough in showing the moral dangers inherent in fascism; he was subtle in exposing the dangers which threatened to pervert the different responses. In presenting his solutions, however, he displayed only a theoretical understanding. This was partly because he was concerned with the values involved and with fostering awareness among catholics. But it also sprang from his lack of a clear global analysis of fascism and from his relative lack of contact with those forces which were actively fighting it.

War and peace

Mounier was among the first to realise that the immediate effect of Munich, far from ensuring peace, was to make war highly probable in the near future. The same realisation struck the whole of France within a few weeks, provoking intense discussion of the problems of war and peace. Mounier's contribution was a detailed study of the problems from a christian point of view, entitled *Pacifistes ou Bellicistes?*,[3] and published in pamphlet form during the summer of 1939. Defining peace as a spiritual state, not simply the absence of military warfare, Mounier pointed out that peace could not be said to exist when hatreds and armaments were proliferating, nor so long as politics remained a continuation of war by other means. Christian peace was not synonymous with tranquillity, docility or immobility, he argued, it demanded courage, sacrifice and action, and in some situations it might require the use of force, if that were the only way the christian's inner strength could express itself.

He equated peace with the affirmation of the human person in all its dimensions. Peace as an eternal order had to be based on justice, generosity and love, he said.

Examining the church's declared doctrine, Mounier emphasised its condemnation of general and obligatory conscription, of armed peace, of economic imperialism, of the militarisation of youth and of the disregard for treaties; he stressed the two constructive principles of arbitration and disarmament. If all failed, he argued, there were limited conditions in which the use of force was legitimate. War was a catastrophe both spiritually and materially, he said, and in the context of 1939, it pointed to the failure of western christianity, but he emphasised that there were other, worse, catastrophic eventualities. The problem of war was a choice between relative failures, he said, in which the Christian was faced with a cruel dilemma. The only solution, in Mounier's view, was to refuse the dilemma until such time as one or other failure was forced on him, hoping at the same time that God would resolve the situation in the best possible way. Although, in a theoretical sense, Mounier evaded the issue by refusing its obvious terms, in the context of 1939, the practical consequence of his analysis was clear-cut: war was admitted as a possible, even probable, course of action, and one which should not be shirked if it became necessary. It served as an authoritative answer to the new-found pacifism of the right while avoiding any charge of war-mongering.

In the frenzied months following Munich, French and British diplomacy was everywhere conceding before the intransigence of German, Italian and even Spanish demands. Each concession was excused as being necessary for the avoidance of conflict, with the result that it became increasingly apparent that war was increasingly likely, and on increasingly unfavourable terms. The policy of a firm stand, even at the cost of war, was finding growing support on the political left. Hitler's invasion of Czechoslovakia and the fall of Prague in March 1939 marked the end of the last illusions generated by the Munich agreement. Simultaneously the behaviour of General Franco in snubbing the French ambassador to Spain, Marshal Pétain, in joining the Rome-Berlin axis, in demanding and receiving financial and military aid, awoke the traditional nationalism of the right, who now reluctantly joined the chorus of those who wanted a firm stand. From this time onwards France urgently prepared for war as crisis succeeded crisis, so that when it was eventually declared in September 1939, no-one, least of all Mounier, was surprised. *Esprit*'s analysis of the developing situation tended to consolidate its stature on the political left. Mounier revealed himself as a perceptive political commentator, but his success was a personal one, based on the acuity of his intelligence rather than the solidity of his professed ideology. And once again, the undoubtedly high quality of *Esprit*'s analysis failed to find any effective correlation in the concrete forces at work in the world around it.

The phoney war
From September 1939 until May 1940 the *drôle de guerre* plunged France into a strange half-world with all the discipline and appearance of war, but with little of its reality. Most of the action during these nine months was on the level of propaganda. A large section of the population was under army discipline, and the remainder were being exhorted to work to support the war machine. The communications media were under the strict supervision of the government information service, and critical comment was firmly discouraged. Most writers not on active service were quite willing to give their energies to promoting the war effort in whatever way they could, and much of what was published was entirely subordinated to this end.

Mounier, being deaf in one ear and almost blind in one eye, had not previously done any military service; with universal conscription he was called to join the Auxiliary Service in the region of Grenoble. His duties were clerical and undemanding so that he was able to devote some of his time to writing. Despite the considerable difficulties involved he succeeded, with the help of friends, in continuing to direct *Esprit,* which was allowed to continue publication. The work was mainly done by P.-A. Touchard and his wife, both in Paris. The independent publication of the *Voltigeur* was discontinued. To add to the material difficulties, Mounier's only daughter, Françoise, developed an incurable encephalitis following a smallpox injection. The child, aged two, was reduced to a vegetable-like existence till her death in 1954. This added a testing personal ordeal to the already difficult situation. In the situation which he had largely foreseen a year earlier, Mounier determined to carry out his intention of providing a haven of truth and lucidity amid the propaganda, lies and confusion of war. His primary task, Mounier felt, was to do full justice to the complexities of the various issues, thereby countering the oversimplification and easy emotivity of officially encouraged sources. He attempted to analyse the situation coolly, opposing the total militarisation of life, resisting the imposition of aggressive values of war in place of the spiritual values of peace, rejecting a crude and nationalistic anti-Germanism in favour of determined anti-nazism, keeping an open and constructive attitude to the preparation of the post-war period, and affirming the ultimate supremacy of love against the expedient fostering of hate. The personalist-spiritualist offensive was no longer appropriate, he realised, and he saw his work as a defensive action. In a sense, he believed, western civilisation was entering the beginning of a new middle ages. *Esprit,* he felt, could play the role of a monastery which would preserve the best part of the culture of the past to contribute to that of the future. He did not renounce the attempt to participate in and influence the events and thoughts of the day, but in the face of a massive war effort, he recognised that he could not hope to do any more than keep alive a small current of purity and integrity. The process of dehumanisation, necessary to the successful prosecution of the war, he knew could not be reversed; at best he hoped not to be tainted by it. Mounier did not believe that the axis powers would triumph, but at the same time he could not foresee a rapid allied victory—his perspective was of a long, grim, exhausting struggle. At the same time as asserting the primacy of spirituality, Mounier stressed the importance of commitment. Spirituality did not mean a detached cultivation of purity, he argued; on the contrary it demanded openness to events and a sustained, active presence in the world. The world was in more than usual need of assistance from the resources of the spirit, he suggested, and the menace which threatened to swamp spiritual values would not be evaded by surrendering to the temptation of withdrawal into exaggerated otherworldliness.

Despite his apparent assurance, the generality and vagueness of Mounier's writings at this period betray an underlying uncertainty. He was no longer sure what the main ideological enemy was, or how far he could oppose an undesirable propaganda which was nonetheless aimed at mobilising the nation's morale so as to defeat the axis powers more effectively. Although he was experienced in ideological struggle after seven years with *Esprit,* now that the government was seriously directing its attention to propaganda in pursuance of the war effort, Mounier was unsure of his response, and divided in his own mind about the war. Like the whole of France, he could only with difficulty believe in the reality of it; he was just old enough to remember the Great War, and tended to anticipate a conflict which would pose essentially the same problems. He assumed his country would win and one of his major preoccupations was the preparation of a peace treaty which would avoid the errors and excesses of the

Versailles Treaty of 1919. A resurgence of patriotism moderated his criticisms of the conservative and nationalistic government. In part this was a spontaneous desire to mute any comments which might impede the war effort, but in any case he had to show prudence under the constant threat of censorship. He dare not damage army morale since such an action would automatically deprive him of the readership he had built up in the armed forces, and perhaps bring about unfortunate consequences on a personal level since he was himself a soldier.

An important example of Mounier's readiness to accept the war as a priority was his reaction to the dissolution of the French communist party.[4] Since the signing of the Soviet-German pact of non-aggression in August 1939, the party had suppressed its previously vehement anti-nazism in favour of a blanket opposition to the war. This policy reversal had provoked fearful division in its ranks, but the official line had been accepted with varying degrees of reluctance by many militants. Eventually the French government, recognising that the party offered a potential danger to the war effort, declared it illegal. The measure provoked widespread protest in liberal circles, and the first result, as Mounier acknowledged, was to deprive a large section of the working class of any form of organisation or political expression. In a time of peace, he might well have denounced the move as a measure directed against the working class, but now he accepted it as necessary and approved it unreservedly. Not only did he not shed any tears, he also saw a golden opportunity to win the working class over to a personalist ideology while they were in a state of confusion. Clearly it was a tenable position to hold that the dissolution of the party was a necessity of war, but Mounier accepted the argument with surprising alacrity at a time when he had declared that the war could not be an absolute priority. Under pressure of circumstances the progressive political stance which *Esprit* had come to take in the late 1930s was gradually eroded. Within six months the war and its immediate problems brought the review to a position of confusion and near-collapse ideologically. In the Spring of 1940 Mounier was inevitably involved in the increased military activity. He was beginning to see a modified role for *Esprit,* owing to the difficulties of publication and diffusion facing most reviews, as a platform for writers who had lost their usual tribune, and he himself took a decreasing part in the review's activities. Its future now posed more questions than there were answers available, so that it was fitting and perhaps merciful that the catastrophe of events imposed its own solution.

The occupation

France fell in six weeks before the German onslaught. A demoralised national assembly transferred all its powers to the ageing Marshal Pétain, who dissolved the third republic and became *Chef de l'Etat Français*. France was overrun and divided up. Pétain as head of state was allowed to establish his administrative capital at Vichy and to have effective rule over a large area of southern France. The remainder of the country was under the direct rule of the occupying forces. At this moment there seemed little chance of Germany not conquering Europe, few people expected England to hold out, Russia was apparently in league with Hitler, America would not be committed, France was humiliated, continental Europe was overrun. The sensible thing seemed to be to make the best of a bad job, which was precisely what the Vichy régime at first seemed to offer. The Vichy government installed a right-wing, catholic administration under the motto *Travail, Famille, Patrie*, and called for France to repent of its sins and work for a spiritual renewal. In proposing a 'National Revolution', while leaving the terms vague, Pétain allowed a wide variety of people to believe that this was the revolution they had been calling for since the early 1930s. He also appeared to have wrested a degree of autonomy for his government, although in reality he was obliged to acquiesce in whatever the German authorities wanted.

After the *débâcle*, Mounier spent a short period in a prisoner-of-war camp but by early July he was demobilised and back in Grenoble with his family. His immediate concern was to discover what possibility he had of continuing *Esprit*, and to this end he established himself in Lyon, a natural centre of intellectual activity in the unoccupied southern zone. Along with several colleagues, Mounier hoped that the ambiguities in the new state philosophy might be made to permit true spiritual and human values to be smuggled in beneath the counterfeit. The ambition of subverting Vichy from within was encouraged by the fact that many of the official declarations were couched in terms analogous to those of his own personalism. It was clear to him that nothing was possible in the north, which was directly under nazi occupation, but in the south he was prepared to publish *Esprit* openly and to participate in the government-sponsored youth movements in order to propagate the gospel of the personalist revolution more effectively. After consultation with as many of his old associates as possible, it was agreed that *Esprit* should reappear, the first number coming out in November 1940.

Some of his friends warned him that publishing the review was likely to compromise him, whereas others were delighted at his courage. Mounier stood by his decision throughout, but he became less certain as the months passed.

The arguments levelled against him revolved around how far he might be construed as giving his tacit consent to the Vichy régime, and how far he allowed it to camouflage its essential totalitarianism under an apparent liberalism. No one, it is true, seriously saw Mounier as any sort of collaborationist, but there was deep division over the tactical wisdom of his action. In his own defence he deployed a number of counter arguments. Initially, he suggested that it might be possible to save Vichy from its own worst tendencies by working to assert its best aspects. It is true that he could not propose such a plan with much hope of success, but he felt it as a moral obligation. It would be illegitimate to condemn Vichy, he argued, without giving it a fair chance, however unpromising it appeared.

By temperament and by experience Mounier was fitted only to operate publicly and by a process of debate and persuasion. He relied on the media of publicity: widely-circulated publications, lectures, debates, discussions, none of which would function successfully in clandestinity. For this reason he was convinced that if any thing was to be done during the reign of Vichy, it had to be done in the open, and with the constant aim of keeping the channels of communication open. This, he felt, was possible in a mixed and chaotic régime, where it would be impossible in a disciplined and monolithic dictatorship. Moreover, since he situated his action primarily on a non-political level, he calculated that there was less chance of being seen as a dangerous influence. In his own view, however, the non-political influence he might hope to wield was ultimately more profound and therefore more effective than any political action he might undertake towards his subversive ends. He insisted that within France under Vichy, it was still possible to maintain true values openly in certain sectors, and to a certain extent. In some of the youth organisations and in some intellectual circles there was a real degree of independence, he argued, and it should be fostered despite the inevitable compromises it involved. In other words, against the 'all-or-nothing' argument he proposed the 'half-a-loaf-is-better-than-no-bread' one. The people needed spiritual food, he argued, and if he could for the moment supply their needs without too much sacrifice of integrity it would be negligent to refuse. He was acutely conscious of the battle for the minds of the French population, particularly the youth, and insisted that they should not under any circumstances be abandoned until it was impossible to continue fighting.

Esprit and Vichy

In November 1940, therefore, *Esprit* reappeared, reduced to a slim volume of 64 pages. Much had changed with the defeat and Mounier was as yet unsure of the possibilities offered by the new situation. For this reason, the November edition was somewhat timid. His leading article acknowledged the failure of the third republic and reiterated all the general positions *Esprit* represented. Of the new régime he said he expected it to be excessively authoritarian, but affirmed his willingness to submit to the discipline of events. Despite its moderate tone, the article deployed a wide range of subtle implications and deliberate ambiguities intended to convey a position of substantial reservations to the informed reader. One example will illustrate the point. He concluded:

> La France s'est suffisamment confessée, mes amis. Laissons maintenant les morts enterrer les morts. Laissons la France morte enterrer la France morte. Comme chacun, voici que nous avons regardé notre passé. Ne nous attardons pas dans une mauvaise conscience morbide. Il y a plus de travail que jamais. Commençons-le de bonne volonté.[5]

The conscious imprecision of the passage permitted several different interpretations according to the inclination of the reader. A Vichy censor might have seen in it a sincere determination to adapt to the new government. A neutral observer would perhaps have read it as an exhortation to shrug off the unhappy memories and make the best of a bad job. The initiated reader, however, would have recognised a number of blows struck against the new order. Possibly the passage contained incisive allusions to specific events or declarations which must remain opaque to a later reader, but even in the general context of the time the attacks can distinctly be discerned. Vichy saw defeat as an act of God and consequently demanded that the nation should repent and purge itself of the past errors which had provoked it. In effect, this implied a disavowal of the third republic, particularly the *Front populaire* and all it stood for, in favour of a conservative and authoritarian state. Mounier, in calling for an end to the continued self-reproach and sterile lamentation officially encouraged by Vichy, implicitly resisted the consequent conversion to the values of the catholic right. In discouraging a morbid preoccupation with past errors, he conveyed his reluctance to abandon much that was valuable in the third republic, as well as a refusal to renounce the substance of his own previous positions. Finally, he implied that if there was more work than ever to be done, it was because the new régime would be harder to 'save' than its predecessor. The bulk of this issue of the review was in a similar vein, with the general theme that harsh reality must be faced, but that it must not lead to despair or acquiescence. In another article the concrete implications emerged more clearly.[6] On a political level, Mounier admitted that the only acceptable response to defeat was a massive and dignified silence; but he insisted it should be supplemented by constructive effort in the non-political sector. Hence he felt that attention had to be concentrated on youth organisations, trade unions, religious associations, intellectual circles and public education.

It is difficult to assess the effect of this style of intellectual combat, presented as it was in highly opaque form. Mounier's supporters have tended to assert that his unshakeable opposition to any kind of acquiescence to nazi Germany or Vichy was transparently clear to them at the time, though time and forgetfulness have eliminated much of the clarity. Other, less sympathetic, commentators have taken his ambiguous writing as clear evidence that he flirted with the régime. Post-war polemic has tended to over-simplify the issue in order to assert one or the other point of view more forcibly. Mounier obviously felt his first month's attempt to be unsatisfactory in that his opposition should have been more firmly expressed. Accordingly he became bolder the following month and was rewarded by severe censoring. The resulting areas of blank page were both satisfying and evocative; but on the one hand they were effective in eliminating controversial comment, and on the other, if *Esprit* were to continue, they would not long be tolerated by the authorities. In subsequent numbers, therefore, he struck what he hoped was an effective balance.

Publishing substantial quantities of uncontroversial or highly theoretical articles, Mounier also introduced a system of highly allusive criticism. One section, for example, merely reproduced particularly outrageous or ridiculous statements from government officials and the puppet press, under the title 'Pour servir à une histoire de notre temps'. Usually these extracts required no comment and the implied judgement was clear; occasionally the point was emphasised by witty juxtaposition with other extracts or by a pungent title. The book-review section hid a number of barbs, and took every opportunity to attack works by Vichy supporters.

Mounier also won many minor victories over the censors, inducing them to cut out quotations from Pétain, to allow articles by Jews, to permit quotations from banned books, to miss references to potentially subversive material, and the like.

A battle Mounier fought with great vigour was against the sudden promotion of Péguy to the role of patron of the national revolution. In a highly selected, expurgated version, Péguy was presented as a ferocious peasant patriot in love with a traditionalist catholic France, eulogising mother-earth as the fount of solid virtue. Such a Péguy was well adapted to the ideology now in command at Vichy, and Henri Massis in particular was active in promoting the cult, which gained considerable momentum. Mounier was not entirely displeased at Péguy's popularity, but tried to point to the side of Péguy about which Vichy was silent—for example, his admiration of Jews, embarrassing during the campaigns of anti-semitism. Péguy was an eminently ambiguous writer who could be construed as attacking or defending quite contradictory positions. Mounier hoped to turn the ambiguity to his advantage, just as Vichy did. Significantly, Péguy also appeared in a later edition of the clandestine *Editions de Minuit* series, with selected passages supporting the resistance cause.

The total effect escapes a modern reader, but it is apparent that, after the first two unsuccessful numbers, *Esprit* won the respect and loyalty of many readers who could not be presented as supporters of Vichy. The fact alone of presenting calm and intelligent discussion was sufficient to ensure the review a wide readership at a time when calm and intelligence were so conspicuously absent. In a sense, the mere stimulation of thought was felt as a concrete liberation. In addition, *Esprit,* along with Stanislas Fumet's liberal progressive catholic review, *Temps nouveau,* was probably at the furthest point in opposition that any publication was allowed to reach without risking suppression and worse: it therefore attracted the support of a dissenting public which would otherwise have nothing to read to suit its taste. Within five months the review had reached a circulation in the south equivalent to its total circulation before the war. Its opposition was also recognised by the true mentor of Vichy, *Action française,* which made slashing attacks on it as early as December 1940.

The question arises why the authorities allowed *Esprit* to appear. A first reason is that it was recognised as a catholic review. Since the régime gave the church a position of considerable privilege, and in return received from it considerable moral support, *Esprit* was probably considered unlikely to adopt an ultimately dissident position out of harmony with the declarations of the church hierarchy. A second reason is that *Esprit* shared much of the vocabulary of the national revolution. The twin inspirations of Vichy were Maurrassian nationalism and catholic personalism. Personalism, less influential than nationalism, stemmed largely from the doctrines elaborated by *Ordre nouveau* and the reviews of the *Jeune Droite* in the early 1930s. Three influential figures, René Belin, as Minister of Production and Labour, Gaston Bergery as an ambassador, and Robert Loustau as head of the Foreign Affairs office under Paul Baudouin's ministry, were among those who contributed to the elaboration of the national revolution and who had received some of their earliest training in these movements. Much of the critique of society proposed by these movements had been shared by Mounier and *Esprit* and for a few months there had existed a degree of unanimity in rejecting the totalitarian state, parliamentary democracy, liberalism and individualism, and in demanding absolute respect for the person, pluralism, corporatism and the implementation of catholic values in public life. Though firm distinctions became increasingly apparent after the events of February 1934, the different movements continued to express their positions in the same terms. Whereas the renewed vogue for these terms gave Mounier hope that he might subvert their official meaning by imposing his own content on them, the Vichy ideologists may equally have hoped to draw Mounier into effective support for their objectives by means of the same ambiguity. A third reason why *Esprit* was permitted is perhaps that an appearance of liberalism would be encouraged by the visible toleration of dissent. Provided it remained relatively mild in its attacks, *Esprit* could serve as a channel of recuperation, focussing discontent in a way which implicitly accepted the form of the régime, and hence forestalling more radical opposition. The question remains as to who was more successful in achieving their objectives, Mounier and his colleagues, or the Vichy authorities. To answer this it is necessary to examine Mounier's other activities, which were the logical and necessary adjunct to his activity at *Esprit,* but which were potentially far more compromising.

Ambiguous action
Pétain, following Hitler's example, saw the need to impress the new values of the régime on the nation's youth, and to that end formed a special Youth Ministry, charged with the task. Mounier

was a qualified teacher, and experienced as an organiser and leader, so that when plans were announced concerning the formation of various official youth movements, he was able, with a little discreet help from friends in the civil service, to offer his talents. *Jeune France* was a movement set up and sponsored by the Youth Ministry for the purpose of fostering cultural and artistic activities among young people. On the advice of friends, Mounier agreed to participate in it, and for a short time was one of its directors. His rôle was to ensure that the potential élite had a thorough cultural formation, to encourage the growth of regional cultural resources and ultimately to prepare the establishment of a series of *maisons de culture*. In this, Mounier seems to have enjoyed a high degree of autonomy; most of his energy was spent organising lectures, discussions and conferences with little or no intervention from official sources. The relative abundance of funds allowed him to travel freely and organise meetings with whomsoever he saw fit, and he was therefore able to make contact with many intellectuals and artists who shared his own perspectives. The most prominent of these were the four poets, Pierre Seghers, a contemporary of Mounier's, Pierre Emmanuel, who later shared Mounier's refuge in Dieulefit, Loys Masson and Max-Pol Fouchet. All were connected in some way with the literary resistance.

The *Ecole des Cadres* at Uriage in the Alps was a school blessed by Vichy in the hope of forming new leaders and administrators within the régime. Run by a determined ex-army officer, Pierre Dunoyer de Segonzac, it retained a consistent spirit of fierce independence and invited guest lecturers who were often firmly opposed to the politics of collaboration. Not all those associated with Uriage were connected with any kind of opposition: Paul Claudel, Henri Massis and Gaston Bergery were involved in varying degrees, and were all convinced supporters of Vichy. Nor was the school entirely free from the Vichy ideology: Segonzac had a great admiration for Pétain, and he taught a respect for leaders and authority—being referred to himself as 'le vieux chef'. Several of the staff and students of Uriage later went into the resistance, but in the meantime it operated on a basis of official sponsorship from Vichy allied with a maximum of autonomy in its workings. From the beginning Mounier paid regular visits as a part-time lecturer and soon established solid links with its staff, including the future director of *Le Monde*, Hubert Beuve-Méry. Mounier was convinced that it was a bastion for the kind of values he stood for, and did all he could to support and defend it. He also participated for a short time in *Compagnons de France,* a government sponsored variant of the boy-scout movement. It published a magazine to which he briefly contributed, but he soon felt its totalitarian and para-military spirit to be unconducive to the promotion of personalist values and by mutual agreement withdrew.

In the early spring of 1941, Mounier was at the height of his success. *Esprit* was acquiring a wide following, particularly in the youth movements. He himself was in constant demand for talks and lectures, and he felt that his philosophy was winning an increasing acceptance. As time progressed, however, his growing enthusiasm was accompanied by a growing unease. He was enthusiastic because *Esprit* seemed to him to be the only serious opponent to *Action française* in the ideological battle for the soul of France. This was something of an over-estimation on his part and ignored the influence of other personalists, mainly from *Ordre nouveau,* and of other liberal catholics such as Fumet. It also ignored the ideological forces which could not be publicly expressed, but which were nonetheless present: particularly the various forms of socialism and Gaullism. In the confused circumstances, however, Mounier's optimistic assessment was understandable. On the other hand, he was uneasy because his continued presence in Vichy organisations and the continued appearance of *Esprit* began to awaken fears of seeming compromise and increasingly drew criticism from his close friends.

In April 1941, Uriage was ordered to dispense with Mounier's services, mainly in an attempt to keep so obviously influential a project as the education of a future élite in the hands of more orthodox teachers. Mounier also detected the hand of Henri Massis, who held an influential post at the Youth Ministry and had supervisory responsibility for the school. Nonetheless he continued to visit Uriage on an informal basis for some time, as did several more active resistance leaders, including the dynamic leader of the *Combat* network, Henri Frenay.

Throughout the Spring and early Summer, *Esprit*'s opposition to Vichy became more overt. Alongside uncontroversial and often deliberately childish articles, Mounier included denunciations of false values and attacks on the *Action française* orientation of the régime. At the same time, the Maurrassian campaign against *Esprit* intensified and it is likely that a more efficient system would have banned the review more quickly. In July, however, Mounier, increasingly anxious to avoid appearing compromised, published a hilarious mock fairy-tale by the young writer Marc Beigbeder in which Pétain was lampooned in the figure of a donkey, and the whole of Vichy savagely ridiculed. The local censor missed the point, but not many readers did so, including the Vichy authorities. One final issue appeared before, in August 1941, *Esprit* was officially ordered to cease publication because of its general tendencies. One month previously, Mounier had been definitively excluded from Uriage, and a month later, he was dismissed from *Jeune France*.

The suppression of *Esprit* came as a relief; the strength of Mounier's relief was indicative of the extent to which his activities had been ambiguous. He felt that he was now publicly declared a genuine opponent of Vichy, and saw the event as a kind of accolade. Later he professed surprise at having been tolerated so long, and attributed the fact of publishing ten issues to the stupidity of the censor, though the matter was clearly not so simple. His later defence of his activities rested on two achievements: having applied a brake to the growth of totalitarianism and having established a connection between his own generation and the rising youth. It is doubtful whether *Esprit* can claim to have made a significant contribution to combating the creeping fascism which Vichy represented. Any hopes of influencing the new régime were soon dashed as it revealed itself wholly docile to the orders of the occupying power. *Esprit's* effect on the population as a whole is more difficult to assess, but within its self-imposed limits it was clearly a force for the anti-totalitarian opposition at a time when sullen acquiescence had not yet crystallised into active resistance. Mounier's activity in the official organisations reinforced its effect and arguably provided a degree of lucidity and intelligence which might impede the progress of fascism. Most of his efforts were directed at a small but important catholic élite concentrated in the sphere of education, both inside and outside school. In this way his influence, wherever it was exerted, tended to multiply itself automatically. The second point follows from this: Mounier's major success was to have gained a firm foothold in the rising generation. Nine years had passed since *Esprit* first appeared; the review was marked by the 1930s and those who had been young then. To retain its relevance it had to receive a new injection of youth. This was successfully operated both in the editorial team and in the readership by the considerable impact of the review and its director between November 1940 and August 1941.

Esprit was privileged in being the most dissident of the non-clandestine reviews, in being one of the few reviews to appear at all, and in having retained a solid body of support from before the defeat. It was therefore able to command a large potential audience otherwise uncatered for; it was also able to draw on a large number of young intellectuals with few other means of expression. Mounier was privileged in being one of the most dissident of those intellectuals who were allowed to lead a public life, in being given positions which provided exceptional opportunities to communicate his ideas, and in having retained untarnished his pre-war reputation for courage and integrity. He was therefore in a strong position to qualify as a symbol on which youthful idealism could focus. At a time of extreme confusion he articulated an ideology of constructive opposition which had not been discredited and which offered hope and direction. The importance of these achievements became apparent after the liberation. The only remaining question is whether Mounier's action had the immediate effect of channelling dissatisfaction into forms acceptable to Vichy, thereby detracting from a more militant resistance. In the short term it is highly likely that such was the tendency. However, militant resistance was only beginning to emerge as a tangible alternative for most people and was determined much more by the overall course of the war than by local cultural activities. Mounier's elimination from Vichy was probably a stronger source of persuasion to resist than his ambiguous presence had been a dissuasion. The effect of his activity under Vichy was therefore negligible in the efforts of building a resistance movement. In the history of the war, *Esprit*'s intellectual operetta in the face of the enemy, as one contributor called it, was largely irrelevant. In the history of *Esprit*, it provided a vital base on which to build Mounier's ideological rôle after the liberation.

Resistance
Complex as Vichy was, the resistance was even more complex. Even to define the resistance poses difficult problems. There is no ready criterion for what the resistance was, much less for who can be said to have been in it. The *maquisards* and the more flamboyant leaders of the underground movements were a relatively minor part of the whole, and even the more militant resistance workers spent most of their efforts on relatively humdrum business. The majority of those who later claimed to have resisted did little more than practice a sullen non-cooperation with the Germans until very late in the war. Besides those whose resistance was expressed in action, there was a whole category of intellectual or spiritual resistance which is far harder to assess, and to which Mounier belonged. The fact that northern France was under German military occupation provoked instinctive opposition from the vast majority of the

population there. It was expressed in a multitude of small gestures but serious resistance was from the outset a hazardous undertaking. The earliest organisations were fragmentary and uncoordinated. They succeeded in producing ephemeral underground newspapers from around December 1940, but were ruthlessly suppressed by the Germans, and from early 1941 a steady stream of executions and deportations began. The many small organisations gradually merged so that from about the end of 1942 three major networks were in operation in the north: the socialist, trades-union based *Libération-Nord*, the predominantly middle-class *Organisation Civile et Militaire*, and the communist-dominated, largely working class *Front National*. Even at this stage the number of militants involved was quite small, but as the tide of war turned against Germany during the course of 1943 the movements grew rapidly.

Resistance in the south was different, at least until November 1942. The presence of the ambiguous Vichy government, the absence of German soldiers and the lack of contact with the north created special conditions. Dissent was not immediately perilous and the crystallisation of clandestine movements was slow. From the middle of 1940 Henri Frenay began organising his *Combat* movement gathering together a number of left-wing catholics who, after some hesitation, rallied to de Gaulle in mid-1941. Little by little the network developed a wide variety of subversive activities and published its own paper from December 1941. Sharing Lyon as a base were *Franc-Tireur*, centred on refugee intellectuals from Paris, and the southern branch of *Libération*. With the occupation of the south in November 1942, conditions became similar to those which the north was accustomed to, and from scattered and half-hearted support, the southern movements progressed to more integrated and dedicated series of networks which eventually linked up with the north.

The composition of these early resistance movements was largely left-wing. The bulk of the membership of the right and centre parties solidly supported Vichy, while the non-communist left, including more progressive catholics and christian democrats, tended to oppose it. The communist party, already clandestine, held an uneasy and reluctant neutrality until the German invasion of the Soviet Union in the spring of 1941, after which it threw all its very considerable forces into resistance. Added to this were a number of nationalists in the old anti-German tradition and many uncommitted individuals who resisted by personal decision rather than on ideological grounds. Although there was always a great deal of internal disagreement, the major movements were gradually unified under the ultimate, if precarious, authority of de Gaulle and the *Conseil National de la Résistance* which first met in May 1943.

Much of the activity of the resistance naturally took the form of acts of subversion, increasingly so as time went on. But in addition to the immediate task of liberating French territory, winning the minds of the people and planning the post-war period were high priorities that resisters were anxious not to leave in others' hands. The substance of this ideological combat was undertaken by two main methods: study groups and clandestine publications. The study groups were usually composed of prominent intellectuals and aimed at drawing up projects and plans of action to be implemented upon liberation. They also contributed to the underground press. The press existed for the purposes of information and propaganda in the first instance, but in the long term aimed to stimulate discussion and to prepare a climate of opinion in which a reconstruction could most successfully be carried out. Apart from the regular radio broadcasts from abroad, the secret press was the only effective means of communication. Its printing and diffusion were carried out at considerable risk and sacrifice, which placed a particularly heavy responsibility on the intellectuals who wrote for it.

With his experience of ideological struggle, Mounier was apparently well equipped to participate in the ideological resistance. In some respects his public activities under Vichy might be placed in this category, but there was also a clandestine side to his action which more clearly belongs to the resistance. Initially it was a simple extension of the broad ideological struggle he was leading at the time. In late November 1940 he organised the first of a series of large gatherings of catholic intellectuals who had sought refuge in Lyon. Not all those present were opposed to Vichy, but this was deliberate policy, both to legitimise the gatherings and to try to exert some pressure on the pro-Vichyites. Many of those who attended became prominent names in the history of the resistance: they included the progressive journalists Hubert Beuve-Méry and Louis Martin-Chauffier, the economist François Perroux and the political scientists André Philip and François de Menthon. Also present were less militant catholic laymen such as Gabriel Marcel, Stanislas Fumet and Jean Lacroix, and several influential and militant priests: the Jesuit Fathers de Lubac, Chaillet, Daniélou and Fessard among them. Not all the participants were of one mind, though most of the divisions were on the level of tactics, depending on each man's view of the Vichy government. Mounier received some harsh criticism for publishing *Esprit,* but the majority were unanimous in their long term aims. Whether or not these meetings could be called early manifestations of the resistance, they did have the effect of establishing a loose liaison between all the dissident catholic intellectuals of the southern zone, and of diffusing opinions and information that could not be expressed openly.

Militant resistance was only just beginning at this time, either in the north or in the South. A handful of clandestine pamphlets had appeared, but these early attempts were essentially individual gestures, and no concerted organisation had yet asserted itself. The *Combat* movement was beginning to emerge more strongly during the early months of 1941, and Mounier kept in contact with its activities so that soon after the suppression of *Esprit* he began, with the blessing of *Combat*'s leader, Henri Frenay, to organise a clandestine study group. Its first task was to draw up a new declaration of rights which would serve as the preamble to a new constitution. For a month the group of half-a-dozen intellectuals worked to complete a first draft, entitled 'Déclaration des droits de la personne'. It was a highly theoretical task with a long term intention, arguably more appropriate to a later stage of the war. Its relevance to the *Combat* movement is ambiguous, particularly since most of *Combat*'s activities were more concrete at this stage. However, events cut short the group's further projects.

Imprisonment and trial
Though he was not actively engaged in militant resistance at this point, Mounier was on close terms with some of the leading resistance figures, and more than once acted as an intermediary putting potential workers in touch with one or other of the local organisations. It was at this period that the clandestine *Cahiers du Témoignage Chrétien* began to appear. Though he did not personally take part, he was in close contact with its Jesuit editors, so that the police for a time mistakenly suspected him of having written the first issue. In reality, Mounier was devoting much of his time to the preparation of his next book, dealing with the French working-class tradition, a project which occupied him for some time, but was never brought to fruition. The extent of his clandestine activity is difficult to establish with certainty, but the Vichy police suspected him of belonging to the *Combat* resistance movement. On this suspicion, Mounier and forty-six others were arrested on 15 January 1942. From then until the end of October, excepting a short period on parole, he spent his time in prisons at Clermont-Ferrand,

Vals-les-Bains, and Lyon. In mid-June, he and several others undertook a hunger strike in protest against their detention without charge. After a battle of wills with Vichy lasting twelve days, and amid considerable publicity, the government relented; the detention order was lifted and Mounier and his friends were transferred to hospital. The victory was unfortunately brief, for three days later they were all charged and imprisoned in Lyon gaol, where they remained until the trial took place in late October 1942.

Fifty *Combat* militants were charged with various anti-governmental activities, but only Frenay and seven other leading figures, all of whom had escaped, were given severe sentences, the remainder receiving light penalties. Mounier was accused of being the spiritual leader of *Combat*. The only real evidence against him was confined to the text of the 'Déclaration des droits de la personne', to surmise based on the occurrence of his name in association with other known resisters, and to suspicion that the *Esprit* group system was part of a resistance network. Through the brilliant conduct of his defence by his lawyer, through an impressive array of witnesses to vouch for him, and through the lack of any concrete evidence, he was given the benefit of the doubt and released.

It is difficult to tell how justified Mounier's acquittal was, since the evidence is ambiguous. He later claimed that the leaders of the three southern resistance movements were due to meet at his house on the day of the arrest, but that the rendez-vous had been retimed at the last minute. If he had engaged in such subversive activity, Mounier must have covered his tracks remarkably well, for it was not discovered by the prosecution. At all events he received, for the duration of the war, a small allowance from *Combat*. In the long term, his arrest, imprisonment, hunger strike and trial were more significant for the effect they had on people's minds than for the rights and wrongs of the case.

The hunger strike in particular aroused a wave of support which established it as a symbolic act of opposition sufficiently important to be discussed on the resistance radio. The apparent victory gave rise to a feeling of triumph out of all proportion to the ends achieved. In the universities of the south, men of moderate views and considerable prestige felt able to protest at the injustice of Mounier's detention without committing themselves to a particular political stance; writers and artists wrote to Vichy, confident that their dissent need not be ascribed to complicity in *Combat*; diplomats, notably the Swiss embassy, considered that their pressure for his release did not violate their political neutrality. But for many people this protest was a rare chance openly to declare an opposition which went much further than this limited issue. The imprisonment and trial which followed had an effect of making people more aware of the degree of opposition which existed and the extent to which it was organised. Mounier's presence helped to confer on this opposition an aura of respectability, which Vichy strove to eliminate. Whether he willed it or not, his reputation for intellectual integrity and seriousness of purpose was in part at least reflected on the resistance. In return, Mounier was established as a resister and acquired prestige in the eyes of those who considered that to be the direction of a Frenchman's duty. The full implications of this became clear in the post-war period. In the meantime, his imprisonment consecrated him as an acceptable model to many young catholics who were determined to resist, but had few catholics of stature to look to for inspiration. It also made his thought a serious force among the ideologies which were contending for the mind of the resistance.

Clandestinity
On Armistice Day, 11th November 1942, scarcely a fortnight after Mounier's release, the German army occupied the southern zone. Any pretence of French independence was finally shattered and the south enjoyed roughly the same conditions of life as the north. The relative leniency of the police and the courts towards resisters was at an end. Prudently, Mounier took an assumed name, Leclerc, his wife's maiden name, and retired to a small village, Dieulefit, in the Drôme region, where he remained until the summer of 1944. Since the area was nominally under Italian occupation it was relatively sheltered from the German authorities. Most of Mounier's time, when not spent in ensuring basic subsistence for himself and his family, was spent in reading and working on two major studies: one on the future of christianity; the other, begun in prison, a treatise on human character. He was not entirely cut off from his old contacts, for Dieulefit had become something of a refuge for writers wanting to escape attention. Among its residents were the poet Pierre Emmanuel and the catholic journalists Andrée Viollis and André Rousseaux, who had all worked with Mounier before the war. Several guests stayed there for short periods, including the poet and novelist, Louis Aragon, and his wife Elsa Triolet, and the poets Loys Masson and Pierre Seghers. At Dieulefit, Mounier organised two *Esprit* conferences in 1943 and 1944, uniting friends from both zones in a series of short study session to prepare for the post-war reconstruction. In addition to the established participants, the

journalist Hubert Beuve-Méry, the publisher Paul Flamand, the journalist André Mandouze and the student leader Gilbert Dru were also present. The last two names are particularly significant in that they represent the young catholic intellectuals who became closely associated with Mounier, and also the development of the two movements which could claim an affinity with his thought—christian democracy and *progressisme*. Little enough sprang directly from the meetings, though Mounier did take the opportunity to express his determination that *Esprit*, under his direction, should reappear after the end of the war.

Since the winter of 1942–1943, the prospect of a German defeat had become increasingly apparent, and the French resistance began to grow rapidly. Its activities diversified and on the intellectual side, the preparation for a new post-war France was its major preoccupation. To this end, de Gaulle's envoy, Jean Moulin, the famous 'Max', set up a weighty study group, the *Comité Générale des Etudes*. The group's task was to publish a review of serious political reflection and to prepare itself to act as adviser to an eventual provisional government. Its regular members were Paul Bastid and Alexandre Parodi, who had both held pre-war government posts, the political scientist François de Menthon, the socialist trade unionist Robert Lacoste, a professor of law Pierre-Henri Teitgen, and the distinguished marxist historian Marc Bloch. With the exception of Bloch, who was shot by the Gestapo, all went on to hold government office after the war. Mounier was invited to join the group, and although there is no record of what part he played in its deliberations, he contributed a substantial article to the clandestine review, *Cahiers politiques*, which expressed the *Comité*'s positions and researches. It is the only surviving piece of clandestine writing Mounier published, and it appeared in July 1943.[7] Few of the key words of personalism were present, but that is explained by the desire to evade identification and by the possibility that the article may have been retouched by another hand lest the style be too revealing, a common practice. Nonetheless, all the basic themes of Mounier's political theory were expounded, emphasising those parts which were common to all catholics, particularly the refusal to assimilate the catholic faith to any specific form of régime. He outlined the catholic values which any regime should respect, and in conclusion recommended a radically new republic, free from the errors which had vitiated the third republic, as the best way to embark on a reconstruction. Relatively free from polemic, the article was an example of Mounier's lucid, though committed, intelligence.

Apart from the *Cahiers politiques,* Mounier's name has been associated with the clandestine publications *Combat, Témoignage chrétien* and *La France intérieure.* He was certainly in contact with the first two, and probably the latter, a substantial review produced in the Grenoble area. If he wrote anything for them then no trace remains. The only other article by Mounier's hand to have appeared was a brief extract from a pre-war article attacking the right-wing press and the cowardly defeatism of the bourgeoisie. Towards the end of the war Mounier was involved in planning at least two projected newspapers, but events prevented the realisation of his planned contributions. During the eighteen months following his release from prison Mounier decided that he had no vocation as a man of action or as a politician. He declined to serve on any of the provisional committees being set up, and carried his decision even to the point of refusing an invitation to join de Gaulle's Consultative Assembly in Algiers in January 1944. Following the Normandy landings in June of that year, all the adult males in the Drôme lived in a state of semi-mobilisation until the eventual liberation of the area at the end of August. Dieulefit was of little strategic importance and therefore largely escaped the savage battle which was going on around it, though it was only a few miles away that the *maquis* were decimated in the Vercors region. Within a month of liberation Mounier was back in Paris and ready for the hard battles confronting him in post-war France.

Politics of the resistance
With the ignominious fall of the Vichy government and the collaborationist factions, the political right within France was, for a time at least, eliminated in disgrace from public affairs. The most coherent single force to emerge from the resistance was the communist party. Although since Hitler's rise to power it had been the most strenuous opponent of nazism, the signing in August 1939 of the Soviet-German pact of non-aggression had split the party by forcing its leadership to denounce the pending war as 'imperialist'. The party was in disarray and subjected to savage persecutions throughout the war months. Despite tentative approaches both to Vichy and to the German occupiers, this persecution was continued and increased after the French defeat and the party, demoralised and decimated, continued a precarious underground existence. June 1941, when Hitler invaded the Soviet Union, was the turning point. From this date onwards communists flocked enthusiastically into clandestine organisations and, although under more severe

oppression than other branches, soon became the most dynamic wing of the resistance. Whether they formed a numerical majority is impossible to ascertain, but it is beyond doubt that they showed remarkable dedication, organisation and effectiveness. Communist preponderance in the resistance enabled the occupying and collaborating authorities to use the well-established fear of bolshevism to hinder the growth of support for the resistance in general. Particularly among catholics, many potential recruits were deterred from joining, at least in the early stages, lest they might be contributing to a communist take-over which might be worse for them than the German occupation. On the other hand, and in the long term more important, their rôle won for the communists a degree of respect, trust, and, eventually, influence among resisters of every political complexion. Non-communist intellectuals in particular were often highly impressed by their first real contact with a powerful ideology they had previously dismissed. Many conditioned fears were allayed by close personal relationships. No one who had fought in the resistance could contest the communists' claim to an important part in the decisions of the post-war. This was a serious inconvenience in some quarters, but nonetheless a fact which had to be taken into account.

Much ambiguity surrounds the activities of the catholic church during these years. Since Vichy was dominated by the political right and since the right was almost entirely catholic, it is not surprising that the church was accorded a place of privilege in the new order. For the church there was no question of dissidence in the first instance, since catholic doctrine traditionally stipulates loyalty to the established civic powers. Although the church hierarchy could not contemplate any sort of profane authority over it, it amply compensated Vichy by a thoroughgoing cooperation with the régime, sometimes bordering on positive subservience. In return the church was offered a considerable degree of power, mainly visible by the appointment of traditionalist catholics in political office; Jacques Chevalier, for example, was for a time Minister of Education. By tactical error Chevalier failed to achieve his objective of total clericalisation of the education system. But in other fields, particularly in youth organisations and social work, those responsible were more successful, to the extent that many clerics thought of Pétain as the instigator of a great new christian revival, and gave their wholehearted support. The hierarchy, finding itself in greater harmony with the government than at any time for more than a century, was not conspicuous in its protests. Indeed one member, the ageing

Cardinal Baudrillart, was embarrassingly pro-German. Beyond its charitable work on behalf of prisoners, refugees and other war victims, the official church's participation in resisting the occupation amounted to a handful of protests at the worst nazi atrocities, isolated protests against the persecution of Jews and a refusal to make forced labour in Germany an obligation of conscience.

On the level of individual action, it was a different picture, though among the higher clergy only the Archbishop of Toulouse and a small number of bishops made more than a derisory contribution to the resistance. Despite the general discouragement of their superiors, many priests and laypeople were militant resisters, taking part mostly in non-confessional activities. The production of such clandestine publications as *Témoignage chrétien,* the number of catholic *maquisards,* and the relatively strong catholic representation in the *Combat* movement helped lend respectability to an otherwise inauspicious record. The immediate effect of the hierarchy's position was generally to discourage resistance and encourage compliance with the demands of Vichy even until late in the war. A conscientious catholic could not do other than hesitate before engaging in subversive action, though many did not hesitate long. One result of this was the emergence of a greater spirit of independence among the laity and the lower clergy, who felt that their moral position was stronger than that of their slightly discredited spiritual superiors. It became an urgent necessity for the church to rehabilitate itself in the public mind. As a result, those catholics who did resist were given a prominence which the intrinsic value of their actions did not always merit. On the one hand they wielded considerable influence, on the other hand they were used as a means to retrieve the church's lost authority and ultimately to prepare the return of the catholic right as a political force.

After a long period of disarray, the non-communist left asserted itself in the latter half of the occupation as a major ideological current. Less monolithic than either the catholic church or the communist party, it was a product of the resistance in a sense that they were not. On a political level it was expressed in a regenerated socialist party and a greatly enlarged christian democratic movement. The socialist party had split in confusion at the fall of France. Despite the courageous public stand of Leon Blum and one or two other prominent figures, the party had effectively ceased to exist. Many socialists had spontaneously joined the various resistance movements as individuals, and after the communist party had entered the resistance as a unit, it was not long before socialists began to prepare a reconstituted SFIO party structure. Under almost entirely new leadership, the party drew support from its traditional sources, but also from many otherwise uncommitted resisters. The catholic left in general, including Mounier, was for a long time disoriented under Vichy, and reactions varied widely, though by 1942 many were won over to resistance. Of these, a small proportion found an acceptable expression in orthodox socialism, a handful were attracted to the communist party, but many felt a rethinking of christian democracy to be more appropriate. These latter, including a large section of the rising intelligentsia, laid the foundations of what was to become the *Mouvement Républicain Populaire* (MRP).

The influence of personalism

Since the war, many attempts have been made to establish the resistance as predominantly belonging to the non-communist left. If christian democracy can be termed left-wing, which until the liberation it generally could, it is true that those resistance workers who were not communists were mostly left-wing. What they shared was a desire for a renovated democratic republic, social reform and peaceful international cooperation. Within this loose grouping is situated the substance of Mounier's influence. Distinct from catholicism, to which he owed spiritual loyalty but whose temporal representatives he often had to resist; distinct from communism, to whose social programme he owed broad cooperation but whose philosophy he considered nefarious; distinct from the ideologies of the pre-war years, in which his own thought had originated but which the war years had largely discredited; distinct from these, Mounier strove to crystallise an ideology based on the principles of personalism. This personalism was intended to express and direct the aspirations of the new men which the resistance had formed.

The impact of personalism is difficult to assess. On a specific level it is possible to point to individuals who were animated by it. Perhaps the most energetic of these was Gilbert Dru, a leader of the catholic student movement, who before the war became attracted to Mounier and *Esprit*, and who attempted in his own activity to implement the ideals of personalism. A determined resister, he played an important rôle in shaping the christian democratic resistance and laying the foundations of the MRP before his death at the hands of the Gestapo. Another energetic resister and close friend of Dru, Jean-Marie Domenach, shared a similar enthusiasm and survived to join the staff of the resurrected *Esprit*, whose director he eventually became. On a general level, the impact of personalism is visible in the ideas which dominated the resistance, though they formed rather a mixed bag. A revolution was broadly accepted as being necessary for a satisfactory regeneration of France after the defeat of Germany. It was widely accompanied by the insistence on a spiritual regeneration, without which a material revolution would be in vain. The means for achieving this comprehensive transformation was a form of socialist humanism which would renounce the use of totalitarian methods, adopt as its axiom the respect of the human person, and implement the republican ideals of liberty, equality and justice. These themes, all commonplaces of *Esprit*'s canon in the thirties, now became commonplaces of the resistance canon, although a direct causal link is impossible to establish.

At the liberation, the need was widely felt for a new and effective ideological force, and for a time it seemed that the historical conjuncture might have singled out personalism to fill that need. The need for a political ideology was produced by the failure of the old ones. Liberalism as embodied in the third republic was discredited by Munich and the fall of France; nationalism and monarchism had fallen with Pétain; conservatism had become enmeshed in Laval's *double jeu;* fascism had frankly collaborated with the invader. Patriotism was too diffuse to stand as a coherent ideology, and communism had too many enemies to command a consensus. Socialism and christian democracy seemed to hold the key to the future, and a synthesis of the two into a democratic and libertarian socialism based on the values of christian humanism was what personalism offered.

If events conspired to make Mounier's ideas so potentially applicable, events also conspired, and were used, to make Mounier an appropriate agent to communicate the ideas. His stature as a public figure and as a symbol was considerable. He was already known to a broad section of the population as editor of *Esprit,* a prominent review which had tried to continue under Vichy but had been suppressed. He was known to many of the rising generation as a teacher and organiser who had been eliminated from Vichy's youth movements while at the peak of his popularity. He was established by virtue of his imprisonment, hunger strike and trial as a member of the *Combat* movement. For having adopted or been forced into these crucial positions, Mounier received absolution for any ambiguity which may have surrounded his actions: his public image was that of an intellectual leader of the resistance. The significance of this is hard to overstate, since post-war France required resistance credentials of any public figure who aspired to power or influence. Mounier had also acquired the reputation of being a just man of unimpeachable integrity. His name was not associated with any of the squabbles or less savoury incidents which had occurred during the occupation years. His hands were clean and free to undertake the task of building a new France on the fresh and untried principles of personalism.

His appeal was not limited to the resistance. As a loyal catholic he could hope to win the support and assent of many whose mediocre record owed something to the church's excessive deference to Vichy, but who were prepared to work in the new spirit of regeneration, provided their religious convictions were not an object of recrimination. In addition, the complexities and ambiguities of his thought exposed him to the constant risk of misappropriation. Some whose dubious past obliged them to seek new channels of expression saw Mounier as an apparently progressive model which could be safely imitated on a formal level, but which could be used to serve objectively retrogressive ends. By blurring essential distinctions, by shifting crucial emphases, by neglecting vital reservations, these newly found disciples hoped to use him as a cover for the stealthy reintroduction of conservatism, and rallied to his support.

As a result of all these factors, at the time of the liberation, Mounier was well-known in most sections of the community, and widely looked upon for a variety of motives as a spiritual and intellectual leader. His personal reputation and the opportuneness of his personalism left him poised to become a major ideological influence in the development of post-war France.

Notes

1   E. Mounier, 'Lendemains d'une trahison', *Esprit*, no 73, octobre 1938, p1–15.
2   E. Mounier, 'En interrogeant les silences de Pie XII', *Le Voltigeur*, no16, 5 mai 1939, reprinted in *Bulletin des Amis d'E Mounier*, no23–24. décembre 1964, p28–33.
3   E. Mounier, *Pacifistes ou Bellicistes?* (Paris, 1939), reprinted under the title 'Les chrétiens devant le problème de la paixs', in *Oeuvres* I p785–834.
4   E. Mounier, 'Sur les décombres du communisme', *Esprit*, no90, mars 1940, p428–430.
5   E. Mounier, 'D'une France à l'autre', *Esprit*, no94, novembre 1940, p1–10, p10.

6   E. Mounier, 'Les nouvelles conditions del la vie publique en France', *Esprit*, no94, novembre 1940, p60–64.
7   Unsigned article: 'Pourquoi je suis républicain: réponse d'un catholique'' *Cahiers politiques*, no2, juillet 1943, p4–9. Reprinted in H. Michel and B. Mirkine-Guetzévitch, *Les idées politiques et sociales de la résistance* (Paris 1954), p88–94.

Bibliographical Notes

Useful studies of France at this period are: A. Werth, *France and Munich, before and after the Surrender* (London 1939); A. Werth, *France 1940–1955* (London 1956); A. Zévaès, *Histoire de six ans (1938–1944)* (Paris 1944). A valuable source is the *Revue d'histoire de la deuxième guerre mondiale*, particularly the issues of October 1964 on Vichy youth policies, January 1966 on Uriage and *Témoignage chrétien*, April 1964 on the occupation generally. The *Revue française de science politique* has useful analyses: in January 1956 on the Vichy régime, and in December 1959 on Uriage. The Vichy regime is well analysed in R. Aron, *Histoire de Vichy* (Paris 1954); on a more general level in H. Amouroux, *La vie des français sous l'occupation* (Paris 1961); and on a regional level in H. Amoretti, *Lyon capitale, 1940–1944* (Paris 1964). The controversial question of catholic activities during the occupation is discussed by: P. Vergnet, *Les Catholiques dans la Résistance* (Paris 1946); Mgr E. Guerry. *L'Église catholique en France sous l'occupation* (Paris 1947); R. Garaudy, *L'Église, le communisme et les chrétiens* (Paris 1949); J. Duquesne, *Les Catholiques français sous l'occupation* (Paris 1966).

Among the many studies on the resistance, the most useful are those of M. Henri Michel who has written on many aspects of it. His compact *Histoire de la résistance française* (Paris 1965) is particularly useful. Also useful is H. Noguères, *Histoire de la Résistance en France*, 2 vols (Paris 1969). The problems and achievements of the intellectual resistance are well described in J. Debû-Bridel, *La Résistance intellectuelle* (Paris 1970); Vercors, *La Bataille du silence* (Paris 1967); and Alban Vistel, *La Nuit sans ombre* (Paris 1970). On the clandestine press the most useful works are R. & P. Roux-Fouillet, *Catalogue des périodiques clandestins diffusés en France de 1939 à 1945* (Paris 1954); C. Bellanger, *Presse clandestine 1940–1944* (Paris 1961). On the intellectual content of both press and study groups the main published sources are H. Michel, *Les Courants de pensée de la Résistance* (Paris 1962); and H. Michel & B. Mirkine-Guetzévitch, *Les Idées politiques et sociales de la résistance* (Paris 1954). Studies of particular topics can be found in: J. -P. Gault, *Histoire d'une fidélité, Témoignage chrétien* (Paris 1964); M. Granet & H. Michel, *Combat, histoire d'un mouvement de résistance* (Paris 1957); F. Rude, ' "La France intérieure": une revue clandestine née dans la région Rhône-Alpes', *Annales de l'Université de Grenoble*, section *Lettres-Droit*, tome 22, 1946, p51–96; J. Fauvet, *Histoire du parti communiste français*, vol 2 (Paris 1965) esp p11–44; D. Mayer, *Les Socialistes dans la Résistance* (Paris 1968). There is valuable material on the Liberation period in R. Aron, *Histoire de la Libération de la France* (Paris 1959); A. Dansette, *Histoire de la Libération de Paris* (Paris 1958); J. Chapsal, *La Vie politique en France depuis 1940* (Paris 1966).

CHAPTER FIVE

Battle for the Minds
(1944–1947)

Liberation
In the autumn of 1944, liberated Paris was in an atmosphere of euphoria; the sense of victory was fuelled by the progressive retreat of the German forces on all fronts. At this early stage it was tempered by the difficulty in assuring the basic material needs, but not even the acute food shortages could stifle the general feelings of relief. France seemed unified as rarely before, though already signs began to emerge that the relative unity would be short-lived. Those forces which contributed to the liberation all thought of themselves as the resistance, but their differences, patched over for the sake of defeating a common enemy, soon reappeared when faced with the task of fashioning a new France. Everyone knew what they had been fighting against; there was sharp disagreement as to what they had been fighting *for*, and each group insisted on its right to a part in the reconstruction. The end of four years of occupation and puppet government had left the country in a state of turmoil. The war was still being fought and the economy had to be lifted from its total collapse, daunting tasks in themselves without the additional problem of creating new political, social and cultural structures. Although it sought ostensibly to unite all movements and tendencies which had played a part in the liberation, the provisional government of General de Gaulle was divided between various tendencies which were slowly beginning to crystallise.

The foundation congress of the christian democratic *Mouvement Républicain Populaire* (MRP) and the reconstituting congress of the socialist party, held in the winter of 1944, both joined with the communist party in pledging their commitment to the charter drawn up in March 1944 by the *Conseil National de la Résistance* (CNR). This charter, intended as a programme of government for the new republic, was the basis of the revolution which many resistance workers confidently expected to follow the liberation. It offered a clear index for situating men and movements on the political spectrum. Briefly it provided for the setting up of an independent republic, the punishment of collaborators and Vichyites, the expropriation of traitors and all who had profited by the war and occupation, universal suffrage, full civil rights and liberties, and economic and social reforms. The economic and social reforms were the main point of contention since they provided for widespread nationalisations, workers' participation in management, producer and consumer cooperatives, economic and social democracy, the right to work and rest, a protected and adequate standard of living for all, full social security, independent trade unions, education based on ability rather than privilege, and full political, economic and social rights for the colonies. It was a left-wing programme reminiscent of the aims of the *Front Populaire* of 1936 and coincided most closely with the general line of the socialist party. But it was a reformist rather than a revolutionary project, and therefore the communist party regarded it as a minimum programme, the first step towards a socialist society. Within the ranks of the MRP it was diversely received, and although the progressive wing gave its enthusiastic commitment, there were many who paid no more than lip service.

Though they had introduced new elements into their action, neither the communists nor the socialists were new to the political scene. Both parties had been heavily depleted by executions and deportations, but the new élites which replaced the pre-war leaders followed closely on their predecessors in their approach to political action. Of the three major parties, only the christian democrats were substantially new, and they did not fail to emphasise that the MRP was born in the resistance. Although it was not a new conception, christian democracy had never acquired a large following in France. It drew its inspiration from many sources, ranging from the social catholic Albert de Mun, the *Sillon* movement, the catholic youth organisations and the small *Parti Démocrate Populaire* which had been a minor political force between the wars. In its new form as the MRP, it sprang directly from the war, corresponding to the realisation of many catholics that they had a legitimate and important duty to participate in the political life of the nation in a positive and constructive sense. The parties of the right, to which catholics had traditionally given their allegiance, were now discredited, and the time seemed ripe for the establishment of a progressive party built on specifically christian principles.

BATTLE FOR THE MINDS (1944–1947)

The MRP could not claim any formal ties with the church, but the abundance of informal links with the hierarchy and the various catholic organisations ensured that in its early years at least, it could rely on the church's blessing. It was also able to use the network of contacts and organisational resources of the catholic organisations. The party's clientele was drawn almost entirely from practising catholics and from a wide spectrum of opinion. It included at one end those who looked for genuine social reform and even revolution, but were not prepared to risk the possible erosion of christian values which communism and socialism might involve. At the other end it included those who, with the dissolution of the traditional right, gave their support to the movement as being the most likely to further the reactionary ends they could not yet publicly profess. The ambiguity implied by this broad range of support was the party's strength, in that it initially ensured a strong electoral support, and its weakness, in that it led to division and loss of direction. But in the early days after its foundation in November 1944, the MRP could still claim both to be direct descendant of the resistance and to embody the progressive aspirations which the CNR had laid out in its charter.

If the MRP received most of its support from catholics, it was nevertheless not the only party catholics supported. As time passed and genuine right-wing parties began to emerge, the MRP lost many of those who had supported it only as a temporary expedient. Also during the first months following the liberation, a small number of catholics supported the communist party, and a rather larger number the socialist party. An important minority had been won over to the kind of revolutionary socialist humanism which emerged as a dominant current of the resistance. In the temporary absence of prohibitions from the church, they constructed their own relationship with the two major parties which embodied it. Both parties had the advantages of long political experience, a proud resistance record, and a coherent political doctrine. These factors, coupled with the muting of their once virulent opposition to religious belief, made them particularly attractive to progressive catholic militants and to the catholic working class.

Within the catholic church itself, changes had taken place. By virtue of its ambiguous rôle during the occupation, the catholic hierarchy had been widely criticised and as a result lost much of its moral authority. With it, the conservative and traditionalist wing of the church had suffered a temporary eclipse. In the years after the war, therefore, responsibility for maintaining the church's influence fell to younger, more progressively minded catholics. As a result, pressure was felt by the upper reaches of the hierarchy, which responded by calling for a renewal of the church's apostolic mission. The call was welcomed and interpreted as a new openness and flexibility in answer to which renovations were initiated both within the priesthood and in the auxilliary organisations. The *Mission de Paris* began to extend its experiment with worker-priests; the religious orders in their different fields re-examined and increased their action in the world, as for example the Jesuits in the spiritual direction of youth movements or the Dominicans in the communications media; experiments with community living and a new emphasis on missionary work began to emerge at a parish level; certain sections of the catholic action movements, such as the *Mouvement Populaire des Familles*, abandoned their strict denominationalism, preferring a broad and effective action to doctrinal purity; study groups were being set up throughout the country to examine the possible reforms in liturgy and education with the help of which the church might more effectively fulfil its rôle in the post-war world.

The atmosphere was one of readiness to change within the structures of the church, though this tendency was not to flourish unchecked. In their temporal activities too, catholics no longer felt so bound to traditional patterns. There was the hope of an end to the prickly formalism which had always limited the action a catholic could take to obtain social justice; likewise there was the expectation that the recent upheavals had blown away the ingrained sectarian reactions which had always restricted catholic participation in political life. An example of this was the evolution of the catholic-inspired *Confédération Française des Travailleurs Chrétiens*. This trade union had always been considered as docile to the employers and bound by strict observance of papal encyclicals, which generally excluded militancy. After the war, however, it relinquished its explicit dependence on the church and, while remaining pledged to christian principles, gradually evolved to a position of accepting non-christian workers and of taking its place alongside the other unions as militant defenders of working class interests. In all this the church authorities acquiesced and continued to encourage catholics to associate themselves with the CFTC.

If France was in a turmoil of reappraisal politically and institutionally, it was also going through a similar upheaval on a cultural and intellectual level. Throughout France, the ways in which people thought of themselves, each other, and their relation with the world, had been called into question by events. Of the pre-war ideologies which sought to give structure and coherence to people's reflexions, none had emerged unshaken. But out of the wreckage of dead ideas, two powerful secular ideologies were asserting themselves as contenders for the nation's minds: marxism and existentialism.

Existentialism
Existentialism was in many ways a new phenomenon and a product of the war. Associated above all with the philosopher, novelist and playwright, Jean-Paul Sartre, it was a diffuse and often complex movement. At its widest it included a broad, non-conformist sub-culture which ranged from anarchistic young social drop-outs to the sophisticated expression of disillusionment in various art-forms. It expressed a mood of amoral individualism, most often founded on bitterness and disillusion, but often enough giving birth to a surprising intensity and imagination. It was a middle-class phenomenon, even the social drop-outs had mostly dropped out of middle-class families. And it was largely centred on the generation which had come to adulthood just before, or during, the war.

The mood on which the existentialist vogue was based was not of Sartre's creation. It was a product of the historical conjunction, a reaction by the rising generation to the years of occupation and the post-war austerity. Sartre expressed a similar mood. He was therefore appropriated and, as often as not, misappropriated. Many disparate phenomena were associated with existentialism once the label had been established. A taste for jazz, American films and fiction, Juliette Greco, unkempt appearance, unconventional behaviour, iconoclastic views, all qualified in the popular press and the popular imagination as existentialist. Whether or not it was initially due to a misrepresentation, Sartre and his colleagues undoubtedly owed much of their influence to the success of existentialism at this level. The centre of the sub-culture was the Parisian Latin Quarter, the traditional centre of French student life. It was there too that the more consciously ideological supporters of the movement were to be found, among the students and the educated young middle class, mainly Parisians, who were filling the lower ranks of the professions, education, the media and the civil service.

For the most part, even those who read Sartre and the others were not especially concerned with the intricacies of phenomenological existentialism. What they took was a way of looking at themselves and the world and a way of behaving in it. In many respects it was an expression of attitudes they already felt appropriate. The main features were the denial of any kind of philosophical or moral absolute, the affirmation of the free individual as the only point of reference, a disillusionment with the world, and a determination to face the worst, and if possible change it, with courage and honesty. Politically, existentialism was a less than cohesive force in the non-communist left. There was no clear continuity between the substance of its message and its political positions, but there was a strongly asserted, if often unspecified, insistence on the need for commitment to progressive political change.

The philosophers and theorists of existentialism were, of necessity, drawn from those sections of the middle class which dealt with ideas and had the leisure to devote themselves to study: writers, journalists, teachers in senior secondary or higher education. To them might be added a few students and a sprinkling of intellectually inclined people from other sectors. Many of the best-known names in French culture were associated with the movement, and the intellectual organ around which they gathered was the monthly review *Les Temps modernes*. Sartre directed the review, closely assisted by Simone de Beauvoir and Maurice Merleau-Ponty, both of whom were writers of considerable stature. They were joined by writers and critics like Jean Genet, Michel Leiris, Violette Leduc, Boris Vian, Georges Bataille, Etiemble, Francis Jeanson and Maurice Blanchot. From the beginning they were divided by a succession of debates and quarrels of varying gravity which had them almost all set against one another at some time. As a result it is difficult to find a precise characterisation of their common features, but they would probably all have acknowledged that their most basic concerns were most typically expressed in Sartre's own writings.

Sartre, Merleau-Ponty and Simone de Beauvoir drew their philosophical inspiration mainly from the German-based school of phenomenology. Following its leading theorist, Edmund Husserl, they held that any account of the world had to take its starting point in the act of perception. Since all experience was received through the senses, they argued, nothing could properly be said to exist except in terms of a perceptual relationship, and therefore existence was constituted in the mutual interdependence of the perceiver and the perceived. Many consequences followed from this initial position; they were explored at length by Sartre in his *L'Etre et le néant* (1943) and by Merleau-Ponty in his *Phénoménologie de la perception* (1945), but from an ideological viewpoint only the general implications were influential. The heavy and complex analyses phrased in technical language, borrowed directly from the German, roused few people to examine the difficulties posed by Husserl and Heidegger, the fathers of Sartrean existentialism. What was communicated was a serious attempt to face the problems of human isolation, both metaphysical and psychological, of guilt and anguish, of freedom and responsibility. Although Sartre's was an uncomfortable vision which raised many problems and solved few, his determination to deal lucidly and honestly with real human experiences in purely human terms found strong echoes in a generation which had just emerged from a war into a difficult post-war period. It was less the philosophical cogency than the emotive and imaginative power of existentialism that was its strength.

Marxism
The other contender for the minds of the French people, marxism, was a far more concrete and far more powerful movement than existentialism. Like personalism but unlike existentialism, it sought to be a total ideology. That is, it claimed to describe the world comprehensively and to formulate a complete practical response to it. Socially, marxism had its main base in the working class, where it was virtually unchallenged. The reasons for this are not difficult to find, since it was an ideology whose analysis of history and society was based on the class-struggle and it committed itself both practically and theoretically to the victory of the working class. Despite the strong influence which marxism enjoyed on the non-communist left, its most energetic and influential defender was the French communist party, which dominated political thinking and activity, especially on the left, as well as broader theoretical discussions. The influence of marxism therefore extended at least as far as the party's influence, which meant that it was felt in every aspect of working class life. The structure of the party itself was closely knit. Its stress on education was supported by a network of communications comparable in scope to that of the catholic church and certainly more efficient.

Its influence in the middle class was more tenuous, but marxism was making striking progress even there. Following the war, the middle class was conscious of the failure of traditional liberalism as a viable ideology. Many still held to the political and religious authoritarianism which had traditionally been the major alternative, but the generation which had grown to maturity in the resistance, along with many of their elders who had been active in it, were drawn into close contact with the communists. Such contact would, for the majority, have been unthinkable five years earlier, and it forced them to assess their position in relation to the party and the ideology it offered. The respect and sympathy which its resistance record commanded, the unaccustomed presence of communists in government posts, and the high regard in which the Soviet Union was for a time held, ensured an unprecedentedly receptive audience for marxist ideas. Among catholics there were relatively few who took the step of embracing marxism, though many felt a clear need to come to terms with it. Among non-christians there were many for whom it resolved satisfactorily the ideological disorientation they felt. The major rival to marxism in this social sector was existentialism, but both overlapped sufficiently into the church's territory to forbid any complacency on its part. The leading marxist intellectuals in France were more varied in their social origins than their rivals, but they were nonetheless dominated by the same social group of teachers and journalists. The important difference was that as an older and international ideology, marxism could call on a body of theory and practice which existentialists could not hope to equal, and which seriously rivalled that of the catholic church.

Catholic personalism
Within catholicism there was no current which combined a comparable degree of coherence and comprehensiveness with the high prestige and wide audience which personalism commanded. With his team in *Esprit* and his network of supporters and associates, Emmanuel Mounier led the strongest of the catholic ideologies in post-liberation France, and occupied a vanguard position in the church's spiritual and intellectual struggles against its ideological rivals. The other main religious group in France, protestantism, was not sufficiently organised or widespread to present an ideological challenge to personalism. In any case, many protestants, like the politician André Philip or the critic Denis de Rougemont, were happy to subscribe to personalism, which was generally compatible with their own beliefs.

Mounier faced several tasks: to defend the central values of catholicism against its two major opponents; to stimulate a renewed confidence and sense of purpose among catholics; to extend the influence of personalism; and to find an effective means of political expression. He saw that the gestation of a new order presented enormous difficulties for anyone wanting to influence its formation, but also that the opportunities offered were unprecedented in their scope. The basis of experience and influence which he had now acquired gave him every reason to hope to play a large part in the creation of a new France.

Despite the material hardships of 1944, Mounier succeeded, with the help of influential friends, in getting the first post-war issue of *Esprit* into print for December, earlier than most other reviews. It regained, and rapidly surpassed, the readership it had already established. Subscriptions were taken by many catholic institutions and by a wide range of non-catholic individuals and establishments. Although its positions were still considered 'advanced' among catholics, it was respectable enough for the French government to take five hundred subscriptions for the purposes of its diplomatic and cultural services. Outside *Esprit*, Mounier and his editorial team contributed widely to other publications both as spokesmen of the review and in their own right. Mounier himself was particularly close to *Combat*, writing some twenty articles for it between late 1944 and spring 1947; he also wrote several for the socialist daily paper *Cité-soir*. His colleagues were as active, if not more so, in a wide variety of publications. Most prominent was Jean Lacroix, who took over the regular philosophy column in the newly founded and influential daily *Le Monde*. They were also active in other media, and Mounier himself was given a regular weekly radio programme on the national network, speaking on topics of his own choice. The number of books produced as well as the lecture tours, debates and public discussions all added to the means available to Mounier and *Esprit* in pursuit of their aims.

The basic editorial team had not changed significantly since before the war. Jean Lacroix, Edmond Humeau, Henri Marrou, Georges Zérapha, Paul Fraisse, Pierre-Aimé Touchard, Jacques Madaule, François Goguel, Henri Queffelec and Adrien Miatlev still formed the backbone of the review. They were joined gradually by younger writers like Claude-Edmonde Magny, Marc Beigbeder, Paul de Gaudemar, Joseph Rovan and Jean-Marie Domenach, who were still establishing their reputations. The cohesion of the editorial team was assured by regular meetings to hammer out points of theory and policy, and by annual conferences to gather together as many readers and contributors as possible. Mounier still felt that some organised movement of friends of the review was needed but, learning from pre-war experience, he insisted that such personalist centres as were set up should be surrounded by sufficiently demanding conditions of entry to prevent them from degenerating into directionless talking shops. These centres were animated by *Esprit* militants of long standing and kept in close contact with the review's regular activity. Although editorial policy encouraged a large number of articles from specialists outside the personalist milieu, from the autumn of 1945 onwards there was an increased emphasis on establishing the positions of basic doctrine. This meant that new contributors were expected to serve their ideological apprenticeship before being accepted as regular members of the team. However, Mounier did much to encourage the recruitment of new, young writers, which he rightly saw as an indispensable condition for the long-term success of personalism.

Call to renewal
Aware of the serious crisis the war had faced the church with, Mounier had spent part of his war-time retreat in examining the moral and spiritual consequences of it. He considered this a necessary precondition for any broad movement of renewal. He focussed on the writings of the nineteenth-century German philosopher, Friedrich Nietzsche, who had been misappropriated as a patron of nazism. Nietzsche's fierce attack on received morality and his often savage polemic against christianity made him an ideal point of departure for Mounier's attempt to face and conquer the most serious criticisms to which the church could be subjected. In his book *L'Affrontement chrétien* (Neuchâtel 1945), Mounier called to arms a decadent and slumbering church. History, he said, dealt ruthlessly with the weak, and if very much of Nietzsche's attack was justified, the church could be in imminent danger of destruction. From having rested too long under the wing of the ruling class, and from having fed off the fat of the land, he declared, it had grown unused to battle and appeared to have lost many of its heroic virtues. In view of the many powerful critiques and the many-fronted attack under which it was coming, Mounier thought that the church needed to recover the strength of its early struggles if it was not to risk historical oblivion. Christianity was accused of being a coalition of the weak and fearful, and of haunting the centres of decay; though he felt that the church must assuredly be victorious in eternity, yet in history, he warned, the victory was not assured. The first step was to diagnose the weakness: was it inherent and inevitable, or was it a foreign germ caught from a sick era?

In answering these critical questions, Mounier tried to carry the offensive to the enemy. The church was accused of lacking virility, but the reality, Mounier argued, was that it combined both virility and femininity so as to avoid making an idol of either. The church was accused of complacency but, he replied, it was right to avoid the debilitating excess of anguish with which the atheistic existentialists were afflicted, and right to refuse hysterical and unconvincing melodramatics when dealing with the great questions about man and the universe. Part of the trouble, he suggested, was that atheists failed to distinguish between despair and tragedy. Despair, he explained, was empty, destructive, individualist, and foreign to christianity, whereas tragedy, however painful, allowed hope, offered spiritual riches and lay at the heart of catholic doctrine. He admitted that some christians failed to rise out of a comfortable complacency, but then so did some atheists. The remedy was already in christianity, he said, and not to be found in the frenetic nihilism of post-Nietzschean atheism.

Having made that point clear, Mounier admitted that the failure of christians to live up to their faith was sufficiently widespread to require more than a casual dismissal. This malaise was, he claimed, the product of the church's temporal expression. Naturally, since the church was in the world, it acquired many imperfections from its environment; these defects did not invalidate the spiritual essence of christian teaching, he insisted. Nonetheless, he said, they urgently needed to be combated so that when Western civilisation collapsed, as Mounier considered it likely to in the near future, christianity would not sink with it. On a smaller time-scale, but no less seriously, the christian malaise also operated, he said, on the sociological level. The take-over of the church in France by the bourgeoisie had led, he pointed out, to a sharp decline in its presence in the working class. The result, he argued, was that the church had come to be identified with the mediocre and conservative values of the decaying twentieth century bourgeoisie, shored up by the anaemic apologetics of dull clerical hacks out of touch with the real world. Mounier then examined in some detail the spiritual castration which the bourgeoisie had imposed on christian education. The excessive emphasis on restraint and austerity; the negation of natural instincts; the cultivation of moderation and submissiveness; the resulting dissimulation and shame, tortuous self-analysis and casuistry; the morbid negation of sexuality; the cloying possessiveness of the family; obsession with sin and guilt; all these and many more faults besides could be ascribed, Mounier affirmed, to the bourgeoisie deforming aspects of christian education. Often, he said, the result no longer resembled the original stronger and more demanding teachings of the scriptures and saints. The mediocrity of nineteenth century bourgeois values was passed off as christian truth, he warned, and against these perversions the denunciations of Nietzsche held good. He added that there was even no originality in the denunciations, at least not in 1945, since *Esprit* had already been saying the same for a dozen years.

In addition to attacking its bourgeois accretions, Nietzsche had accused christianity of fostering a slave mentality. Mounier probed the distortions which had been perpetrated on christian doctrine so as to lay it open to such charges. The stress on humility, authoritarian methods of teaching, moral intimidation, Mounier agreed, now produced brow-beaten individuals without strength or joy, whereas in their medieval formulation they were intended to temper the brutal manners of a violent age. The exaltation of obedience in and out of season robbed the young christian of his rightful spiritual autonomy, he continued, and a morbid obsession with suffering for its own sake maimed sensitive temperaments. He added that even the christian virtue of charity could be perverted into a lukewarm sentimentality, a spineless refusal to stand up for the truth, and a neurotic retreat into childishness. None of this, Mounier claimed, was compatible with the words or the intentions of the great catholic educators, who were aware of the dangers lurking for their pupils, and who would have considered the bourgeois perversions of their doctrine as nothing less than blasphemy.

Having lengthily expounded the faults which, he conceded, existed in modern christianity, Mounier returned to the offensive. Despite the deformations, he asserted that it was capable of creativity and adventure. Christianity had its aggressivity and power, its boldness and daring, he said; it feared neither life nor death and held the key to self-transcendence. These virile qualities were, he affirmed, fundamental to a faith which claimed to have the way, the truth and the life, and only such a faith could have the necessary strength and completeness to provide an adequate response to the upheaval of the modern world, always provided it could find and express its own true nature.

In his analysis, Mounier was using Nietzsche as a means of inoculating the church. First he was arguing that the attack only held good against the perversions of christianity; then he was warning christians against just those perversions; finally he was pointing out the ways in which the perversions could be overcome. He was preparing the ground for his defence of christianity against atheistic existentialism, but he was also calling christians to confront the changed conditions of the modern world as they existed in post-war France. In these concerns Mounier was adding his contribution to the widespread movement towards renewal and reappraisal which was beginning to stir throughout the church.

A fighting science
Personalism was recognisably one of the most healthy and combative currents within the church, but it needed to support its moral certainties with scientific knowledge. Although *L'Affrontement chrétien* was an exhortation and a moral appeal, at the same time Mounier had been preparing a substantial work of psychology to give a more solid theoretical basis to the work of personalist education. The theoretical developments of before the war had led to the concept of the person taking a central place in the new personalist humanism. As a moral and metaphysical category it aimed to provide the essence of a philosophy of man, both as he exists and as he should be. The pre-war period had also seen the rapid development of psychology, which was striving to construct a scientific framework for understanding the human mind. These developments offered very considerable resources for a more precise exploration of the crucial psychological dimension of the human person. They also offered the dangers inherent in a science in its early stages: that the valuable additions to human understanding were often ill separated from extravagant speculation and charlatanism, and that the field was vulnerable to an excess of untrained, though often well-intentioned amateurs.

During the enforced leisure time of his imprisonment and later concealment, Mounier took the opportunity to extend his study of psychology, and wrote a long treatise on the human character. This *Traité du caractère* (Paris 1946) attempted to synthesise the new knowledge, provide a scientific basis for the notion of the person, and offer pedagogical advice on how best to encourage the fullest development of the human person. Much of the technical and conceptual apparatus was drawn from the writings of the French clinical psychologist, Pierre Janet, a near contemporary of Sigmund Freud. The analytical methodology was based on the work of the Dutch characterologists Heymans and Wiersma. To this was added a wide range of material from French psychologists of the 1920s and 1930s, notably Wallon, Dupré, Minkowski and Baudouin; a selection of German and Austrian characterology, dominated by Kretschmer, Klages and Künkel; psychoanalysts Freud, Jung and Adler, taken largely from second-hand sources; and a broad spread of literary, philosophical and religious references.

Although his approach was avowedly scientific, an exercise in characterology, Mounier was quick to point out that any such exercise embodied, openly or covertly, philosophical and ethical assumptions. He argued that it was illusory for a psychologist to pretend to dissociate his science from its human attachments, and that if it were true that the human person transcends its empirical manifestations, any scientific approach could only be approximate, because its object was incommensurable. He insisted that the person was always more than any characterisation of him, but that this did not completely invalidate such an exercise, it only set its limitations. Equally, he argued, to know a person was only possible for another person in a personal relationship and all that that implied in terms beyond the scope of science. Moreover, he suggested, a person exists in the dimension of time, developing and shifting, so that no single view of him can be adequate, since he can only be grasped in the context of a past, present and future. Clearly, he concluded, this introduced a would-be science into fields where it could not legitimately operate, involving ethics, values, ambiguities and the ultimate nature of man. For Mounier, the person was fundamentally a mystery, and psychology bore the same relation to the person as did theology to God.

His project was to examine in turn the forces operating in the formation and development of the person, and the different effects which in different circumstances they produced. The underlying assumption was that the external and internal determinants of the person were ultimately at the service of the free centre around which they turned and which gave them meaning. Mounier explored the effects of the material and social environment and the physical condition of the body; the forces of emotive energy, receptivity and the perception of reality; the capacities of action in the world, interaction with other people and self-assertion; the higher faculties of intellectual, moral and spiritual life. Each chapter demonstrated the forces at work and sought to suggest how they might be observed and used to develop the person to the highest and richest degree within its inherent possibilities. In this sense it was explicitly educational, for Mounier continually offered advice on the correction of various maladjustments. The advice was, as he had made clear, based on a preconceived model of what the human person was and should be; from the descriptions and prescriptions a composite picture emerged of what constituted this model. The key was balance. At every step the person, said Mounier, was at the centre of a play of tensions between which he must arbitrate, avoiding excess, to create himself. He suggested that there was an area of leeway between opposing excesses within which the person should strive to maintain himself, and that once having attained a given balance, he should maintain it in a positive, resolute and creative way, always seeking to improve it and explore its possibilities. This applied, he insisted, whether the person was considered in his internal structure, his external relations, his prospective and transcendent development, or any other perspective.

The person as a reality and as a value was indivisible for Mounier, and founded on a commitment of faith. The model, always implicit, was the conception of God expressed in the catholic dogma of the Holy Trinity. In this conception, God was held to be both a living personal reality and an absolute norm, in harmony within himself. God was also held to be present in all men both as their most central reality and as source and criterion of value. The human person was therefore a fragment of the divine person incarnated through man in the world. It followed from Mounier's acceptance of this account that what began as a scientific examination of human character, ended by establishing a hierarchy of human characters, and a hierarchy of human activities, rising from those most closely tied to material conditions to those most associated with religious and spiritual conditions.

The way in which Mounier deployed his material reveals a great deal about his method of thought in general and shows both its strengths and weaknesses. Beginning with the fundamental assumptions which he largely inherited from his catholic faith, he established a hierarchical structure of norms and values into which empirical observations had to be fitted. The structure was rigid in its outline but allowed a certain flexibility within its detail in order to accommodate and benefit from observations. As far as possible, all relevant material was collected and processed for inclusion. The processing consisted of accepting all data and interpretations which appeared to be in general harmony with the structure; those which did not fit were either separated from their original context and adapted, or taken as an illustration of the errors arising from an incomplete understanding, or rejection, of the structure he proposed. By this method Mounier aimed to achieve a personalist synthesis. As before, what emerged was an eclecticism which never quite succeeded in becoming an integrated synthesis. The *Traité* itself was an enormous rag-bag of material, often suggestive, often illuminating, containing some of Mounier's best writing as well as some of his worst. The central structure was there, but it often had little bearing on the substance it had to carry, much of which transferred ill from its original context. His analysis had no basis in practical experience, but was entirely theoretical; the major theorists in the field were incompletely understood, he therefore did not come to terms with them; the portion of rigorous analysis was eked out by generous helpings of received wisdom, speculation and prejudice.

Despite its deficiencies, Mounier's work was well geared to the aims set for it. Other writers made more useful contributions to the study of character: René Le Senne's authoritative *Traité de caractérologie* (Paris 1946), for example, was a more scientifically researched and more technically coherent account of the same subject matter. But the value of Mounier's work lay in its eminent usefulness for people trying to practise an informed and sophisticated method of christian education, whether inside or outside of pedagogical institutions. It offered a comprehensive psychological account of man which was compatible with a non-deterministic metaphysic, and a handbook of information, argument and advice for those who shared its assumptions. Although in many respects it has become old-fashioned, more than thirty years later it is still being reprinted, read widely and even set as required reading on more than one French course in education.

Political options
In his moral and educative work, Mounier was attempting to effect long-term changes within the christian community, with the express intention of altering the course of western civilisation at a deep level. Profound transformations within the catholic church since that time have generally confirmed the direction in which Mounier was pointing, at least on a moral or spiritual level. But if these were Mounier's most cherished concerns, he nonetheless recognised that, in the immediate future, it was hard political questions that were the most urgent. His assessment of France and Europe as a whole in 1944 was that history was moving towards a radical material upheaval.[1] He felt that this historical moment could be used to precipitate a moral renewal which eventually could generate a spirituality appropriate to the new social order which was in gestation. He argued that christians ought to accept the implications of social revolution even if it led to the transformation of their traditional values. In practical terms he called for boldness, strength and decision in destroying the former bourgeois, capitalist structures and replacing them with new, popular, socialist structures. Unless this was quickly done, Mounier argued, the revolution would fail on all fronts, including the spiritual front.

The main danger he feared was that the new and energetic MRP, with all its high moral tone and civilised moderation, would allow its legitimate scruples to shelter a wide range of reactionary elements. For reasons they could never understand, the christian democrats received only criticism and scorn from Mounier, whom they regarded as a spiritual patron of their movement. Despite the sympathy he had for many christian democrat militants, Mounier realised that the MRP was laden with a deadweight of conservative catholic supporters, and that too close a relationship between himself and such a movement would be fatal to his wider ideological ambitions. He also knew from experience that almost no amount of overt hostility on his part would undermine the respect and attention which the christian democrats accorded him. Mounier's position in this was mostly a tactical necessity, but on one major point of principle he was adamant. The MRP presented itself, often cynically, as the only political expression of catholicism. It was therefore guilty of confusing the spiritual and the temporal, an offence which Mounier had strongly attacked in the pre-war right. He was not going to condone it in the MRP. As time passed and the christian democrats emerged as increasingly reactionary, Mounier's insistence on this point of principle also increased. He was able to observe similar situations in Italy and Germany where, for comparable reasons, christian democrats were proving to be the new right-wing in politics.

It was, however, the communists and the socialists who caused Mounier's most difficult problem. If he was to avoid being swallowed up by christian democracy and if he was to establish personalism as a viable political ideology, he had to maintain support within the socialist party and at least gain tolerance from the communists. His political ideology was constructed to command the assent of what Mounier considered to be the best elements among the socialists and christian democrats. In practice, this meant the progressive wing of the MRP and christians in the re-constituted SFIO. These elements, he supposed, would be all the more receptive since they lacked the kind of solid doctrinal foundations which gave communism so much of its force and direction. While he could not hope to supplant communism, he could certainly hope to introduce coherence into the muddled mixture of ideas and habits which passed for doctrine on the non-communist left.

Until the late spring of 1945, it seemed possible that united action might be initiated by the three major forces, crystallising the aspirations of the resistance. Mounier encouraged this as far as he could, particularly insisting that the communists should not be isolated or excluded. He even went so far as to support the attempt of the *Front national* group to set up a broadly based organisation of the left on the model of the British labour party.[2] The *Front national* was a group based on a resistance movement which united communists and the old radicals, among others. It even included a priest on the central committee. During 1945 it merged with other small ex-resistance movements to form the *Mouvement Unifié de la Renaissance Française* (MURF). Mounier felt that this movement could resolve the problem, already acute, of the split between the government and the resistance, and the incipient division in the ranks of the resistance itself. He may even have entertained hopes of establishing himself as a major ideologist of the projected party. He tried to encourage the various constituent elements to build a common synthesis on personalist lines. During this period of ferment it seemed entirely reasonable to work in the perspective of an imminent revolution which would usher in a new era. A large number of French people shared this view. The word 'personalism' was on everyone's lips, as a synonym, quite often, for 'socialist humanism', and for a time Mounier's hopes appeared to be in the process of realisation. The apparent success of the resistance movements in preparing a harmonious liberation suggested that Mounier was about to wield the kind of ideological influence for which the war year shad prepared him.

Despite considerable goodwill and restraint, particularly on the part of the communists, the fusion of the three major forces failed to occur. The immediate reasons behind this were the deep-rooted reservations against cooperation with the communists felt by large sections of the socialists and the MRP. The decisive reasons are to be found in the lack of an integrated social and economic base for the proposed union, as the old class divisions painfully reasserted themselves. The three parties emerged from the 1945 elections with their characters sharply distinguished, but still prepared to work together despite their differences. Mounier was in difficulty: his major hope had been for a new organic union which would find in personalism the ideological expression of its fundamental aspirations, the synthesis which would transcend the individual ideologies of its constituents. This hope was now dashed, but its failure held lessons. The establishment of a political ideology required a strong social base, he realised. The required broad base did not exist in society, and personalism on its own had not the social extension with which to challenge its rivals, however strong its intellectual position. In particular it lacked any real hold within the working class. Mounier took the MRP to task for its fear of popular forces, but for all his goodwill, the larger part of his own followers were open to the same criticism.

The remedy for this situation might have been the creation of an *Esprit* movement to make contact with the working class, but Mounier's pre-war experience gave him every reason to be sceptical of its practical effect. He therefore had to reassess the situation to find a more modest means of insertion. Modesty was also encouraged by the growing fragmentation of the resistance movements despite their earlier apparent agreement. Their adherents had seemed to profess a kind of revolutionary christian or near-christian socialism very close to personalism, but even this common orientation, admittedly vague, could not hold together the political unity which social and economic reality contradicted. Although an organic union of communism, socialism and christian democracy had failed to materialise, the three forces continued throughout 1945 and 1946 in the uneasy cooperation of 'tripartism'. The more modest rôle Mounier now looked for was as a sympathetic observer with no partisan commitment, but who would have the ear of all parties. It was in the light of this strategy that he produced his major political work of the post-war period, *Qu'est-ce que le personnalisme?*[3]

Call to commitment
A year had passed since the heady days immediately following the liberation, when Mounier had thought utopia to be on the brink of realisation. He now explained personalism as being complementary to existing political ideologies, and suggested that:

> On peut être chrétien et personnaliste, socialiste et personnaliste, et pourquoi pas? communiste et personnaliste.[4]

The only difficulty with this daring conception was that although a communist personalist was a hypothetical possibility, none existed in reality. Personalism, Mounier explained, supported the socialist revolution but was also opposed to any oppression of the person by totalitarian forces. He realised that his formulation was vulnerable to misappropriation by reactionary elements, but felt that important values were at stake which could not be abandoned. Acknowledging the danger of theoretical purism, Mounier pointed out that pre-war experience had proved to him how important were commitments made in imperfect circumstances not of one's own choosing. He put forward a theory of political practice which accepted that the precondition for influencing events was in the first place to understand them, that the only way to understand them was to take part in their development, and that only by taking part in them could one hope to implement the changes decided on the basis of that understanding. Mounier acknowledged that in his attempt to find a satisfactory balance between the retention of fixed principles rooted in the eternal, and the introduction of history as a primary determinant, he had come close to the marxist concept of *praxis*. He avoided, however, suggesting that he had taken the concept from Marx. The difficulty, he saw, was that it became impossible to avoid compromising principles unless they were stated in the most flexible terms. The answer he proposed was to undertake a radical work of education, in the broadest sense. Personalist education, he said, would be directed towards eliminating, especially among catholics, the illusory stance of neutrality and objectivity, the excessive cultivation of scruple, the narcissistic conscience-searching, the selfish protection of individual integrity, and the extreme perfectionism which ultimately inhibited decision and action. He felt it was inadmissible that catholics were so often absent from the hardest battles on grounds of conscience.

Mounier's call to commitment, while echoing his earlier analyses, contained a note of urgency previously lacking. In common with the existentialists of Sartre's school, who shared many of the same political objectives, his preoccupation with commitment reflected the realisation of a generation of intellectuals that they were confronted with massive change which would transform the conditions of their lives. They understood that they and their contemporaries were at the height of their ability and presented with a unique opportunity to exercise a decisive effect on the events of their time. The experience of helplessness which had until then been their lot was now replaced by a determination to make use of the new possibilities of power and influence that seemed to be held out. The satisfaction of these ambitions was incentive enough to make them impatient of the constraints which had traditionally kept so many intellectuals from involvement in political action.

While insisting on commitment, Mounier was careful to emphasise the necessity for recognising transcendent absolute values, without which, he warned, temporal action could only lead to servitude. He felt that while he himself had the prophetic task of asserting the rights of the absolute, his readers should not interpret this as a call to defend any specific embodiment of the absolute. Rather, he said, they should seek a progressive and inventive response, creating where necessary new forms of temporal action and new institutions more appropriate to expressing spiritual imperatives in the modern world. First, however, Mounier considered that spiritual values required a new form of expression as a result of the dislocation of the classical conception of man proposed by optimistic liberal rationalism. He presented his personalist humanism as the alternative. But he pointed out that the only way personalism could be put into practice was by destroying the oppressive structures of capitalism and by constructing a socialist society which would enable the new, liberated, whole man to emerge. And this, he emphasised, could only be done by fighting alongside the working class and those who were advancing the cause of socialism.

Mounier's difficulty was that those whose political aims he shared, the working class and their main representatives, the trade unions, the communist party, the SFIO socialists, and their allied organisations, these bodies were largely indifferent, if not hostile, to his spiritual values. On the other hand, those whose spiritual aims he shared, the catholic church, and French catholics as a whole, were generally suspicious of, if not repelled by, his political commitments. The novelty of 1945 was that the war had done much to reduce the contradictions between the two, and increase the area in which they overlapped. This area of overlap was the one in which Mounier worked, hoping to expand it. In many respects the socialist humanism which personalism now came to represent was assimilated into the common fund of catholic thought. The moral and spiritual base of personalism ensured that it appeared as one of the most vigorous forms of catholicism. *Esprit* was established as one of France's major political and cultural reviews, and Mounier's personal prestige was at its height. There remained, however, one issue on which Mounier's position was not easily assimilated, the one which demanded of him determination and courage in the face of hostility from all sides: the question of relations with the communists.

Confronting communism
The position of the church on the matter had in theory not changed, although, in the immediate months following the liberation, few leading catholics had felt it opportune to speak out publicly against communism. However, by the end of 1945 orthodox catholic circles were beginning to point out more firmly the dangers inherent in communism for catholics. In February 1946 Mounier drew up a precise account of his attitude towards communism. Tripartism was

still at its height and the communist party was officially still considered a respectable expression of political aims. Mounier initiated in *Esprit* an investigation of the fascination which the party seemed to hold for people of the new generation, the vital twenty to thirty age group.[5] The individuals consulted in this enquiry were all young intellectuals, mostly from the Paris area. As with one voice they acknowledged the strong attraction of the communist party, and almost as often the powerful effect of marxist analysis. The christians among them, however, mostly drew back on the brink of commitment either in distrust of the party or because they felt that marxism excluded a spiritual dimension which they would not abandon. Significantly, a minority of christians were not deterred by these considerations. Perhaps not surprisingly also, several were convinced of the need for a coherent alternative, not to be found in the existing political parties, but along the lines of the personalist inspiration.

Summarising *Esprit*'s position, Mounier insisted that it was a fraternal attitude towards the communists generally and emphatically refused the anti-communism which was preparing to sweep the west.[6] First he recognised that, whatever its good excuses, anti-communism was the consolidating bond behind the various reactionary forces and as such had to be resisted. Second, he observed, it was an undeniable fact that the communist party had the confidence of the majority, and certainly the militant wing, of the working class. This fact was decisive, he explained, since no one could seriously plan a revolution in which the working class was not the major force. Consequently he considered that any attack on the party was also an attack on the working class. Third, he saw the attraction of the communist party as springing from its virile solidarity, its commitment to action, and the near-religious self-discipline it required of its members.

Despite these attractions, Mounier argued, there were important points of principle which made communism unacceptable. In the first place, he said, marxism sought to reduce everything to a function of economics. While it was undeniable that economic and social factors operated in spiritual affairs, he emphasised that spiritual factors also operated to disrupt any economic determinism. Hence, he claimed, although marxism's social analysis was penetratingly acute, it was in other respects a crude philosophy. Primarily, it failed to accept the necessity for a guiding conception of man, without which, he argued, revolution could disastrously fail to produce the expected liberation. He concluded that until marxists treated such considerations seriously they could not expect to gain the support of those for whom the spiritual dimension was vitally important. On a political level, he was sure that there was room both for the marxist, more concerned with material conditions, and for the personalist, more concerned with human problems. But whereas the personalist was prepared to work with the marxist, each dealing with his own sphere, the marxist, he complained, saw the personalist as unnecessary, if not actually harmful, and refused to listen to him.

While he did not wish moralism to weaken revolutionary action, he felt that a moral standpoint was a necessary safeguard against new forms of social alienation, and therefore called on the communists to practise a greater degree of intellectual integrity, to encourage a liberalisation of conditions within the Soviet Union, and to encourage greater frankness in Soviet propaganda. In making these points, Mounier said, he was not participating in the growing anti-communism, but only expressing reservations which were in theory open to be dissolved. He agreed that his reservations did not exclude christian membership of the party, but felt that they did impose a long hesitation at least. In effect, Mounier was saying, he could only embrace a communism which conceded the acceptance and implementation of personalist values, but he claimed that such a concession was compatible with the spirit of marxism.

Dialogue
Mounier's statement of position was a calculated mixture of praise and blame. It was an attempt to give a balanced assessment, from a catholic standpoint, of how communism should be regarded in the changed conditions of 1946. More important, it was a first attempt to draw the communists into a dialogue. Dialogue, for Mounier, meant a contact between two distinct and separate positions. It offered the possibility of changes of position on either side, but aimed principally at eliminating possible confusions. It involved an acceptance of peaceful co-existence and even co-operation, but implicitly it was a means to strengthen his own side. Several young communists took up the offer of dialogue on the terms offered, and pointed out the misunderstandings in Mounier's picture of marxism, or tried to allay his fears about the party and the Soviet Union. The most weighty response, however, came from one of the party's leading intellectuals, Roger Garaudy, who was a *député* and member of the party's central committee.

Writing in a party review, Garaudy welcomed the intent of the dialogue, but could not appreciate why Mounier drew back from joining the party.[7] He thought Mounier was mistaken in his analyses of the relationship between communism and the working class, and between thought and action. He accused him of asking marxism to embrace a platonic idealism, such as characterised personalism, criticised Mounier's thought for being divorced from action and attacked his concept of liberty for its lack of any material substance. He suspected him of reworking all the worn anti-communist slogans of the last twenty years and concluded:

> Tel est au fond le véritable révélateur de ces pensées impuissantes: l'échec devant les problèmes pratiques. Lorsqu'une pensée est incapable de déterminer les conditions actuelles de son efficacité, et de situer son point d'insertion, elle n'est plus que machine à moudre du vent.[8]

In short he raised the one ghost Mounier had been trying earnestly to lay: his lack of practical efficacity.

Stung, Mounier replied attacking Garaudy for his intellectual dishonesty and prejudice.[9] He refused to recognise himself in the caricature which identified his thought as anti-communism, and accused his critic of misrepresenting his position on thought and efficacity. Sadly, he concluded that there was a long way to go before a true dialogue became possible. There, for the time being, the conversation rested, with neither side much closer to a common understanding. While Garaudy was less than just to Mounier's intentions, the barb directed against his ineffectiveness went deeper than Mounier was prepared to admit. And although Garaudy exaggerated Mounier's anti-communist reflexes, it was true that Mounier had little more than a forced sympathy for communism.

There were a number of possible consequences which Mounier could hope to provoke by his dialogue. The first, a modification in the party's philosophy, was obviously unlikely. The second, a heightened awareness of moral and spiritual values among party militants, was more feasible. The third consequence, a new dynamism injected into the entire left by the example of the best elements in communism, was the one Mounier most earnestly wanted to promote. The points on which he specifically praised the party—solidity, efficacity and working class roots—were those he constantly urged on the personalist movement. The fourth consequence, an immunisation of the rest of the left against the temptation of communism, was one he did not and could not formulate publicly. While they did not amount to the obsessive anti-communism of many socialists, which Garaudy thought he detected, Mounier's objections to communism were strong enough and deep-rooted enough to drive him to counter the spread of its influence beyond the unavoidable minimum.

These consequences help to explain why Mounier was so often accused by catholic critics of contaminating the catholic left with communism, and accused by communist critics of undermining the party's support within the catholic working class. That such contradictory allegations could be made was the logical result of his trying to occupy a position between two forces, both of whom assumed no-man's-land to be in the hands of the enemy. Communists demanded nothing less than total support, anti-communists nothing less than complete rejection. It was Mounier's first task to refuse the dilemma of choice. To establish this middle ground was the indispensable condition for a generalised growth of personalism as an effective element in the political ideology of a revolution, however far away its realisation might be.

Mounier's efforts at dialogue were received with caution in more traditional catholic circles. Although more trust was placed in him than before the war, a journal like the Jesuits' *Etudes* was not slow in giving alarmed warnings to *Esprit* against the dangers it was courting.[10] In particular, Mounier was advised not to underestimate the efficacity of christian social doctrines, and not to concede too many virtues to the communists. No one thought that Mounier was seriously tempted to join the communist party. But one of the most difficult problems of Mounier's position was whether or not he was prepared to condone any catholic membership of the party. He only became fully aware of the problem during his visit to Poland in the spring of 1946, when he met men who, by the nature of their country's government, were being obliged to think out their attitude in the knowledge that a great deal hung on their decision. In the France of 1946, Mounier realised that many catholics were in fact members of the party, and at that stage he did not feel it to be illegitimate. His lack of concern was encouraged by the fact that the church judiciously refrained from any disciplinary measures over the issue.

By mid-1947, as the mounting pressure of the cold war began to temper his relative permissiveness, Mounier was obliged to write more carefully worded explanations of his position.[11] While communism was a legitimate political option, it was not the only possible political stance, he insisted, and those who embraced it should be aware that alternatives existed. If they persisted, he said, they must be exceptionally watchful that their christian faith be not eroded.

Under no circumstances should they abandon their ultimate reservations on spiritual matters, and indeed they should try as far as possible to impregnate their action as communists with a true and thorough spirituality. On the level of theory, he stressed, catholicism and communism were deeply at variance, but practical considerations were also part of a spiritual life, and important concrete realisations ought not to be jeopardised for the sake of purely theoretical differences, provided the differences were constantly borne in mind.

The effect of Mounier's analysis was to safeguard the right of a catholic to join the communist party, but to make that step more difficult and less attractive. Unfortunately, from Mounier's point of view, this one aspect of his thought aroused passions which the rest did not. No one much minded ostensibly revolutionary ideas in non-political matters, and if they did they could always reply within the conventions of intellectual debate. Catholic participation in the MRP and the socialist party was hardly controversial, even to those who disapproved of it; but support for the only serious revolutionary force in French politics was not taken lightly. Mounier's position in 1947 was accepted by the catholic authorities only temporarily. As time passed it became apparent that it was not going to be permanently tolerated, however many reservations accompanied it, and however many criticisms were made of marxist theory.

Confronting existentialism
In relation to marxism, Mounier was playing an avant-garde rôle within French catholicism, and a rôle which took him into dangerous territory. In relation to the other major ideological challenger, existentialism, Mounier adopted a much more aggressive stance. In many ways it was nearer to his own moral and philosophical concerns, and its sphere of influence overlapped threateningly into the christian or near-christian middle class youth who formed the social constituency for personalism. In its first months, existentialism's phenomenal popularity was accompanied by an equally widespread and passionate opposition, amounting at times almost to a crusade. Catholics as a whole were hostile to the militant atheism of existentialism. Conservatives of the older generation were shocked at the comprehensive rejection of established values, fearing the erosion of the influence and prestige which now seemed within their own grasp. Both groups thought it urgently necessary to stem the rapid advance of the existentialist movement among the young. Both were prepared to use their powerful position in the community,

and the considerable channels of communication to which they had
access, in order to achieve this end. Reviews and newspapers began
carrying hostile examinations, books appeared in a similar vein.
There was a widespread reaction of backlash against existentialism,
and although Mounier did not wish to appear a middle-aged
reactionary, he found a fertile soil waiting for his ideological
alternative and was not inclined to refuse it. As existentialism
asserted itself during 1945, Mounier followed its different manifestations and was careful to publish adequate analyses, reviews and
summaries, so that he and his readers had a basic understanding
of its principles and their implications.

Reviewing the first issue of Sartre's review, *Les Temps modernes*,[12]
Mounier welcomed the several points on which they shared a
common view, particularly the importance of a philosophy of man
in which the human person was both free and yet committed to his
situation. Pointing out that Sartre's place was only on one branch
of existentialist thought, he suggested that existentialism, along with
marxism and personalism, was one of the three great doctrines of
the time. Sartre's version, however, he regarded as excessively
pessimistic and felt it displayed the moral ambiguity common to all
forms of stoicism. Already Mounier had decided that Sartrean
existentialism was radically unacceptable and even went so far as to
suggest that despite similarities of language, he was further from
Sartre than from marxism. As always with Mounier, the test was
seen as the conception of man implicit in the philosophy. Sartre's
conception was stated succinctly in the first issue of his review:

> Nous concevons sans difficulté qu'un homme, encore que sa
> condition le conditionne totalement, puisse être un centre
> d'indétermination irréductible. Ce secteur d'imprévisibilité qui
> se découpe ainsi dans le champ social, c'est ce que nous nommons
> la liberté, et la personne n'est rien d'autre que sa liberté.[13]

This passably non-technical summary of Sartre's position was close
to Mounier's in that it asserted both the autonomy of the person and
the limitations imposed by his environment. What Mounier could
not accept was that the person was given total freedom and defined
in terms of it. This knocked the bottom out of his own view that the
person was a nodal point in a network of forces. In particular, the
dimension of interiority, crucial for Mounier since it led to God, for
Sartre led to nothing. In a word, it was the irremediable atheism
at the centre of Sartre's philosophy which determined Mounier's
reaction to it. During the following months he devoted himself

to preparing a major response which would take account of the importance of existentialism as an ideology and at the same time challenge the value of Sartre's atheistic brand.

The result of Mounier's labours appeared in *Esprit* between April and October 1946, and was published in book form at the end of that year under the title *Introduction aux existentialismes* (Paris 1947). His main aim was to describe existentialism in such a way as to reduce to a minimum the importance of Sartre within it. Anxious to give as wide a meaning as possible to the term, he defined existentialism as a philosophy which was primarily concerned with the existence of man, and suggested that, for christian existentialists, it was simply another way of approaching christianity. Mounier saw that the wider the meaning given to the notion of existentialism, the more its centre of gravity could be shifted away from the atheistic branch, presenting Sartre as out on a limb. He therefore included in his analysis a wide variety of christian 'existentialists', including Pascal, Maine de Biran, Kierkegaard, Laberthonnière, Blondel, Bergson, Péguy, P.-L. Landsberg, Scheler, Barth, Buber, Berdyaev, Shestov, Soloviev, Gabriel Marcel, Jaspers and personalism itself. Some of these had only dubious claims to be included. The atheists were limited to Nietzsche, Heidegger and Sartre. In addition, Mounier decided to deal with existentialism thematically. The utility of this approach was that it dislocated the intellectual coherence of any individual thinker and allowed Mounier to propose his own principles of coherence. He thereby avoided having to confront Sartre on philosophical terms and neutralised the intellectual power of his system.

Analysis of existentialism
In Mounier's view, the existentialists' first step consisted of a philosophical awakening, shaking men out of their indifference and provoking them to a vital and passionate appraisal of their existence. They thereby overturned the traditional relationship of knowledge between man and the world, he said, seeing man as a perceiving subject rooted in mystery and opaque to itself, in a world which was inexhaustible, full of mystery, and could not be grasped in its totality, much less expressed in a systematic formulation. He suggested that this led to a dramatic conception which held that: man was contingent in that he existed at all and in that he had one specific existence rather than another; his reason was inadequate to cope with the world; he was dynamic and restless, always moving on into the future; his existence was precarious and never assured,

so that he was in a constant state of anguish, dizziness and danger, confronted with the necessity to choose himself at every stage; he was out of harmony with the world, threatened and alienated; he was faced at every moment with the dreadful awareness of his own inevitable death and had to come to terms with it; he was isolated and cut off from his fellow men and his own true nature was hidden; finally, though for Sartre alone, man was ultimately nothingness. Mounier took the opportunity to attack Sartre's nihilistic view of the frenetic dynamism of consciousness and his paranoid reaction to the contingency of being. He isolated Sartre's concept of *le néant* for particular attack. It entailed, in his view, an impoverished, humiliating and purely negative conception of man.

Mounier admitted that the historical situation had been instrumental in the spread of existentialism, but he believed that its roots went deeper. He saw it on the one hand as a christian response to the over-complacent attitude of the church, which had led to a widespread dechristianisation. On the other hand, he saw it as the atheists' attempt to replace religion, leading more often to despair and nihilism. Mounier warned that the ontology of despair was destructive and unacceptable to the christian and must be corrected by an ontology of hope, which alone could situate man in his true nature and dignity. Locating the problem on a spiritual level, he therefore saw atheistic existentialism as the expression of a malady of the soul, and its christian counterpart as the remedy for such a malady. He pointed out that existentialism shared with personalism a common recognition of the need for interiority, counterbalanced by a self-transcendence and an exteriorisation which prevented it falling into individualism. Existentialists, he said, saw man as torn between this true mode of existence and the false mode, its polar opposite, which had many names—*divertissement* (Pascal), inauthenticity (Heidegger), *mauvaise foi* (Sartre) or aestheticism (Kierkegaard)—all designating the same selfishness, indifference and lack of lucidity. In each case, he explained, the inauthenticity had to be overcome by a conscious choice and a radical transformation on the part of the individual.

Complementary to the value of interiority, Mounier agreed, was the existentialists' stress on involvement in the world. They saw man, he said, as born into a situation which he had not chosen, but which he had to come to terms with and assume responsibility for. This, he felt, led to a complex and even contradictory theory of action which emphasised the conflict between the assumed present and the different chosen future, and between individual freewill and historical necessity. Action in the world, he went on, tended to become objective and impersonal, but refusal to act meant a retreat into unreality, solipsism and the dissolution of the self in pure subjectivity. He regretted that early existentialists had tended to this refusal, probably as an over-reaction against the menace of nineteenth century materialism.

Fortunately, Mounier thought, modern existentialists seemed prepared to restore the balance, although very often they tended to a cultivation of different forms of action only for the intensity of the subjective experience procured. For the atheists, he suggested, this was not surprising, since, despite their protests to the contrary, they had no positive force to nourish effective action in the world, and furthermore no external point of reference by which to direct it. Since moral responsibility fell, in their view, entirely on the individual, and since every least act was taken to be universally normative, he pointed out, human acts carried a debilitating load of responsibility which would tend more often to paralyse than to catalyse into action. The christian existentialists escaped this charge, he claimed, by inserting human freedom into a network of forces in tension, and by offering an external scheme of reference. The total freedom allowed by Sartre in particular could, he said, be no less than arbitrary, leading to a disorientation in a world where everything was possible, where no effective limits were placed on freedom, and where there was nothing and no one to be responsible to. The danger Mounier saw in this was a total moral relativism in which there would ultimately be no firm grounds on which to condemn even nazi atrocities provided that they were undertaken with subjective intensity.

Mounier went on to examine a characteristically existentialist concern: the existence of other people. Existentialists, he said, had raised the problem of alienation which occurred in the relationship between two minds, denying the possibility of communication other than by indirect and unsure means. The atheistic existentialists had been particularly tormented by the problem, he suggested, and ultimately could only see consciousnesses locked in conflict. For Heidegger, he explained, the individual attained authenticity only in total solitude and dereliction, other people being only a temptation to sink into servitude or inauthenticity. Mounier analysed Sartre's view of personal relationships as a battle between hostile freedoms, committed to trying and failing to enslave each other. He admitted that it was accurate up to a point, but as a partial account only applicable to an inauthentic mode of being. He suggested that Sartre in his paranoia had disregarded the possibility of human relationships as a mutual enrichment in which shame, fear and hatred could be replaced by respect, fidelity and love. But he added that only christianity could show the way out of his ontological dereliction, replacing the total isolation of the individual, inescapable in Sartre's view, with a divine inner transcendence. However, Mounier conceded that the existentialists as a whole laid an excessive emphasis on the priority of the individual existent, to the detriment, very often, of general truths. Perhaps the best way to understand this, he suggested, was as part of a total dialectic, needing to be completed by the older essentialist doctrines which had become fossilised and needed to be shaken and challenged in the interests of truth.

Finally, Mounier found in existentialism the intuition of a presence in the world which was not altogether explicable. Atheists were troubled by the experience, he argued, and ascribed it to an illusion of the mind projecting its hidden preoccupations into the world, hence the disquieting experience of the Double. Christians knew, he said, that it was the revelation of the superabundant source of being. However, he considered that the irremediable separation Sartre introduced into being was a false and pernicious one produced by a mind unable to stand outside its own impoverishment. To divorce man from existence, he asserted, was the inescapable consequence of refusing living being, and in this sense Sartre represented the honest and lucid working out of the initial refusal. Mounier declared that christian existentialism offered a positive answer to Sartre in the notion of an authentic transcendence which was that infinite movement within being which drove it on to be more than itself, and rather than a negation, was an affirmation of something beyond. He added that this 'beyond' called for a response which rational thought could not encompass, the model of which was an act of faith, and thought that only in this way could human existence reach outside itself to a reality which could transform it. Thus, Mounier concluded, existentialism offered a kind of prophetic revival, capable of shaking the church into a healthy reappraisal and of revitalising western rationalism to face the challenge of the new world.

Objectives
Throughout his book, Mounier's aim was to defend christian doctrine and to discredit atheism. The aim was carried out first by setting up the christian existentialists as the true form of exis-

tentialism. Marcel, Kierkegaard and Pascal were constantly recommended, though Kierkegaard was occasionally reproached for the more distinctively protestant features of his thought. Jaspers could be regarded as an honorary christian, Mounier implied, since he was striving for a truth which he never fully perceived, and his analyses always suggested a possible religious solution which was never embraced. Heidegger, with whom Mounier was clearly not familiar, was shown as a lost soul, working to come to terms with the loss of God and signally failing, a sad rather than a dangerous figure. So far Mounier had no difficulty in showing the harmony of the existentialist school and the obvious superiority of its christian members; he even emerged as something of an existentialist himself on these terms. With Sartre, however, the situation was different. He was caught in three impossibilities. First, he could not ignore Sartre because without him his account of existentialism would be both incomplete and ideologically irrelevant. Second, he could not base his account on Sartre, since this would make the job of refutation immeasurably more difficult and ideologically ineffective. Third, he could not be over-selective in his presentation of Sartre, since, Sartre being already widely known, that would have laid him open to the charge of misrepresentation and would have been ideologically counter-productive.

The result was a compromise. Mounier grappled with Sartre from different angles, seeking leverage wherever he could find it, but without gaining a decisive victory. Pitching the approach sometimes on philosophical, sometimes on emotional grounds, he tried first to present Sartre as an aberrant, almost illegitimate member of an otherwise valuable school of thought, second to suggest deficiencies in his ontology, third to neglect important areas of strength in his thought. Though Mounier gave a lucid analysis of the christian current of existentialism in its broadest sense, and although he offered many perceptive and serious criticisms of Sartrean existentialism, he failed to give any coherent explanation of existentialism as a social or cultural movement, he failed to consider Sartre's thought as a distinct, systematic, rational philosophy, and he failed to account for its popularity. Nevertheless, the book succeeded in its aims and became a much reprinted study. Resisting, but also accepting some of Sartre's points, Mounier conducted his argument on a level which was never drily technical, often richly expressive and always of some intellectual complexity. In short, the book was tailored to appeal to the anticipated audience of informed catholics with a sympathetic interest in new ideas, whether the older personalists of Mounier's vintage, or the leaders of the new generation of young catholics. To the educated, middle-class public as a whole, it offered a clear general survey of a complex and varied area, an accessible introduction and an intelligent appraisal of one of the dominant intellectual movements of the period.

Mounier's success in articulating an adequate response to existentialism was quickly recognised in catholic circles. He was seen more generally as a prominent figure in the debate over existentialism which was widely pursued in the press and elsewhere. One organised public discussion in mid-June 1946, in which Mounier spoke together with the philosophers Maurice Merleau-Ponty, Maurice de Gandillac, Jean Wahl and Jean Daniélou, attracted a Parisian audience of several thousands. Mounier was in great demand to contribute to books, magazines, papers, radio programmes and public meetings on existentialism. Apart from the opportunity, thus offered, of combating an influential atheistic ideology, perhaps the most significant development, from Mounier's point of view, was the upsurge of public interest in christian existentialists, who had hitherto slumbered in relative obscurity. Such interest, broadly confined to christian circles, may have led some to personalism, but in any case it helped to sensitise the catholic population to the change, questioning and rethinking which was running through the old structures. Against this background of growing awareness, Mounier's personalism appeared as a firm and respected doctrine and as an open window on to the intellectual unknown. Even if they did not embrace it whole-heartedly, there were many, even cautiously progressive catholics, who looked to personalism for a lead.

Post-war achievements

The two years following the end of the war were in many ways the pinnacle of achievement for Mounier and *Esprit*. Personalism was widely accepted as the most dynamic and fertile current of christian thought. The central value of the human person was generally acknowledged as the keystone of catholic social thought. *Esprit's* socialist humanism brought together much of the political theory which had emerged from the resistance. Mounier's dialogue with the communists did a great deal to map out the possibilities of an important and controversial field of action. His study of existentialism helped to counter the effects of an attractive form of atheism. It was not, therefore, without justification that personalism was widely regarded as one of the three major ideologies of post-war France. At the liberation, when hopes were green and new, everything seemed possible. The enormous intellectual effort furnished by Mounier and his review ensured that no opportunity was missed of taking full advantage of the situation as it developed.

But if personalism's achievement was to become permanent, it needed a secure base in social and political reality. At that point, however, it came into contact with the powerful forces of history which were beginning to make Mounier's ambitions impossible in the foreseeable future. In face of the developing class struggles and the cold war, *Esprit*'s middle class catholic support was not able to spearhead the looked-for personalist revolution on a social and political level. Personalism became confined to the less widereaching, but still important task of transforming the attitudes, ideas and sympathies of the catholic middle class. And even that was only done in the teeth of increasing difficulties.

Notes

1 E. Mounier, 'Suite française aux maladies infantiles des révolutions', *Esprit*, no105, décembre 1944, p19–33. Reprinted in *Oeuvres* IV p76–90.
2 E. Mounier, 'Front national', *Esprit*, no108, mars 1945, p620–621.
3 E. Mounier, *Qu'est-ce que le personnalisme?* (Paris, 1947), was written as a series of articles in *Esprit*, janvier & mars 1946, février 1947. It is reprinted in *Oeuvres* III p179–245.
4 *Oeuvres* III p179.
5 E. Mounier, 'Ceux qui en étaient, ceux qui n'en étaient pas: enquête sur le communisme et les jeunes', *Esprit*, no119, février 1946, p191–260.
6 E, Mounier, 'Débat à haute voix', *Esprit*, no119, février 1946, reprinted in *Oeuvres* IV p114–137.
7 Roger Garaudy, 'Impuissance et malfaisance du spiritualisme politique', *Cahiers du communisme,* mars 1946, p212–223.
8 Ibid, p223.
9 E. Mounier, 'Autour du communisme (suite)', *Esprit*, no 122, mai 1946, p855–867.
10 See J. Daniélou, 'Tentation du communisme', *Études,* avril 1946, p116–117, and L. Barjon, 'Quand les chrétiens s'accusent', *Études,* mai 1946, p214–220.
11 E. Mounier, 'Réponse à une enquête sur le communisme', *Confluences,* no 18–20, 1947, p191–206, reprinted in *Oeuvres* III p611–620; and E. Mounier, 'Communistes chrétiens?', *Esprit*, no135, juillet 1947, p116–121, reprinted in *Oeuvres* III p620–625.
12 E. Mounier, 'Le message des "Temps Modernes" et le néo-stoïcisme', *Esprit*, no117, décembre 1945, p957–963.
13 J.-P. Sartre, 'Présentation', *Les Temps modernes,* no1, octobre 1945, p17.

Bibliographical Notes

Useful studies of the social and political situation of post-war France are: A. Werth, *France 1940–1955* (London 1956); C. Gavin, *Liberated France* (London 1955); P. Williams, *Politics in Post-war France*, 2nd ed (London 1958); J. Chapsal, *La Vie politique en France depuis 1940* (Paris 1966); J. Ardagh, *The New France* (London 1970); M. Beaujour & J. Ehrmann, *La France contemporaine* (Paris 1966); O. M. Taylor, *The Fourth Republic of France* (London 1951); J. Fauvet, *La IVe République* (Paris 1959); H. W. Ehrmann, *Politics in France* (Boston 1968). Good analyses of the changes within French catholicism are given in W. Bosworth, *Catholicism and Crisis in Modern France* (Princeton 1962); A. Dansette, *Destin du catholicisme français (1926–1956)* (Paris 1957); R. Rémond, (editor), *Forces religieuses et attitudes politiques dans la France contemporaine* (Paris 1965); G. Mury, *Essor ou déclin du catholicisme français* (Paris 1960).

Informative accounts of the christian democratic movement are given by: M. Vaussard, *Histoire de la démocratie chrétienne* (Paris 1956); M. Einaudi and F. Goguel, *Christian Democracy in Italy and France* (Notre Dame 1952); and F. Spotts, *The Churches and Politics in Germany* (Middletown, Connecticut 1973). R. W. Rauch, *Politics and belief in contemporary France* (The Hague 1972) gives a comprehensive survey of Mounier's relations with the French christian democrats. Helpful studies of more left-wing currents of catholicism are: G. Suffert, *Les Catholiques et la gauche* (Paris 1960); and I. Lepp, *Espoirs et déboires du progressisme* (Paris 1956).

Useful material on French marxism and communism can be found in: A. Kriegel, *Les Communistes français* (Paris 1968); D. Caute, *Communism and the French Intellectuals* (London 1964); G. Lichtheim, *Marxism in Modern France* (New York 1966); F. Bon and others, *Le communisme en France et en Italie*, vol 1 (Paris 1969); G. Walter, *Histoire du parti communiste* (Paris 1948); J. Fauvet, *Histoire du parti communiste français* (Paris 1965); R. Tiersky, *French Communism, 1920–1972* (New York 1974). Relations between the communist party and catholics are examined, from opposing standpoints, in J. Kanapa, *La Doctrine sociale de l'Église et le marxisme* (Paris 1962) and J. Marteaux, *L'Église de France devant la révolution marxiste* (Paris 1958–1959).

There are many accounts of existentialism, few of which give a clear definition of their subject. The most useful philosophical accounts are J. MacQuarrie, *Existentialism* (London 1973); J. Wahl, *Philosophies of Existence* (London 1969); and M. Warnock, *Existentialism* (London 1970). The political aspects of existentialism are dealt with at length in M.-A. Burnier, *Les existentialistes et la politique* (Paris 1966).

In connection with the psychological aspect of personalism, the following books are useful: G. W. Allport, *Personality* (London 1938); R. Le Senne, *Traité de caractérologie* (Paris 1946); I. Gobry, *La Personne* (Paris 1961); and Semaines Sociales de France, *Socialisation et personne humaine* (Lyon 1961).

CHAPTER SIX

The Struggle for Survival
(1947–1950)

Political decline
Since General de Gaulle's departure from the government in January 1946, the system of tripartism had given France the appearance and the possibility of a national consensus. For more than a year the uneasy coalition of communists, socialists and christian democrats lurched from one disagreement to another, with tensions increased by domestic and foreign pressures. At home, economic difficulties led to a disenchantment with the governing parties. The problem of constructing an acceptable constitution took its toll in disharmony. Shifts in the balance of electoral power, coupled with the emergence of a Gaullist right-wing party, the *Rassemblement du Peuple Français* (RPF), made the concept of three-way cooperation seem less unequivocally necessary or even desirable. Abroad, the first decisive moves in the cold war made it difficult for France to continue a system of 'national unanimity' increasingly in contradiction with the international disunity.

At the crux of the problem were the communists who, as the strongest individual party, had every claim to their share of power. They excited the fear of France's Anglo-American allies, of the conservative and moderate elements within France, and of their politically weaker partners in government. In May 1947 they were excluded from the government following their protest against its economic policy. At approximately the same time communists were excluded from government in all the western European countries where they had participated in governing coalitions. In France they became the permanent opposition, which served to underline what had only been disguised by tripartism: that of all the differences which separated the parties, those existing between the communists and the others were the most substantial. Whatever conclusions may be drawn from this, it infallibly meant that the communist party, with the consistent support of one fifth of the electorate, became the major point of reference in economic, political and ideological matters, whether in order to oppose it, to support it, or to find some other kind of relationship with it.

Throughout 1947 the anti-communist campaigns intensified, while the living conditions of the working class worsened. These tendencies were sharpened by the crisis which broke during the winter of that year. Economic deterioration led to widespread strikes and demonstrations. The government's response was to unleash the full force of its repressive machinery to restore order. The working class, divided in its response, was defeated and the trade union federation split in two. France henceforth slipped into the orbit of the United States, the communist party was isolated politically, and the working class weakened.

More than ever Mounier was under pressure to adopt a position of anti-communism, and more than ever he asserted his refusal. The communist party, threatened, began to close its ranks and tended increasingly towards the intransigent and illiberal reflexes which Mounier most regretted in it. To add to this, a series of political trials in Eastern Europe had begun with that of Petkov in Bulgaria. The rôle of the Soviet Union in Czechoslovakia seemed to confirm Mounier's fears about its intentions. Although he refused to change his stated position, Mounier was led to assert more emphatically his reservations about communism.

An important factor in Mounier's development was the founding in late 1947 of the *Union des Chrétiens Progressistes,* who declared that spiritual and political matters were entirely separate and that in their judgment the only feasible means of defending the working class and the ideals of popular democracy was to work in conjunction with the communists. Commenting on their manifesto, Mounier criticised them for their unseemly haste.[1] He felt that their uncritical adulation forgot or ignored the negative side of communism's record, and that they lacked a strong and independent position, which alone could prevent their merely being assimilated into the party. He took care not to condemn their efforts as such, but also not to identify himself with their line. Religiously, he argued, they were perfectly within their rights as far as he could tell, but politically they were being naïve. As the *progressistes* defined their attitude more precisely, it appeared that they were less unconditionally bound to communism than had at first seemed the case. Particularly, they were not for the most part members of the party. Mounier felt more confidently that they might be a promising movement, though he knew that too close an involvement with communism was unacceptable to the catholic hierarchy, and that the hierarchy was bound eventually to assert its view.[2] For himself, he was careful to keep contact with the communists to purely verbal exchanges.

By 1948 Mounier was finding it difficult to sustain his revolutionary political posture within the framework of existing political forces. The communists were becoming intractable, the socialists sterile and centrist, the christian democrats increasingly reactionary. The only apparently dynamic group was the Gaullist RPF, and he wanted nothing to do with what he considered to be its neo-fascist tendencies. He began to look for a new socialist force, free from the contaminations of the existing parties. Only at one moment did this hope come anywhere near fulfilment. Towards the end of February 1948, after several months of preparation, a new political movement was launched: the *Rassemblement Démocratique Révolutionnaire* (RDR). Its *comité d'initiative*, dominated by the figure of Sartre, included the psychologist Paul Fraisse as *Esprit* representative among the nine journalists, four members of the National Assembly and seven trade unionists. The RDR's foundation appeal declared its independence from liberal democracy, weak-kneed social democracy and Stalinist communism. It proclaimed its determination to struggle for human rights, liberty and social justice, and affirmed its fidelity to the working class and the spirit of revolutionary democracy.

Concrete proposals were not precisely stated, but the RDR's declaration coincided closely with the principles and aspirations which Mounier held. He greeted it with cautious optimism as the first sign of a new socialist revival, and urged his readers to lend their efforts to ensuring its success. He felt that it offered a possible answer to the problem of finding a concrete political expression for his personalism. He had become conscious that despite his attempts to lever the major parties in a personalist direction, he was failing to exert more than a piecemeal influence which could not be fashioned into a cogent political force. The RDR offered the promise of a movement which might embody a near-personalist ideology, and he detected in it the youthfulness and seriousness which might command success.

To his credit, however, Mounier also saw the embryonic faults which might vitiate its action: a temptation to mere rhetoric, a lack of economic and political rigour, and an excess of leaders with too scanty a base. Sadly, his fears were too well grounded. The RDR soon foundered in theoretical squabbles and a surplus of good intentions over political realism. Disavowed by the socialist party, which furnished most of the troops, and strongly criticised by the communists and their allies, on whose cooperation they had counted, the movement had no substantial group left to turn to for support. It eventually died a natural, though ignominious death. Possibly the only serious achievement of the RDR was to stimulate a wide-ranging reappraisal of socialist theory. As part of this reappraisal, Mounier initiated an attempt to reinvigorate the European Marxist tradition, timed, appropriately enough, to coincide with the centenary of Marx' and Engels' *Communist Manifesto*.

Marxism revisited
Although marxism was the major ideology he had to face from 1932 onwards, Mounier never addressed himself to it in the same way as he had done to anarchism before the war, or to existentialism after the war. When he died in 1950 he had just begun to read a French translation of Marx's *Capital* for the first time, possibly with a view to a major confrontation. In effect, his most serious attempt to face marxism publicly is represented by the May-June 1948 issue of *Esprit*. The issue, with the general title of 'Marxisme ouvert contre marxisme scolastique', devoted almost 300 pages to articles and montages on various aspects of marxism, and set out to offer a fund of reflection and criticism. In this very substantial work, Mounier's own contribution was largely editorial. The contents included an anthology of Marx' and Engels' writings; articles on Marx and Proudhon; articles on marxist theories of morality, history, religion, revolution, consciousness, materialism, economics, and culture; and an enquiry into whether marxism was becoming a scholastic philosophy. The contributors ranged from committed communists to Dominican priests and through a selection of nationalities.

Mounier's declared intention was to try to understand the obvious power of marxism, examining its strengths and limitations without falling into the confusions which assisted polemic but not truth.[3] Refusing to expurgate marxism for easy consumption, he also refused to father on to marxism disguised versions of his own thought, understanding that the task of elucidating marxism was a long, difficult one which was only worth doing honestly. Mounier felt that this kind of exercise might encourage marxism to cast off some of its rigidity and develop its inventive forces to the point where it would recognise its own inadequacies. In particular, Mounier argued that marxism erected a system of explanation which was valid in a limited context into a universal explanation. The hope that marxism would go beyond its own limitations was founded, Mounier said, on the dynamic and open principles which were built into it. If these principles were adhered to, he hoped, a genuine dialogue would be possible which could be to the ultimate benefit of both personalism and marxism itself. The openness Mounier wanted to encourage in marxism was a greater readiness to concede the autonomy of consciousness in relation to the economic infrastructures. From this concession the way would be open to introduce the possibility of spiritual forces playing a decisive rôle in events. This was Mounier's eventual aim, though in the process of achieving it he was prepared to adopt much of the marxist analysis of the social and economic spheres, where he had consistently admitted its superiority.

Pursuing the theme of marxism's open, as opposed to its scholastic, tendencies, Mounier had asked a number of writers, communist and non-communist, to comment on the distinction he proposed.[4] The answers were largely predictable. The communists, to a man, replied that marxism was by its very nature open and creative, constantly ready and able to take account of changing circumstances, prepared where necessary to renew defunct or inappropriate analyses. Some of them pointed out that marxists were only human and consequently there were times when they failed to be true to their principles. One of them, Claude Roy, pointed out that there was no reason why they should try to fit the stereotypes formed for them by non-marxists. Moreover, Roy added, in view of the treatment which they had been accorded by everyone else since the beginning, marxists had shown extraordinary lucidity and tenacity in remaining true, though they ought not to be complacent about it. The non-communist contributors, also to a man, felt that marxism had suffered an inevitable loss of vigour, and was tending to a rigidity comparable with the worst excesses of scholasticism. This, they hastened to add, was no one's fault since it arose from the peculiar social and historical conditions in which marxism had to grow. It could be remedied, they suggested, if marxists would only become more ready to criticise their beliefs and open themselves to other possibilities, which they had hitherto disregarded.

Despite the presentation of the enquiry, which suggested a certain coherence and unanimity among the contributors, there was evidently no real agreement between the two sides. Claude Roy came nearest to forging a link between them. Having admitted that marxists do sometimes use their ideology as a simple framework into

THE STRUGGLE FOR SURVIVAL (1947–1950)   151

which everything must be fitted, and fall short of the intelligence and rigour with which the marxist method should be used, he concluded:

> Nous sommes toujours menacés, de l'extérieur et de l'intérieur, en nous-mêmes et en face de nous, de périls et de paresses. Mais le marxisme est aussi une discipline de la lucidité. Il doit préparer *les lendemains qui chantent* avec des aujourd'hui qui parlent clair, droit et vrai. C'est un programme sur lequel je pense que nous pouvons nous retrouver aussi, mon cher Emmanuel Mounier, avec toi, avec tes amis.[5]

It is difficult to see what more in theory Mounier could wish from a marxist. The commitment to honesty, the intellectual modesty, and the openness of his declaration demanded a reciprocal response from Mounier; this was, however, not forthcoming. The same is true of the Italian communist, Remo Cantoni, whose contribution was essentially in the same spirit.[6] While he appreciated their position and always referred to them afterwards as honest, open marxists, Mounier did not try to come to terms with them; on the contrary, he used them as a stick with which to beat their less amenable colleagues.

Among their less amenable colleagues, two party intellectuals, Jean Kanapa and Victor Leduc, soon made it clear that they regarded Mounier's position with suspicion, but were prepared to continue a dialogue now that it had been opened. Kanapa accused Mounier of giving expression to a number of distorted interpretations of marxism and trying to undermine the basic doctrine.[7] But he thought that with vigilance on both sides a dialogue was possible if Mounier were prepared to take fewer liberties with marxist doctrine. Leduc echoed this sentiment and added that Mounier should leave marxism to the marxists and concentrate on the more fruitful line of cooperating with the party on practical issues.[8] Both men took the whole affair as a confused indication that the party was making some headway and could hope to build on this, given the right approach. The right approach, as they understood it, was to take a firm doctrinal position, conceding nothing, and to attempt to establish a limited unity on a practical level.

Mounier firmly repelled their advances, denying, rather dishonestly, that he had intended any dialogue, but agreeing to open one since it had been taken that way.[9] Rejecting their accusations of distortion, he replied to their invitation of practical cooperation saying that the elucidation of basic ideological positions was more

F

important. He suggested that he had as much right as anyone else to examine marxism critically, and that the communists would do well to follow his initiative, as had Roy and Cantoni. The effect of his reply was to draw a sharp distinction between theory and practice in marxism, a separation his interlocutors resisted, but one which permitted Mounier to pursue his study of marxism through a period in which the political implications, if accepted, would have been overwhelming.

During the summer of 1948, he elaborated on his position in some detail for the benefit of the review's annual conference.[10] It was necessary, he suggested, to intensify the relationship with marxism, on the one hand learning more from it, on the other multiplying the reservations provoked by the basic difference between them. Such an intensification, he rightly saw, could not take place without his having to neutralise the proselytising force of communism, and while he felt himself immune to it, he also felt a responsibility to protect those of his associates and followers who might be less secure. In this project can be found the explanation for his attitude to dialogue with communist marxists.

The spur to Mounier's intensified interest in marxism lay first in the need to consolidate the position of catholic personalism among the young catholic élite, facing ideological pressure from the growing number of young people who were turning to marxism. But another factor also emerged imperiously demanding attention: the substantial increase in recruitment of working class catholics both by the communist-dominated trade unions, and by the party itself. Although Mounier could not hope to exercise much direct influence on events there, he was not entirely helpless ideologically. Any aid he could offer in the direction of analysis or argument would be welcomed by those catholic organisations and publications operating in direct contact with the problem. Their prime need was a pertinent, effective critique of marxism which would not appear to run counter to the advancement of the working class, or to contradict those analyses which corresponded with working class experience.

Taken together, these factors compelled Mounier to redouble his efforts to come to terms with marxism without yielding ground, and above all without reaching a peaceful coexistence with communism. Such coexistence, he knew, would inevitably lead to an erosion of personalism as the weaker of the two. The erosion of personalism, he felt, would expose the church to the risk of being undermined. For these reasons Mounier took an intransigent and uncompromising stand against the solicitations of communist intellectuals and at the same time devoted much time and energy to learning from marxism.

Retreat from politics
Though he resisted the political implications of marxism, Mounier had no serious alternative to offer. Following the disappointing collapse of the RDR, it became clear that he was gradually being forced on the defensive. He lacked the political vehicle which might have made it worthwhile for him to formulate practical suggestions. Though he did not despair, he found his attention increasingly taken by his other work. His political declarations became more sporadic. He had, it seemed, nothing to add, and in the face of a great reactionary upsurge he felt politically helpless. Personalism now had no specific political expression, either in one party, or in a coherent group of parties. The most Mounier could do was to encourage the development of a personalist tendency within all parties. For himself, he now emphasised the need to withdraw from specific political commitments:

> Il faut que l'intelligence se donne le recul, les doutes, le champ de réflexion nécessaires pour rendre l'action plus efficace, ou l'accorder à des exigences qui la débordent.[11]

Though not precisely a reversal, Mounier's position had evolved considerably in the year since he had emphasised the need to 'mettre la main à la pâte révolutionnaire'.[12] Without any single concrete objective to pursue, one political party was now as good as another for Mounier's purposes.

Since he could not be sure of finding an audience, sympathetic or not, among non-catholics, Mounier was increasingly addressing himself to christians. His efforts were directed at revolutionising catholics once more, in the hope that eventually as much as possible of their spirituality would penetrate the revolutionaries. In the case of the socialist party, catholics were already a significant minority and, along with a number of protestants, formed a ready audience within the party. Mounier had no longer any need to appeal for a spiritualisation of its doctrines, since most of the unacceptable elements had been removed or muted. He therefore spoke to socialists in a similar way as to christian democrats, emphasising the need for bold revolutionary action with no dogmatic anti-communism. The MRP to all intents and purposes consisted of catholics and had largely slipped into a reactionary political stance. Mounier tried to conduct a rearguard action against the resurgent right-wing and to keep open the MRP's early progressive tendency. He therefore resigned himself to a long term strategy, trying to prepare ideologically for the day when events might again lend themselves to the assertion of personalism as a political ideology. He effectively withdrew from political debate at this point, and it was only an initiative from the communist party that drew him temporarily back into political activity.

The beginning of 1949 saw a serious attempt by the communist party to initiate a wide-ranging peace campaign and to reaffirm its offer of the hand of friendship to catholics. For some months, Mounier's interest in communism had been purely philosophical, he now found himself plunged back into the troubled waters of a political dialogue with them. In April 1949 the party's General Secretary, Maurice Thorez, speaking at the party conference, called specifically on Mounier, Claude Bourdet, the christian socialist editor of *Combat*, and men like them who rejected anti-communism, to join in a common action with them.[13] Thorez presented cogent reasons, based on common attitudes to social, political and economic problems and on a common commitment to the spirit of the resistance. Since it came from Thorez himself, Mounier could not fail to recognise the force of the appeal; he took it seriously and replied in *Esprit*.[14] Without questioning Thorez's sincerity or his courageous attempts to end the party's isolation and the resulting sectarianism, he had, he said, to refuse the invitation, however sad and depressing the refusal might seem. Admitting his irritation at being singled out, he accused the communists of going the wrong way about obtaining left wing unity. They were, he said, intolerant, intractable, and inflexible, and they could not hope to attract serious collaboration from himself or the non-communist left in general until such time as they gave up their insistent attempts to swallow up all who came near to them.

This strong retort, coming soon after Mounier had firmly reprimanded the *progressistes* for their excessive cooperation with the party, drew immediate responses from major communist figures. François Billoux, a *député*, ex-minister, and long-standing member of the political bureau, considered Mounier's position interesting from the point of view of the foundation of a future united front movement, but thought it unfair to attack the firmness of the party's doctrine when this was part of its strength.[15] Roger Garaudy, the party's leading spokesman on dialogue with catholics, felt that Mounier's position was based on a kind of philosophical relativism

THE STRUGGLE FOR SURVIVAL (1947–1950) 155

which ignored class and political determinations.[16] He thought it was illegitimate or at least ill-advised to try to separate Thorez from the party as a whole, or the party from the working class, as Mounier was implicitly doing. On the other hand he felt it was justified for communists to single out individual catholics since the church as a political force was generally anti-communist and anti-working-class. These and similar reactions within the party encouraged the possibility of cooperation on a practical political level, but took a firm stand on the correctness of marxist theory.

The communists' position was based on the well-tested conviction that any eventual ideological changes would tend to follow from practical activity. Mounier's position, on the other hand, was that principles were of the first importance and should determine practical commitments as far as possible. In any case, the intensifying cold war climate made real cooperation with communism a virtual impossibility, and the offer of cooperation a positive embarrassment to him. Clearly, little short term benefit could come from such a dialogue. At this point, with a state of comradely deadlock inaugurated, the church authorities chose to intervene.

A decree

On 14 July 1949, the catholic Holy Office published a decree which forbade catholics to join the communist party or to undertake any activity which might lead to the setting up of a communist state. Though it was scarcely more categorical than the encyclical *Divini Redemptoris* of 1937, it went so far as to threaten excommunication, and was immediately seized upon by the right wing who turned it into ammunition for the cold war. It was far from certain what the exact aim of the decree was: Poland, Czechoslovakia, East Germany, Italy, China, Indo-China, France, all had political situations which might have provoked it. Or it might have been a general response to the world-wide advance of communism. In France it led to a virulent press campaign against the catholic left, with Mounier prominent among the targets.

Mounier was strongly affected by this development, and rapidly produced a lengthy and detailed analysis of its implications.[17] Refusing to dismiss or disobey the decree, he tried to reach a full understanding and assent. But first he insisted that the measure could not be taken as evidence of the church's right-wing sympathies, and that neither he nor *Esprit* were guilty of the activities it condemned. It was, he said, a warning and a guide to the church's avant-garde to exercise an increased caution and rigour. The duty of an avant-garde, he noted, was to venture into dangerous and unknown regions in order to explore and chart them, but it was essential that it should not lose contact with the main body on whose behalf it was operating. The effect of declaring part of this territory out of bounds, he added, was not to prevent exploration, on the contrary it was to encourage a redoubled effort of exploration in the areas still within bounds. In other words, catholics should interpret the decree in a constructive way, using it to become more fully aware of their obligations and responsibilities both to other catholics and to the non-christians with whom they were engaged in dialogue. This said, however, he admitted that some political content had inevitably entered the promulgation, though that need not vitiate the spiritual content.

If a blow had been struck against communism, which was the only serious opponent to capitalism, then, Mounier argued, it was all the more a catholic's duty to assert himself in the fight against capitalism, lest the poor and wretched, the working class, feel itself abandoned by the church. He noted that the church had excommunicated neither the nazis, nor the fascists, nor the exploiters, nor the arms manufacturers, all of whose material crimes were far greater than those of the communists. Perhaps the most appropriate reaction to the decree, he suggested, was to regard it as a measure to prevent the rising forces of democracy and socialism from being contaminated by the risk of tyranny which communism still undoubtedly contained. In the same way, the church had in the past tried to defend reason against liberalism, social reform against materialism, and science against scientism, and each time attempts had been made to throw the baby out with the bathwater. Similar attempts to throw revolutionary socialism out with communism, he concluded, must not be allowed to succeed.

While in this article, Mounier did not ostensibly deviate from his already established political relationship with the communists or anyone else, it nonetheless marked a turning point. His brave words could not erase the fact that he was now obliged unconditionally to reject the possibility of catholics joining the communist party, though he had previously always stopped short of such a rejection. But perhaps more important, for the first time since the war, Mounier was confronted with the danger of disavowal by the church. Of course the climate was now different from before the war, but the shadow of disapproval was still a serious problem, since *Esprit* was still dependent on predominantly catholic support. His criticism of *progressisme* had been undertaken at least partly because

THE STRUGGLE FOR SURVIVAL (1947–1950)

he recognised that their position was ultimately unacceptable to the hierarchy. He was commonly thought of as being close to them, so that any attack on them would by implication cloud his reputation. The decree was widely taken to be just such an attack, and Mounier knew himself to be threatened, however unjust the lack of nuance might be.

Mounier was correct in saying that the decree did not condemn him, but its impact was wider than the precise area of its strict application, and extra prudence was needed. Privately, he considered the decree as extremely unfortunate, probably based on a massive error of historical interpretation and sense, which might in the long term jeopardise the church's survival in a changing world.[18] But since the church had spoken, he had to take its decision as containing a prophetic warning in addition to the immediate practical consequences. It was as if a sharp rap on the knuckles had been administered. Mounier's attitude towards the communists, which had never been enthusiastic and which for some time had been less than warm, cooled rapidly.

Final exchanges
The communists, dismayed at the set-back to their attempts at reconciliation with catholics, and finding their former misgivings confirmed, returned to their hard line. Relations deteriorated. During 1949 a number of international controversies proved highly divisive on the left, serving especially to separate the non-communists from the communists. Mounier had always gone out of his way to give the benefit of the doubt to communists in previous affairs. Even the trial of Cardinal Mindszenty in Hungary had not drawn Mounier to join the righteous howl which was set up in catholic circles. Now, after the decree, he began to take a more intransigent stance against the socialist countries, and against the way in which they appeared to be dealing with catholicism. He published several articles which were sharply critical of the Soviet Union, particularly in relation to developments in Czechoslovakia, Hungary and Yugoslavia. In each case, Mounier felt that the Soviet Union, and the French communist party with it, was deliberately suppressing or falsifying important information. He insisted that he did not want to damage the interests of the international working class, which looked to the communist party as its only serious protector, but could not accept that its aims would be better served by lies than by truth.

The French communists took these criticisms as part of a much broader orchestrated attempt to undermine their position and divide the working class. Their replies were vigorously polemical, taking the attitude that those who were not solidly behind them must be against them, and classifying *Esprit* along with the anti-communist press. Mounier stuck to his position, but refused to be drawn into a generalised attack on the communists, insisting that he and other sympathetic intellectuals had the right and duty to formulate constructive criticism. Since he was no longer able to assume that the communists were amenable to such criticism, and since he himself could not make such concessions as would restore the lost dialogue, he felt that the time had come to reassess his whole position regarding them.

Mounier's editorial in *Esprit* of February 1950 was significantly entitled 'Fidélité' to indicate that he was following the fundamental principles he had always held; but its effect was to modify his political position.[19] He had, he said, never been directly linked with either the communist party or marxist philosophy, however much he might have benefited from their inspiration. If he had been particularly concerned with communism since the war, he said, it was because that had been a basic condition for the satisfactory implementation of the ideals of the resistance. Moreover, he added, he could not contemplate abandoning the mass of the working class, who looked to communism as their only true friend. As long as there had been a chance of a united national movement, he had, he insisted, refused to strike any blow against the communists. However, such a movement, he suggested, required the communists to respect their allies and refuse the dangers of dishonesty, totalitarianism and subordination to foreign models, particularly the USSR. In Mounier's view, since they had failed to meet these conditions, he was faced with three important tasks. First, it was necessary to continue the fight for material security, human and social dignity, democracy, honesty and liberty, regardless of whoever else, even communists, he might be in practical alliance with at any time. Second, it was necessary to take more account of the price and consequences of socialist revolutions, weighing more carefully the incipient dehumanisation they may contain. Third, it was necessary patiently and intelligently to avoid the isolation of communism and therefore the proletariat from the other progressive forces, since experience showed that only if all three were combined could a socialist revolution succeed. As a result, he concluded, the non-communist left had to reject anticommunism, refuse to be excluded from the proletariat by the communists, reject the negative satisfaction of ineffectual purism, and redouble its efforts to create an authentic and just socialist force.

In effect, Mounier was signalling the end of the privileged position which communism had enjoyed in his eyes since the war. No fundamental difference was theoretically involved, but the tactical immunity he had given the party was lifted, and though he did not mean this to herald a concerted attack, it inevitably meant preparing for battle. The cold war was now anyway in full swing, and the left, divided, seemed condemned to a long term of entrenched fighting. The communists, already under severe pressure, adopted a savagely defensive posture. Garaudy's reply to Mounier's new position was vicious.[20] Attacking him as a servant of anti-communism, and as part of an organised offensive in the guise of friendship, Garaudy accused him of using the excuse of spiritual values to cover a crusade on behalf of the interests of capital. With a highly selective anthology of quotations, he attempted to discredit *Esprit*'s action during the occupation. Then, pointing out Mounier's refusal to accept the reality of class or of class struggle, his persistence in trying to set up a kind of third force, his defence of Tito against the Soviet Union, and his rejection of Thorez's offer of cooperation, he suggested that Mounier's real ambition was to lead the left-wing working class youth away from the defence of the working class. Garaudy's attack was over-simplified, and in some respects unfair. Whatever the actual effect of Mounier's position, it was free of any intention to defend capitalism, though it admittedly refused to see history or politics as a product of class struggle. Though Garaudy's interpretation of *Esprit*'s role under Vichy was too categorical, there were sufficient ambiguities lurking in that episode to raise uncomfortable questions. And it was at least true that Mounier wished, if at all possible, to woo the working class away from the communist party.

In his reply, Mounier rejected the unfair suggestions as to his intentions, his war record and his participation in a capitalist plot.[21] He reiterated his firm determination to refuse the polarisation of communism and anticommunism. He did not agree that his ambition to exercise a salutary influence on communism could be equated with an attempt to subvert it. Finally, he reaffirmed:

> Nous restons sur le terrain que nous occupons, si difficile soit-il à tenir aujourd'hui. Il arrive que l'Histoire récompense ceux qui s'obstinent, et qu'un rocher bien placé corrige le cours d'un fleuve.[22]

These lines, among the last he published before his death in March 1950, asserted an ambitious desire to occupy a position which was becoming practically untenable: that of bridge between the communists and the non-communist and mostly anti-communist left. How long he could have held it is impossible to guess. Already his shift over the previous six months had made it extremely precarious. He had on the one side to overcome his moral objections to the political methods of communists both in France and in other countries, the prudence dictated by the church's categorical position and the increasing force of anticommunist pressure among those who had usually been close to him in outlook. On the other side he had to overcome the communists' fierce hostility to criticism from outside, their deeply rooted reluctance to tolerate non-materialist philosophy or religion, and their tendency to make converts among their allies. Dialogue had broken down, but Mounier did not allow himself to be ignored. He determined to carry on trying to do the impossible, since he could not see an acceptable alternative and was unwilling to do nothing at all. The task was all the more difficult for being a long term commitment, and had he lived, it would have demanded a heroism and obstinacy equal to anything he had yet shown.

A man of less determination might quite reasonably have despaired. With the failure of the RDR Mounier's political insertion had been brought to an end, except in so far as his influence continued to be felt in the parties of the pragmatic and conservative *Troisième force* government. The government offered less and less ground for any hopes he had entertained as to its capacity to embody the principles of personalism. Political reality did not lend itself to the implementation of the programme sketched briefly in the last book he published before his death. *Le Personnalisme* (Paris 1949) was a condensed outline of his thought for the popular 'Que sais-je?' paperback series. *Esprit*'s positions on political issues, summed up in a few pages at the end, were intelligible only in the context of a specific political programme. In the absence of one, they appeared as no more than intimations of utopia. Mounier sketched the main lines of his political theory, adding in very general terms what its implications were, and referring to appropriate numbers of *Esprit*. At best it was an invitation to reflection, at worst a succession of vague imperatives devoid of substance, and ignoring the practical questions of means. It was formulated more as an act of duty than of hope, revealing by its brevity the improbability of its being implemented.

Avant-garde catholic ideology

Although in purely political terms, personalism came to an impasse in the later 1940s, it continued to function on a broader ideological level. If it lacked the strength to expand appreciably beyond the catholic milieu which had been its cradle, it did at least maintain its position as an intellectual force within catholic circles. It was an ideology of the catholic avant-garde, seeking to create modes of coexistence with the major secular ideologies, exploring new territory and building a total structure of responses to meet the challenge of new situations and relationships in all areas of human activity. Attempting to give his position a concrete content, Mounier insisted on the dimension of commitment, but constantly stressed that no single political line followed necessarily from personalism. Its broad objectives must, he said, include the destruction of the western bourgeoisie and the coming of socialist structures as a result of working class action. Divorced from these implications, he warned, it would turn into 'une idéologie à tout faire'[23] and be taken over by reformist or conservative interests to become a mystification.

Caught in a cleft stick, Mounier saw that if he refused to work from the social reality of his audience, he was doomed to sterility, and if he allowed his social base to dictate his positions, they were bound to be perverted. His project was therefore to unite the vanguard of the catholic middle classes, a project requiring a fine sense of balance and a strong sense of direction. The relationship between an ideologist and his audience is reciprocal. He both expresses and modifies their consciousness, and cannot separate the two tasks without losing his function. Mounier had aimed at inducing a radical transformation in his followers, so it was all the more essential that he should continue to cater for their particular tastes and needs. However universal he wanted personalism to be, he had always to ensure that it would not be rejected on a large scale by the catholic middle classes. He had therefore to remain visibly loyal to catholicism, and propose an acceptable rôle for the middle classes in the social and cultural transformations he considered to be imminent.

Mounier's fidelity to catholicism was basic to his personalism, though he consistently refused to allow it to appear as an exclusively catholic, or even christian, philosophy. In this regard he tended, more than before the war, to adopt a dual position. While always making it clear that personalism was one of a number of possible choices for a catholic, he increasingly allowed himself to be represented as a lay spokesman for the church on intellectual matters, whether in international visits and conferences, in books and reviews aimed at largely non-catholic audiences, or in radio broadcasts for the French cultural service. The personal prestige thus acquired contributed to his efforts to establish personalism as an effective defender of the catholic faith. Mounier was always prepared to go to great lengths to safeguard his orthodoxy, as he had proved before the war. It was usually a happy coincidence of personal belief and ideological necessity, but on one occasion the two conflicted: the occasion of the decree of July 1949 condemning catholics who were prepared to work with the communists. Privately Mounier considered this a disastrous step, but loyally swallowed his objections in public. Eventually he might have changed his personal assessment, but he immediately saw that his influence would be undermined unless he publicly accepted the ruling. In this decision, he revealed an awareness of the nature of his audience and his sensitivity to their reactions.

By virtue of his efforts, Mounier consolidated his rôle as mentor to the catholic avant-garde, offering a context in which it could come to terms with the problems facing it. Through *Esprit* he offered serious analyses of current political affairs in France and abroad, contributions to philosophical and moral debates which were occupying the intelligentsia, and reportages on social and economic conditions throughout the world. Linked to this was a loose network of friendships, meetings and discussions which gave sympathisers an opportunity to feel in touch with important developments, and which further consolidated the solidarity which their common interests encouraged. Together these elements helped to create a movement. Other sectors of the church were also working in the same direction, and the movement can be seen as part of a more general movement among catholics to seek new expressions of their place in the world by looking at hitherto relatively unexplored areas.

In its substance, Mounier's personalist philosophy had remained unchanged since its elaboration fifteen years before, offering the same analysis of the person in the world. In its appearance, however, there were differences. His vocabulary had altered in harmony with the climate of the post-war. Much of the *péguyste* rhetoric had disappeared, along with the flowers of bergsonian eloquence, and the unctuous jargon of late nineteenth-century piety. Some of it lingered on, but it was largely replaced by the drier, more precise terminology of social and economic analysis, the unwieldy jargon of germanic existentialism, and the more racy and aggressive polemic of the working class struggle. These were the legacy of Mounier's dialogue with marxism, his confrontation with Sartrean philosophy, and his involvement in the social and political struggles of the liberation. These aspects of Mounier's activity were at their height in the years immediately after the war. As the 1940s ended, the increasing influence of marxist analysis in personalism was counterbalanced by a growing rejection of marxism's political and social implications; the political involvement of *Esprit* was thwarted by the absence of conditions in which personalist principles might have been implemented. The popularity of existentialism began to wane and no longer presented the threat the church had once feared. It increasingly became clear that, for all its atheism, existentialism's moral, spiritual and existential concerns were close to those of the christian community. This belated reappraisal came at a time when Sartre himself was preparing to move decisively away from his early positions, a time when existentialism was ceasing to exist as a social phenomenon and becoming a more modest, left-wing intellectual movement.

As cultural ideologies, both personalism and existentialism had passed their peak by 1948. Within four years atheist existentialism had been torn apart by the tensions of the cold war. Personalism, suffering from similar strains, entered a rapid decline following Mounier's death. Neither was destroyed by intellectual considerations, but simply because the conditions of their functioning as ideologies had changed. Personalism was already destroyed as an effective political ideology. The growing conflicts within France, and the re-emergence of catholic conservatism to challenge the avant-garde, rendered finally pointless any attempt to preserve personalism's coherence as a philosophy, and therefore as a distinct cultural ideology, after the death in 1950 of Mounier, whose work it had been. For existentialism, the increasing political divisions between its major figures and Sartre's own absorption in politics deprived it of the coherence it required to continue as an independent ideology. Social conditions also evolved, young middle-class supporters were growing older and seeking more settled habits of mind. Their younger brothers and sisters were looking for new idols. The intellectual establishment was looking for new debates. The political left was being flung into the brutal polarisations of the cold war. Under these circumstances both existentialism and personalism succumbed.

The mantle of prophecy
The collapse of personalism as an ideology was not a sign of total failure for Mounier. His view of his own achievement was indicated by his analysis in *Le Personnalisme* of the notion of commitment, *l'engagement*.[24] In practical terms, he said, commitment must take account of the prophetic and political modes, the former being contemplative, the latter material. The resulting interrelationship between efficacy in action and adherence to absolute values must be maintained, Mounier insisted, however difficult it might be. He spoke of the many dangers which lurked in such a position and recognised that the dialectic of action could only be authentically conducted if there were profound transformations in the social and spiritual climate. In the meantime, he argued, it was necessary to try to bring the two opposite poles together as far as possible, and summed up:

> Une action non mutilée est toujours dialectique. Souvent il lui faut tenir, dans l'obscurité et le doute, les deux bouts d'une chaîne qu'elle ne peut souder.[25]

It is clear that the two ends of the chain were getting further apart and that for Mounier, attempting to hold both, with the obscurity and doubt growing, the situation was becoming increasingly painful. He considered himself justified in withdrawing from the political pole as a temporary measure, if he could thereby maintain the prophetic pole more strongly. In other words, he intended to stick to his principled position, however ill it accorded with reality, in the hope that reality would one day give it substance.

Mounier's new-found rôle of voice crying in the wilderness was a long-term commitment which would have required exceptional perseverance and courage to sustain. It was a dogged gesture to the future, but it was nonetheless solidly based. The ferocious struggles of nations, classes and ideologies which characterised the cold war made the situation difficult, but not entirely impossible, for those forces which were seeking to bridge the divisions. The catholic community was no longer a monolithic force of reactionary politics, nor was it united in embattled defence against the transformations of the modern world, nor was it closed to the solicitation of new ideas and attitudes. Mounier, who did so much within French catholicism to bring about this evolution, also did much to train and strengthen a new, more adventurous generation to take up the work. He contributed to making catholic socialism an accepted and growing political option. His dialogue with communism was cut short, but the ground was prepared for later, more sustained contact in conditions where both catholics and communists recognised the need. The movement to the left by French catholicism was slowed, but not stopped, by the cold war. The growing awareness of the church's need to adapt itself to the modern world was restrained, but could not be reversed. Mounier's work, which in 1950 seemed to have reached a dead end, proved to have been only a beginning. Though he was not broken in spirit, he was physically exhausted. Personal tragedy, overwork, the consequences of imprisonment and hunger strike, physical frailty, and the strain of events, all told on Mounier's health until, following a worsening series of heart-attacks, he died on the morning of 22nd March 1950, barely ten days before his forty-fifth birthday.

Notes

1 E. Mounier, 'Délivrez-vous', *Esprit*, no141, janvier 1948, p133–139, reprinted in *Oeuvres* III p625–632.
2 E. Mounier, 'Les chrétiens progressistes', *Esprit*, no150, novembre 1948, p744–746, reprinted in *Oeuvres* III p632–634.
3 E. Mounier, 'Marxisme ouvert ou marxisme scolastique?', *Esprit*, no145, mai-juin 1948, p705–708.
4 'Y a-t-il un scolastique marxiste?', *Esprit*, no145, mai-juin 1948, p736–766. Contributors were: communists: Claude Morgan, Henri Denis, Marcel Prenant, Jean Beaufret, Claude Roy, Georges Mounin; non-communists: J. -W. Lapierre, Brice Parrain, André Dumas, Georges Friedmann.
5 Claude Roy, in an untitled article, *Esprit*, no145, mai-juin 1948, p754.
6 Remo Cantoni, 'Mythe et critique dans la culture marxiste', *Esprit*, no145, mai-juin 1948, p767–782.
7 Jean Kanapa, 'Avec les catholiques le dialogue est possible . . . mais il y faut une vigilance réciproque', *Cahiers du communisme*, no8, août 1948, p818–831.
8 Victor Leduc, 'Qui sont les obscurantistes?', *Action*, 22–88 juin 1948; and 'Chronique des revues', *Cahiers du communisme*, no7, juillet 1948, p744.
9 E. Mounier, 'Main ouverte et marxisme fermé', *Esprit*, no147, août 1948, p214–217, reprinted in *Oeuvres* IV p169–172.
10 E. Mounier, 'Les tâches actuelles d'une pensée d'inspiration personnaliste', *Esprit*, no150, novembre 1948, p679–708.
11 From an untitled editorial note, *Esprit*, no146, juillet 1948, p75.
12 In 'Communistes chrétiens', *Esprit*, no135, juillet 1947, p119 (*Oeuvres* III p623).
13 The speech, given to the national congress of the party on 10 April 1949 at Montreuil, was published under the title 'Partisans de la paix, unissons-nous', *Cahiers du communisme*, mai 1949, p623–646.

14 E. Mounier, 'Ne nous demandez pas de ne pas être nous-mêmes', *Esprit*, no156, juin 1949, p849–852, reprinted in *Oeuvres* IV p172–176.
15 F. Billoux, 'Éléments de discussion avec Emmanuel Mounier', *France nouvelle*, 2 juillet 1949, p3 & 8; 9 juillet 1949, p3; 16 juillet 1949, p3.
16 R. Garaudy, 'Le dialogue communistes et catholiques et le marxisme vivant', *Cahiers du communisme*, août 1949, p993–1004.
17 E. Mounier, 'Le decret du Saint-Office', *Esprit*, no158, août 1949, p305–314, reprinted in *Oeuvres* III p654–663.
18 *Oeuvres* IV p821.
19 E. Mounier, 'Fidélité', *Esprit*, no164, février 1950, p177–182, reprinted in *Oeuvres* IV p17–21.
20 R. Garaudy, 'Lettre à Emmanuel Mounier, homme d'Esprit' (Paris 1950): this was a short pamphlet.
21 E. Mounier, three articles in *Esprit*, no165, mars 1950, p545–552, reprinted under the title of one of them, 'L'avilissement ne rend pas', in *Oeuvres* IV p180–189.
22 *Oeuvres* IV p189.
23 *Oeuvres* III p238.
24 *Oeuvres* III p498–506.
25 *Oeuvres* III p505.

Conclusion

Contradictions
In the heady days after the liberation, and even as late as the spring of 1947, personalism had seemed poised to establish itself as one of France's major ideologies. It enjoyed a secure audience which felt itself in harmony with personalist aspirations. It offered a coherent intellectual framework already familiar to many. It enjoyed a creditable resistance record, unlike many other catholic movements. And its leading exponent was one of France's most distinguished intellectual figures. Mounier had produced an impressive and well-judged defence of personalism against the two major opponents which had posed a challenge. He had established a position in which catholics could hope to assimilate what was valuable in existentialism and marxism, leaving catholic orthodoxy intact. He had incorporated into personalism many elements of European thought which increased the subtlety and flexibility of its analyses. He had also conducted a long and difficult campaign to maintain personalism as an agent of communication, if not of unity, on the rapidly fragmenting political left. Within the limitations of his situation it is difficult to suggest what more Mounier might have done to encourage the growth of personalism's influence. Neither his energy, nor his intelligence, nor his personal qualities, nor his skill as an ideologist can seriously be called into question. Yet personalism as such scarcely survived Mounier's own death.

Despite the esteem and interest with which Mounier's works and his review *Esprit* were read, it is clear that, by 1950, personalism was no longer a viable ideology, politically or culturally. It commanded a decreasing measure of assent as a distinct and coherent doctrine even among the middle-class catholic audience which was its strength. There was no significant support for it in the working class or among non-christians. The reasons for this were inherent in its intellectual formation and in the conditions of its social existence. They can be expressed as a series of structural and historical contradictions.

The first contradiction lay in the coexistence of conflicting principles of unity and diversity within personalism, both on a theoretical and a social level. Mounier conceived personalism as a philosophy which should be coherent without being systematic. As a result he took analyses from divergent sources without adequately integrating them into an overall synthesis. Since many of his sources were flatly incompatible, what remained was an eclecticism of juxtaposed fragments. The only principle of coherence was the coexistence of all the different elements in a particular person: himself. It followed that this intellectual structure was not readily transmissible.

In the *Esprit* team, the unifying factor was nominally a commitment to, or interest in, elucidating and defending the human person, of which each member had his own conception. In reality, however, they were held together by much more diffuse aspirations, and ultimately by a common loyalty to Mounier. Although in principle the review's doctrinal coherence was asserted in Mounier's own writings, the strength of *Esprit* lay increasingly in its special numbers on matters of general importance, where Mounier adopted a pluralist attitude, juxtaposing relevant views, with perhaps an attempted synthesis in conclusion. Although this attitude had the effect of making readers think, it no longer offered firm principles on which they might take a common stand. However valuable on other grounds, it did not help to build a fighting doctrine. Where it had once presented solutions, personalism now offered its supporters only contributions to debates. Mounier's pluralism undermined the unity which might have strengthened personalism as an ideology. But without a pluralistic attitude, Mounier would have been obliged to abandon the comprehensive scope of his thought, the wide range of colleagues, and the broad support of French catholics.

A more serious contradiction was the dislocation between theory and practice. Since the earliest days of *Esprit*, Mounier had insisted on the imperative need for action to implement principles. After, as before the war, he spoke out strongly against the tendency of personalism to be purely theoretical. At the same time he refused to formulate any specific form of action, on the grounds that personalism could not necessitate one particular choice of action rather than another. The divorce between theory and practice in politics meant that despite Mounier's exhortations, personalism lacked any serious chance of implementation and could not therefore gain any benefit from practical experience, nor was it of much assistance in defining practical lines of action. The separation of politics and theory was undertaken initially to safeguard the unity of personalism and avoid divisive controversy. To that extent the tactic was successful, and the amicable recognition of political diversity saved it from being torn apart by the tensions of the cold war. Instead it merely drifted apart and lost its power and cohesion as a distinct ideology.

The structural contradictions of personalism were, in themselves, sufficient to subvert Mounier's ambitions. But in many ways they were an expression of, and an attempt to deal with, the historical contradictions of Mounier's position. He was substantially formed in a privileged class during a period of relative prosperity and tranquillity. The first serious situation he had to face as a young adult was an international economic and political crisis which he tried to understand in the framework of his inherited values. Neither his principles nor his training helped him to understand or deal with the events of the early nineteen thirties. As he learned to understand his historical situation, borrowing increasingly from socialist, and particularly marxist, analyses, he found himself in the position of an avant-garde, continually in danger from both sides. He was caught between the catholic middle classes to which he belonged, and the marxist-led working class where his political sympathies lay. Personalism aimed at reconciling the best of both camps, and could only hope to succeed in a situation where the two class groupings had formed an alliance. In the late 1940s, as the class struggle asserted itself with particular intensity, the middle ground which Mounier occupied was severely reduced. As a result, his position became practically untenable. However, in other places and at other times the existence of such a class alliance would cause his central preoccupations to be raised again more urgently, albeit in different terms.

His position in the avant-garde of catholicism put Mounier under further severely contradictory stresses. The margin between transforming the church and being rejected by it was slim. He was therefore obliged to assert his catholicism to such an extent that it became difficult to assert personalism as a distinct ideology. During periods when the catholic rearguard were muted it was possible to take wide freedom for innovatory thought. Such was the case in the late 1920s and immediately after the war. But where the church reasserted its traditional conservatism, as during the Vichy government and in the late 1940s, Mounier's middle ground was once more severely eroded. It was only when, in the late 1950s, the church entered a new stage of development that the progressive ideas of Mounier and his associates were able to re-emerge into the forefront of catholic thinking.

Achievements
In so far as Mounier's aim was to foster the creation of an ideology which would ultimately guide the thoughts and actions of men and women of all conditions in all aspects of their life, it is clear that he did not achieve his aim. As a more or less coherent body of principles, personalism gained currency among catholic intellectuals who were anxious to find an adequate response to the problems posed by the warring ideologies of the forties and who sought to restate their faith in a new relevant form. In their efforts they attracted a few protestants and agnostics to whom neither existentialism nor marxism appealed. As an intellectual matrix it appealed to middle class thinking catholics for whom it represented a convenient scheme of reflexion on spiritual and cultural questions, without involving technical philosophy to any great degree. In that restricted area it continued to exercise a limited intellectual influence throughout the early fifties.

These attainments were much less than personalism's original project, and indeed ran flatly counter to all Mounier's declared aims. But they were obviously in harmony with everything Mounier was, did, and stood for. He himself was supremely the product of the milieu he now spoke to, the largely provincial catholic middle classes. His methods were intellectual and élitist, and therefore tailor-made to operate in the structures these classes had evolved to accommodate their cultural and spitual activities. He stood for confidence in the ability of faith and intelligence to push an adventurous but not foolhardy path through the difficulties of a changing world. He was therefore adopted as a public 'directeur de conscience' by many more than would have called themselves personalists.

Although personalism failed to survive as a distinct and cohesive ideology, the work of Mounier's life cannot for that reason be dismissed as a failure. His early high political ambitions were progressively eroded by hard realities. He failed to make contact with the working class and therefore could not advance the personalist revolution which he hoped the working class would lead. He failed to maintain a working dialogue with the communists, without whose political strength, he recognised, no revolution could take place. These failures were partly of his own making, though not entirely his own fault. His intellectual and élitist methods were not designed to work in a communist, working class milieu, which was foreign to him. The priorities he defended were too remote from working class experience, the language he used was too close to that of the middle class intelligentsia, for him to breach the class barrier, let alone the religious barrier. It was inevitable that the success he ultimately sought should elude him, but in the process he achieved a different kind of success, which was less spectacular but not negligible.

Mounier successfully fulfilled the rôle of the vanguard in establishing positions in the relatively unknown territory of catholic socialism, particularly on the margins of communism. Despite the severe strain under which the events of 1949 placed him, Mounier did not slide into outright anticommunism, nor was he censured by the church. Although he failed to maintain the dialogue with the communists, he did at least succeed in keeping the possibility open on the catholic side. Limited though this achievement may appear, it was nonetheless valuable in the context of the intensifying cold war, the Vatican's increasing intransigence, and the temporary defeat of working class militancy within France. Other catholics more audacious than Mounier came to grief with surprising speed. The *progressistes*, pioneering political cooperation with the communist party; the worker-priests, pioneering new forms of priestly service among the working class; the advanced Dominican theologians, pioneering new theological formulations of the church's insertion in the world; all of these felt the weight of papal displeasure during the late 1940s and early 1950s. In many ways Mounier represented the furthest a catholic could safely move in a progressive direction during these years. As a result he was taken as a point of reference and a point of departure for progressive-minded catholics.

In terms of immediate political change, Mounier had no tangible effect, but in terms of ideological change, his influence is undeniable. The intellectuals of the MRP, and their colleagues in the German and Italian christian democratic movements, among whom he counted many personal friends, borrowed extensively from his analyses, though in attenuated form. He was widely regarded, along with Jacques Maritain, as one of the spiritual patrons of christian democracy. It is doubtful how much of this reflects creditably on Mounier and how much can be ascribed to the christian democrats' search for coherence and intellectual respectability, particularly since it was on the level of political judgements that they diverged from his thought. Other intellectuals, politically nearer to the socialist party, were more faithful to his inspiration. Some of them, less cautious than Mounier, found their activities curtailed by censure from the church, but many more avoided such hazards and continued to pioneer the same paths. For them, Mounier was as much a comrade-in-arms as a spiritual mentor. They had been formed before and during the war, and had shared the same struggles. *Esprit* and the group which Mounier had gathered around it held a leading position among the catholic avant-garde. The progressive catholic newspaper, *Témoignage chrétien*, typified the relationship: it looked upon Mounier as a helpful and respected guide, though not as an authority. Mounier's effective political contribution lay therefore in helping to form a progressive intellectual group of which he was part, and in giving the example of a successful attempt to follow in principle a consistently revolutionary socialist line, while retaining his integrity as a catholic.

Mounier had at one time hoped for more than this, but his chosen method of creating a small active élite to educate and animate the people was of necessity a long term project. He could not reasonably have expected at this stage a more tangible political result than the existence of such an élite. The less tangible success of setting an example fulfilled the ambition of his early years to lay down an act of witness. He believed then that he would act as much by what he was as by what he did, and although his conception of political action underwent a considerable evolution, he finally returned to this earlier notion. In effect, he represented the combination of catholicism and revolutionary socialism. Whatever its defects and whatever his failures, the fact that such a combination could exist in one man without prejudice to his faith was in itself a powerful political statement. In sum, he set up a human paradigm for catholic socialism and the cadres for a continuing attempt to implement it politically.

Legacy
Mounier died at the early age of forty-four. Had he lived as long as most of his own contemporaries, he would have witnessed the transformations in the catholic church initiated by Pope John XXIII and the second Vatican Council. He would also have seen the Cardinal Archbishop of Paris denounced by a right-wing French government as a 'Red' and a dangerous subversive element. From the dark and embattled winter of 1949–1950 it was impossible to foresee these far-reaching changes in international catholicism and in the political complexion of the French catholic church. Nonetheless, the changes were prepared and worked for over long years before

they came to fruition. The efforts of Mounier and his associates can be clearly seen, in retrospect, to have been an important contribution towards making such changes possible on an ideological level.

The radical changes in the post-war world made necessary the innovatory papacy of John XXIII and its consequences in order to secure the survival, let alone the advance, of the catholic church. Within its historical stronghold of western European society, the church was confronted with the dechristianisation of whole classes, the spread of powerful rival ideologies, the erosion of its influence in state affairs, the secularisation of national institutions, the destruction of traditional social structures and moral codes, the changing configuration of social forces, and the revolutionary implications of scientific and technical progress. The growing international strength of the socialist and communist movements could no longer be ignored, while the newly independent and developing countries of Asia, Africa and Latin America were posing radically new problems on a vast scale. The work of creative reappraisal initiated by the second Vatican Council was an urgent attempt to come to terms with these problems after the long, cautious and conservative papacy of Pius XII. Vatican II was a far-reaching collective reflection in which it would be pointless to attempt to isolate the contribution of any one participant, much less to single out the influence of any individual precursor. Mounier's role can best be seen as one of preparing the ground and to some extent defining the terms which the council took as the basis for its discussions. In this work, Mounier was one lay thinker, albeit an influential one, among many laymen and clerics throughout the catholic community who were working and arguing for a thoroughgoing reassessment of the church's place in the world.

Within France, Mounier's contribution is more tangible, but historical movements are never the work of one man. During the twenty years of Mounier's public activity, French Catholics moved from their extreme right-wing ghetto to the point at which they were represented in all significant political groupings. Despite the chill winds of the cold war, this evolution continued after Mounier's death, with catholics increasingly finding their place among the left and progressive forces in the nation. The social and economic factors behind this shift are clearly perceptible in the accelerated industrialisation, the growing proletarianisation of the middle classes, the erosion of the old petty bourgeoisie, the increased concentration of wealth and power, the crises of decolonisation, and the sharpening of social conflicts. Mounier's rôle was ideological and political. He did much to shape the ways catholics saw themselves and their changing situation, adapting old ways of thinking and old doctrines to new realities and new ways of understanding them. He elaborated principles of political change and pioneered new political alliances and relationships, offering a bridge between them and the conservative political thought of an earlier generation of catholics. A man of transition, writing in a time of transition, Mounier developed personalism as an eclectic doctrine which could be many things to many people, a crossroads at which many divergent doctrines briefly met before proceeding elsewhere. In this it closely resembled the early forms of utopian socialism: a mixture of various theories and visions adding up to a kind of average socialism which excited a minimum of opposition. But for all its evident defects, it was nonetheless a form of socialism, based largely on catholic principles and well suited to a French catholic community for whom socialism of any description was a suspicious new discovery.

Like many transitional figures, Mounier is barely recognisable in the new reality he helped to create. His thought had neither the originality nor the coherence to survive intact. The catholic student movement, the catholic action movements, the CFDT trade union organisation, catholic youth organisations, catholic lay movements, industrial chaplaincies, catholic mass media, peace movements, social reform movements, these and other progressive collective enterprises in France bear the marks of the personalist ideas which were an important factor in their development. Yet their leading militants now look to other sources for inspiration, whether to the works of economists, political scientists, sociologists, theologians and other specialised theorists, or to papal encyclicals, the documents of Vatican II or elsewhere. Significantly, *Esprit* continues to play a prominent part in making this material available and assessing its value. Though Mounier's writings are readily available and widely read in the French-speaking world, his thought has been overtaken by events and no longer occupies an avant-garde position. Though his work is often recognised as seminal by progressive thinkers, it is acknowledged in historical terms; and the avant-garde cannot spend too long in looking back.

But if Mounier's work has lost much of its power in the French context, there are other contexts which can and do restore its relevance. In Eastern European countries, especially in Poland and Hungary, where catholics are obliged to accommodate themselves to communist governments, Mounier's thought is consulted and studied with interest. In southern Europe, particularly in Spain and Portugal, where many catholics are trying to change the reactionary political alignment of their national church, Mounier is read with enthusiasm. In Latin America, particularly in Brazil, Chile and Argentina, where Catholics are involved in the struggle against brutal and repressive dictatorships, and where they find themselves in alliance with the non-catholic left, Mounier is looked to as a model and inspiration. Wherever catholics find themselves confronted by the problems of a transition from reactionary and sectarian politics to progressive and ecumenical politics, and wherever catholic socialism is on the agenda, there Mounier's thought can prove a valuable and dynamic source of guidance for reflection and action.

General Bibliographical Notes

What follows is a selection of useful material, which makes no attempt to be comprehensive. A full and detailed bibliography of works by Mounier, along with an extensive list of works on him, can be found in Michael Kelly, 'The Development of the Work and Thought of Emmanuel Mounier: a Study in Ideology' (Unpublished PHD dissertation, University of Warwick 1974).

The majority of Mounier's main writings are reprinted in the four-volume *Oeuvres* (Paris 1961–1963). Volume four contains an extensive bibliography of his work, edited by his widow, Mme Paulette Mounier, but containing a number of errors and omissions. A virtually complete collection of his works and a wide range of related material is kept in a small library at 19, rue d'Antony, 92 – Châtenay-Malabry, under the auspices of the Association des Amis d'Emmanuel Mounier. The Association also publishes a regular *Bulletin des Amis d'E. Mounier* which contains unpublished material and information on activities and studies relating to Mounier.

The following individual works, or collections of works, by Mounier are currently available in French, in paperback form: *Le Personnalisme* (Paris 1949); *Introduction aux existentialismes* (Paris 1962); *L'Affrontement chrétien* (Paris 1963); *Communisme, anarchie et personnalisme* (Paris 1966); *L'Engagement de la foi* (Paris 1968); *Maritain-Mounier. Correspondance 1929–1939* (Paris 1973); *Traité du caractère* (Paris 1974).

Several of Mounier's works have been published in English translations: *A Personalist Manifesto* (New York 1938); 'Catholic Personalism Faces Our Times', in J. T. Delos and others, *Race, Nation, Person* (New York 1944) p 323–380; *The Spoil of the Violent* (London 1955); *The Character of Man* (London 1956); *Existentialist Philosophies* (London 1948); *Be Not Afraid, a Denunciation of Despair* (London 1951, & New York 1962); 'Reflections on an Apocalyptic Age', in various authors', *Reflections on Our Age* (New York 1949); *Personalism* (London 1952).

A great deal has been written on Mounier in French. The following books are devoted wholly or partly to him: Michel Barlow, *Le Socialisme d'Emmanuel Mounier* (Toulouse 1971); Etienne Borne, *Emmanuel Mounier ou le combat pour l'homme* (Paris 1972); Jean Calbrette, *Mounier, le mauvais Esprit* (Paris 1957); Hervé Chaigne and others, *Emmanuel Mounier ou le Combat du juste* (Bordeaux 1968); Jacques Charpentreau & Louis Rocher, *L'Esthétique personnaliste d'Emmanuel Mounier* (Paris 1966); Jean Conilh, *Emmanuel Mounier, sa vie, son oeuvre* (Paris 1966); Jean-Marie Domenach, *Emmanuel Mounier* (Paris 1972); Lucien Guissard, *Emmanuel Mounier* (Paris 1963); Jean Lacroix, *Le personnalisme comme anti-idéologie* (Paris 1972); Jean Lestavel, *Introduction aux personnalismes* (Paris 1961); Jean-Louis Loubet de Bayle, *Les Non-conformistes des années trente* (Paris 1969); Candide Moix, *La Pensée d'Emmanuel Mounier* (Paris 1960); Jean-Marie Roy, *Mounier aux prises avec son siècle* (Paris 1972); Michel Winock, *Histoire politique de la revue 'Esprit', 1930–1950* (Paris 1975); Nouréddine Zaza, *Etude critique de la notion d'engagement chez Emmanuel Mounier* (Geneva 1955). However, the most useful single publication in French is the special number of *Esprit*, December 1950, which contains a number of substantial studies in addition to otherwise unpublished material by Mounier.

Studies on Mounier in English are more sparse. There is a useful chapter in Roy Pierce, *Contemporary French Political Thought* (London 1966). Informative studies of particular aspects can be found in R. W. Rauch, *Politics and Belief in Contemporary France: Emmanuel Mounier and Christian Democracy* (The Hague 1972); and Joseph Amato, *Mounier and Maritain* (Alabama 1975). There is also a small number of articles of varying scope and quality: J. B. Coates, 'The Personalism of Emmanuel Mounier', *The Fortnightly* (London) August 1952, p 109–116; Frederick Copleston, 'Mounier, Marxism and Man', *The Month* (London) October 1951, p 199–208; Annunciata Dunphy, 'Emmanuel Mounier: Personalism and Vatican II', *Compass* (Melbourne) September-October 1968, p 114–120; Peter Hebblethwaite, 'A Prophet and the Holy Office', *The Tablet* (London) 4 April 1970, p 327–328; John Hellman, 'The Opening to the Left in French Catholicism: the Role of the Personalists', *The Journal of the History of Ideas*, July-September 1973, p 381–390; Patrick J. Hill, 'Emmanuel Mounier: Total Christianity and Practical Marxism', *Cross Currents* (New York) Winter 1968, p 77–104; M. H. Kelly, 'The Fate of Emmanuel Mounier: a bibliographical essay', *Journal of European Studies* (London) September 1972, p 256–267; D. L. Lewis, 'Emmanuel Mounier and the

Politics of Moral Revolution. Aspects of Political Crises in French Liberal Catholicism, 1935–1938', *Catholic Historical Review* (Washington) July 1970, p 266–290; Robert Rouquette, 'French Catholicism Confronts Communism', *Thought* (New York) Autumn 1953, p 354–374; Donald Wolf, 'Emmanuel Mounier, a Catholic of the Left', *Review of Politics* (Notre Dame) July 1960, p 324–344.

Index of Names

Adler, Alfred, 123
Alain, 28
Aragon, Louis, 59, 102
Archambault, Paul, 31, 41
Aristotle, 6
Arland, Marcel, 18
Aron, Raymond, 13
Azaña, Manuel, 69

Bakunin, Mikhail, 73, 77
Barrès, Maurice, 22
Barth, Karl, 138
Barthélemy, Georges, 13
Bastid, Paul, 103
Bataille, Georges, 116
Baudouin, Charles, 123
Baudouin, Paul, 93
Baudrillart, Cardinal, 106
Bazin, René, 18
Beigbeder, Marc, 95, 119
Belin, René, 93
Benda, Julien, 19
Berdyaev, Nicolai, 18, 31, 36, 41, 43, 49, 138
Bergamin, José, 69
Bergery, Gaston, 41, 56, 57, 93, 94
Bergson, Henri, 6–8, 14, 22–24, 34, 47, 52, 138
Berkeley, George, 6
Bernanos, Georges, 70
Beuve-Méry, Hubert, 94, 99, 103
Billoux, François, 154
Blanchot, Maurice, 116
Bloch, Marc, 59, 103
Blondel, Maurice, 9, 31, 35, 138
Blum, Léon, 61, 106
Boethius, 46
Bourdet, Claude, 154
Bremond, Henri, 10, 31

Brentano, Franz, 47
Buber, Martin, 138

Cantoni, Remo, 150–152
Chaillet, Pierre, 99
Chamberlain, Neville, 81
Chautemps, Camille, 61
Chevalier, Jacques, 6–9, 14, 17, 21, 47, 51, 105
Chiappe, Jean, 58, 59

Daladier, Edouard, 81
Dandieu, Arnaud, 31, 47
Daniélou, Jean, 32, 99, 143
D'Astorg, Bertrand, 45
Déléage, André, 31–33, 62
Descartes, René, 6, 8–10, 19
De Beauvoir, Simone, 116
De Becker, Raymond, 44
De Castelnau, General, 58, 59, 71
De Fabrègues, Jean, 30
De Gandillac, Maurice, 22, 143
De Gaudemar, Paul, 119
De Gaulle, Charles, 98, 99, 103, 104, 111, 146
De Lubac, Henri, 99
De Menthon, François, 99, 103
De Mun, Albert, 112
De Rougemont, Denis, 32, 43, 118
De Santillana, Georges, 56
De Tocqueville, Alexis, 6
Domenach, Jean-Marie, 107, 119
Dru, Gilbert, 103, 107
Du Bos, Charles, 18
Dunoyer de Segonzac, Pierre, 94
Dupré, Henri, 123

Ellul, Jacques, 45
Emmanuel, Pierre, 94, 102

INDEX OF NAMES

Engels, Frederick, 73, 149
Etiemble, René, 116

Fessard, Gaston, 99
Flamand, Paul, 103
Fouchet, Max-Pol, 45, 94
Fraisse, Paul, 119, 148
Franco, General, 69, 70, 71, 82, 84
Frenay, Henri, 94, 98, 100, 101
Freud, Sigmund, 123
Fumet, Stanislas, 92, 95, 99

Galey, Louis-Emile, 32
Garaudy, Roger, 133, 134, 154, 159
Garric, Robert, 22, 41
Genet, Jean, 116
Gilson, Etienne, 31
Goguel, François, 119
Greco, Juliette, 115
Guerry, Emile, 11
Guitton, Jean, 14, 15, 18

Hegel, Friedrich, 14
Heidegger, Martin, 49, 117, 138–140, 142
Heymans, G, 123
Hitler, Adolf, 47, 71, 79, 81, 82, 87, 93, 104
Hobbes, Thomas, 6
Hume, David, 6
Humeau, Edmond, 32, 119
Husserl, Edmund, 47, 116, 117

Izard, Georges, 22, 31–33, 40, 56, 57

Janet, Pierre, 123
Jaspers, Karl, 138, 142
Jeanne d'Arc, 22
Jeanson, Francis, 116
John XXIII, Pope, 172, 173
Juan de los Angeles, 15
Jung, Carl Gustav, 123

Kanapa, Jean, 151
Kant, Immanuel, 6, 14, 47
Kierkegaard, Søren, 138, 139, 142
Klages, Ludwig, 123
Kretschmer, Ernst, 123
Kropotkin, Peter, 73, 77
Künkel, Fritz, 123

Laberthonnière, Lucien, 138
Lascoste, Robert, 103
Lacroix, Jean, 14, 32, 99, 109
Landsberg, Paul-Louis, 47, 48, 51, 138
Laval, Pierre, 108
Lavelle, Louis, 31
Leduc, Victor, 151
Leduc, Violette, 116
Lefebvre, Henri, 30
Leiris, Michel, 116
Lenin, Vladimir Ilyich, 4
Leo XII, Pope, 9
Leo XIII, Pope, 28
Le Senne, René, 31, 126
Locke, John, 6
Loustau, Robert, 93
Luther, Martin, 10, 46

Madaule, Jacques, 58, 119
Magny, Claude-Edmonde, 119
Maine de Biran, 9, 138
Malebranche, Nicolas de, 9
Malraux, André, 59
Mandouze, André, 103
Marcel, Gabriel, 18, 21, 99, 138, 142
Maritain, Jacques, 10, 17–19, 22, 25, 29, 31–34, 40, 42, 43, 46, 47, 48, 52, 62, 70, 171
Marrou, Henri, 119
Martin-Chauffier, Louis, 99
Marx, Karl, 4, 65, 66, 73, 77, 130, 149
Massis, Henri, 22, 24, 63, 71, 92, 94, 95,
Masson, Loys, 94, 102
Maulnier, Thierry, 30
Mauriac, François, 41, 70
Maurras, Charles, 4, 93, 95
Maxence, Jean-Pierre, 24, 30
Meinong, Alexius von, 47
Merleau-Ponty, Maurice, 45, 116, 142
Miatlev, Adrien, 119
Mindszenty, Cardinal, 157
Minkowski, Eugène, 123
Montesquieu, baron de, 166
Moulin, Jean, 103
Mounier, Francoise, 85
Mounier, Madeleine, 5, 11
Mussolini, Benito, 55, 71, 82

Nechayev, Sergei, 73